VILLAIN, VERMIN, ICON, KIN

Villain, Vermin, Icon, Kin

Wolves and the Making of Canada

STEPHANIE RUTHERFORD

McGill-Queen's University Press

Montreal & Kingston • London • Chicago

ISBN 978-0-2280-1107-1 (cloth)
ISBN 978-0-2280-1108-8 (paper)
ISBN 978-0-2280-1340-2 (ePDF)
ISBN 978-0-2280-1341-9 (ePUB)

Legal deposit second quarter 2022
Bibliothèque nationale du Québec

Printed in Canada on acid-free paper that is 100% ancient forest free
(100% post-consumer recycled), processed chlorine free

This book has been published with the help of a grant from the Canadian
Federation for the Humanities and Social Sciences, through the Awards to
Scholarly Publications Program, using funds provided by the Social Sciences
and Humanities Research Council of Canada.

Funded by the | Financé par le   Canada Council   Conseil des arts
Government | gouvernement   Canadä   for the Arts   du Canada
of Canada | du Canada

We acknowledge the support of the Canada Council for the Arts.

Nous remercions le Conseil des arts du Canada de son soutien.

Library and Archives Canada Cataloguing in Publication

Title: Villain, vermin, icon, kin: wolves and the making of Canada /
    Stephanie Rutherford.

Names: Rutherford, Stephanie, author.

Description: Includes bibliographical references and index.

Identifiers: Canadiana (print) 20210384506 | Canadiana (ebook) 20210384514 |
    ISBN 9780228011071 (hardcover) | ISBN 9780228011088 (softcover) |
    ISBN 9780228013402 (PDF) | ISBN 9780228013419 (EPUB)

Subjects: LCSH: Wolves—Canada. | LCSH: Wolves—Social aspects—Canada. |
    LCSH: Wolves in literature. | LCSH: Human-animal relationships—Canada. |
    LCSH: Animals and civilization—Canada.

Classification: LCC QL737.C22 R88 2022 | DDC 599.7730971—dc23

This book was typeset by Marquis Interscript in 10.5/13 Sabon.

For Mom, and for the wolfy-looking love of her life, Molly

Contents

Figures

Acknowledgments

Sometime in 2015 I was called the wolf lady by a student at a university that was not my own. That's when I knew I was in trouble. I had been working on this book for too long. Anyone even marginally acquainted with the project can tell you that. I gratefully received a Social Science and Humanities Research Council of Canada Insight Grant to support this research and imagined having a book draft by the end of 2017. Other projects, including two edited volumes, intervened, but the wolves never left my mind. I kept thinking and talking about them in my classes, at conferences, and in community settings. Ten years since this all began, the book is finally here. Many things have changed in the interim – my one-year-old is now a ten-year-old, I have secure rather than precarious employment, a global pandemic has reshaped our world – but much remains the same. And I still admire the wolves featured in this book.

But a decade is a long time to work on anything, and I was helped in the process by many people along the way. I have been graced with friends and colleagues, both at Trent and elsewhere, who have provided feedback, encouragement, and conversations that aided specific elements of this project. Many thanks to Jodi Aoki, Tayohseron:tye Nikki Auten, Katie Bellamy, Mike Bellamy, Stephen Bocking, Michael Classens, Rosemary Collard, Darren Dias, Finis Dunaway, Bruce Erickson, Stephen Hill, Tom Hutchinson, Helen Knibb, Dan Roronhiake:wen Longboat, John Marsh, Heidi Nast, Lisa Nisbet, Roger Picton, David Seitz, David Sheinin, Karen Thompson, Jocelyn Thorpe, John Wadland, Tom Whillans, Brad White, Shari Wilcox, James Wilkes, and Asaf Zohar.

A number of graduate students participated in aspects of this study; the work of Carley MacKay, Adam Marques, Meagan Sorley, and Brook Schryer is deeply appreciated. James McBride deserves special mention for conducting comprehensive and meticulously detailed research at the University of Toronto Archives and the BC Archives. As I wrote this book, I was continually reminded of the gift his diligent work has given me.

The editorial support provided by McGill-Queen's University Press has been exemplary. Mark Abley initially sought out the book and, before retiring, offered gentle encouragement, once telling me that "books take their own sweet time to emerge" – he wasn't kidding! Khadija Coxon took on the project after Mark's departure from MQUP and has been unfailingly positive and helpful as we navigated to the finish line together. Khadija also found two truly wonderful reviewers for the book whose generous and insightful comments refined the end result immeasurably. Kathleen Fraser provided extremely helpful guidance once the manuscript was submitted and commissioned the beautiful cover, which I love. Eleanor Gasparik was the much-appreciated expert copy editor added to the team. Her work greatly improved the style and flow of the book. I am also grateful for the indexing work of Alexandra Peace, who offered a comprehensive and detailed catalogue of the concepts and information I explored.

As part of my research, I availed myself of the amazing knowledge base of a great number of staff in archives and libraries across the country. I am grateful for the help (and patience) from the staff at the Archives of Manitoba, the Archives of Ontario, the BC Archives, the Hudson's Bay Company Archives, Library and Archives Canada, the Provincial Archives of Alberta, the Trent University Archives and the University of Toronto Archives. I am also grateful for those people and organization who granted permissions for the images and one of the chapters in this book, including Malcolm Mayes, the Archives of Ontario, Library and Archives Canada, the Trent University Archives, Shutterstock, and SAGE Publications.

My family has been particularly patient with my work on this book, from pedantic outbursts on canid behaviour to my grumpiness about finding time to write. I am grateful for Jen, Sav, Sophia, and Lily for their frequent visits and constant support. My dad has been an unfailing mentor for all my work and has read and commented on multiple iterations of this book from cover to cover. This book would have been much less without him. My stepmom, Margarita, is an astute student of all things canine. She graced my office wall with the photograph of a stunning black wolf that proved helpful to look up to as I wrote. My mom is an enthusiastic wolf lover and even more fervent booster of her kids. She also generously gave her time and expertise to this project by searching historical newspapers for me. My partner Darcy offered the belief that I can do anything, coupled with the gift of time and space to write. He also boasts a sharp editorial eye, which, for this and all other projects, is immensely helpful. And finally, my son Desmond is my heart and a howling little phenomenon. He put up with me dressing him as a wolf for two Halloweens running and is now in the habit of calling me "Wolf Mama." Without him, all else would be pointless.

VILLAIN, VERMIN, ICON, KIN

Introduction

The howling of wolves is a complicated sound. You hear it, but not just with your ears. It is a sound that is felt in the body; it moves the senses. There is something both frightening and compelling about it. Goosebumps rise, the heart quickens; a chill may tremble through you. It may seem both incomprehensible and entirely knowable. The howl can be heard as a threat or an invitation, haunting or hailing, and both would be understood as correct interpretations. It is rich with meaning, but not premised on human mastery and comprehension. It is a force that leaves no listener unaffected.

The polyvalent responses to the howling of wolves serve as a road map for the arguments in this book. For instance, in a 1910 issue of *Rod and Gun*[1], one can read Dorothy Patrick Dyar's account of a particular moment in her life in Western Canada in "Experiences of a Woman Homesteader." One of many such stories that appear in the pages of this magazine at the time, it illustrates the fear that settlers harboured for the ravening wolf as well as the restoration of order, often at the end of a gun. She describes her experiences with a "monster" timber wolf on the Alberta prairie. Left alone with her children while her husband searched for a lost cow, Dyar (1910, 228) recounts being stalked by a lone wolf, coming face to face with it at dusk as she went to the cold storage for butter. At first, she mistakes the wolf for her dog, until "cold fear gripped [her] heart." She manages to chase the wolf away and make it back the cabin, but her terror is far from over: "From the depths of the ravine I now heard a long drawn, weird cry that curdled my blood. I had become accustomed to the howling of the coyotes, but this sound was very different – far more savage and wild" (Dyar 1910, 228, 230). She lights every lamp in the cabin and waits. The wolf continues to howl, tormenting her, unseen in the darkness. After what seems like an eternity to Dyar, her husband returns with the

cow (and their dog) and sets out with his rifle to track the wolf, unsuccessfully in the end, as the "huge" wolf has disappeared into the dark. The
lupine violence that Dyar imagined as signalled in the howl never came
to pass. But Dyar's fear is rooted not only in the potential for physical
harm – though one would imagine the prospect of her and her family
ending up as dinner was likely panic inducing – but also linked to a broader
understanding of wolves as boundary crossers in the attempt to remake
the west as white colonial space. In this story, then, wolves and their howls
become a cipher for the anxieties of settler colonialism (Rutherford 2016).

Juxtapose this with the experience of the Algonquin Provincial Park
Public Wolf Howl, held every Thursday in August since 1965. As part of
Douglas Pimlott's research on wolves in the park in the late 1950s and
early 1960s (see chapter 4), he observed that wolves would respond to
humans, replicating their vocalizations. Park staff decided to test whether
this might be a means for nature interpretation (Strickland 2004). According
to Michael Runtz, park naturalist Russ Rutter (1997, 83) "anticipated
20 cars at most"; he was met with 200. This enthusiasm for hearing wolves
howl has grown in the intervening years, such that a wolf howl held today
routinely draws 2,000 people. Like Dorothy Patrick Dyar, wolf howl
attendees hear wolves calling into the darkness. But unlike her, it strikes
in them wonder rather than fear. This shift has been so complete that
Destination Canada, the Canadian national tourism marketing organization, has named Algonquin Park's Public Wolf Howl one of the nation's
"Signature Experiences" – part of a collection of "once-in-a-lifetime travel
experiences found in Canada," which are "offered by Canadians who are
passionate to share their part of the country with you" (Destination
Canada 2018).

These two ways of encountering wolves, separated by a mere fifty-five
years, show how their fortunes have changed in these lands we now call
Canada. Stories such as these led me to the study of wolves in Canada in
an effort to think through how such a dramatic shift could occur in such
a short period of time. But paradoxically, my initial interest was piqued
by a trip to the United States. As part of the research for *Governing the
Wild* (2011), I went on an ecotour in Wyoming, the focal point of which
was the grey wolves that had been reintroduced to Yellowstone National
Park. I was surprised and intrigued by the way the members of this tour
so single-mindedly sought a glimpse of a wild wolf, even if it was two miles
away and only visible through a spotting scope. I wondered about this
fascination and was curious about what had changed. Wolves were persecuted in the United States and were extirpated from Yellowstone National

Park by 1931. Yet here we were, a mix of Americans and Canadians, getting up at 4:30 a.m. to shiver in the snow in the hope of seeing an animal that, a scant hundred or so years ago, all of us would have likely shot on sight.

When I returned from this trip, I began to read about the history of wolves and came across a compelling piece of folklore in the United States, presented by Jon T. Coleman in his book *Vicious: Wolves and Men in America* (2004). He recounts the legend of a family leaving Batavia, New York – at dusk – to make their new home in what white settlers called the Western Reserve (in what is now northeastern Ohio). The parents and eight children load up on a sled pulled by oxen and depart in snow, already almost a foot deep, falling fast. As night descends, the oxen begin to struggle against the snow, and the howling of wolves begins. The wolves then begin to lunge at the sled. The father tells the mother: "we must protect the oxen; they are our only salvation." While the mother protests, she knows what he means: they must sacrifice one of the children. So the parents begin feeding their children one by one to the wolves. They pitch three toddlers to the wolves and are headed for the fourth when the wolves relent. The remaining family settles in Brecksville, Ohio, near what is now known as Cleveland and lives to tell the tale (Coleman 2004, 102–3).

As I read this rather remarkable tale, I wondered: How might this relate to human-animal relations in the Canadian context? What might such encounters tell us about how people engaged with what they perceived to be a hostile landscape? How might the ways in which wolves have been narrated through time tell us something about the roles and ideas of citizenship, nationhood, and national identity? And how have wolves been actors in historical change? The central thrust of this book is that the history of wolves in Canada offers a particularly interesting way to conceptualize the shifting terrain of nationhood, thinking about how wolves have migrated through space and time in Canada and, in doing so, have moved people in particular ways. Wolves have variously been imagined as villain, vermin, icon, and kin. Strikingly, each of these iterations had a pedagogical intent: to teach the appropriate relationship between humans and nonhumans. Yet, the lessons imparted have changed over time. This book is animated with a consideration of how the wolf has been formative of Canadian national identity. Put differently (and to borrow from Bruno Latour), it asks: what would Canada be without wolves?

"CANIS LUPUS SOUPUS"

To start: what wolves are we talking about? The answer to that seemingly obvious question has been remarkably opaque. If the definition of Canada is up for debate, so too is the definition of the wolf. When I began this book, I approached my research subject in an unscientific way: I assumed that we all know what a wolf is. It soon became clear that I was rather naive. Indeed, some of my own colleagues at Trent University were working on genomic analysis that documented the emergence of a new species: *Canis lycaon* or the eastern wolf (see, for example, Wilson et al. 2000; Grewal et al. 2004; Kyle et al. 2006). Indeed, the messiness of wolf classification in North America led renowned wolf biologist L. Dave Mech (2011) to name it "canis lupus soupus," or a canid soup. Mech (2011) points out that as recently as 1995, there were thought to be twenty-four subspecies of wolves in North America; there are now thought to be three. But it's probably no surprise that there is confusion. Differences between wolves are colloquially made into what seem to be distinct species by appellations like Arctic wolf, coastal wolf, Mackenzie Valley wolf, northwestern wolf, Rocky Mountain wolf, timber wolf, Algonquin wolf, and brush wolf (which is actually a coyote). Despite this confusion, there are now two recognized and distinct species of wolf in Canada: *C. lupus*, the grey wolf, and *C. lycaon*, the eastern wolf. But as Mech (2011, 7) remarks, these distinctions do not really change what a wolf is: "What does all this mean in terms of understanding basic wolf biology and behavior? Actually not much. The aphorism 'a wolf is a wolf is a wolf' is highly appropriate in this regard to anyone except the taxonomist."

Just two hundred years ago, wolves were among the world's most widely distributed mammals, covering the northern hemisphere (Canadian Wildlife Federation 1993; Musiani and Paquet 2004). Their range blanketed almost the whole of North America, except for a slice of the Baja peninsula. While it is unclear how many wolves were found on the North American continent before settler colonial attempts at extermination, their broad range implies that their populations were large; some suggestions are between 250,000 and 2 million animals in the United States alone (Mission: Wolf, n.d.). While wolves in the United States were largely extirpated through systematic programs of extermination, wolves in Canada remain and, in some cases, thrive in large portions of the country that are less densely populated (Musiani and Paquet 2004). The International Wolf Center estimates that in 2018, there were approximately sixty thousand wolves in Canada, and their numbers were stable or increasing (International

Wolf Center 2020). They continue to be found in all the provinces and territories, with the exception of New Brunswick, Nova Scotia, and Prince Edward Island. The grey wolf is not considered threatened or endangered; however, in 2015, the Committee on the Status of Endangered Wildlife in Canada (COSEWIC) assessed the eastern wolf as threatened.

THEORETICAL ARRANGEMENTS:
BIOPOLITICS, AFFECT, AND THE NATION

A disclaimer: while my objects of analysis are largely historical, this is not a history book. This book does owe a debt to the scholarship of environmental historians and historical geographers both in terms of insights and approaches. Indeed, I would have scarcely been able to imagine this book if not for the work of scholars in these cognate fields. I have borrowed from their methods and practices, emphasizing historical contingency in our relationship with wolves in Canada. But I have not set out to write a comprehensive and documentary account of wolves in Canada, although I think this would be a fascinating, if perhaps a lifelong, endeavour. Instead, this book uses relationships with wolves, as demonstrated through historical and contemporary texts and practices, to understand how animals and humans are imbricated, tied together in knots of power. I draw on a range of materials to elaborate these points: archival materials, newspaper articles, trappers' accounts, popular histories of the wolf, predator control manuals, Indigenous teachings, scientific studies, and fictional writing, as well as events and practices like the Algonquin wolf howl, the Fort St John wolf hunt, the death of Kenton Carnegie, and the wolf culls in Alberta and BC. I set out to make an intervention that explores how white settlers, who have been so inobservant – so incurious – for most of the time they have known wolves, have, rather suddenly, chosen to be otherwise in very specific, and often limited, ways. Digging into the specificities of one animal in one "imagined community" (B. Anderson, *Imagined Communities*, 2006) allows for a deeper dive into the particularities of the relationships between humans, animals, and the lands we share, albeit unequally. But I have been selective rather than wide-ranging. I have focused on particular sites, moments, practices, people, and texts to tell the story of wolves in Canada. I have emphasized particular narratives of fear, disgust, love, and loss. I have amplified moments of conceptual instability and indeterminacy. I have traced the threads that run through encounters with wolves, not only to document them but also to explore how they might provide the possibility to live differently with the nonhuman world, how they might teach us to love. In short, I have sought to write a book that makes a more conceptual rather than historical contribution.

More-Than-Human Biopolitics

The primary theoretical intent of this book is to provide a biopolitical account of wolves in Canada. I contend that the story of wolves in Canada is one that picks up this central aspect of Foucault's theoretical oeuvre (Foucault 1979; 1990; 2007; 2008). Whereas sovereignty is bound up in the juridical power to effect death – the "spectacle of the scaffold" (Foucault 1979, 32–69) – and disciplinary power takes as its focus the individual body, biopower takes aim at populations. It is the mode of power that seeks to regulate and optimize a population's health, longevity, well-being, economy, and productivity. This shift from sovereign and disciplinary power to biopower (though all three continue to operate simultaneously) marked the emergence of the modern liberal state and led to new and interesting constellations of governmentality geared toward nurturing particular kinds of life: "One might say that the ancient right to take life or let live was replaced by a power to foster life or disallow it to the point of death" (Foucault 1990, 138). It is, as Nicholas Rose (2006) suggests, "the politics of life itself." Biopolitical mechanisms, then, are those through which the self and others could be governed via invitation to live in particular ways that cause specific kinds of life to flourish. This "making live" was constituted through the establishment of populations of people whose lives were managed – by the state, various agents, or authorities, and by themselves – to their best end.

By now, biopolitical analyses are commonplace across a wide range of disciplines in the social sciences and humanities, so much so that it feels that biopower, like the panopticon, sees all. However, these interrogations almost entirely trained their analytical lens on humans. More recently, geographers, anthropologists, philosophers, historians, and political theorists have put forward a different contention: we need a more expansive view of what constitutes political and social life – that which figures in the calculus of biopolitics – if we are to see the impact of biopower in its fullest extent. It is here, of course, where the intersects between biopolitical and nonhuman occur. Much of the early scholarship that sought to apply Foucault to the nonhuman world – including my own (Rutherford 2007) – saw this as a labour of extension. For some, Foucault's emphasis on discourse, insistence that power was primarily social, and conception of agency as only ever human made his work incommensurate with a return to the material (Barad 2003). But recent scholarship has made the opposite argument, suggesting instead that Foucault's work, particularly around biopolitics and governmentality, always already considered the constitutive role of matter in the operation of rule. For instance, Thomas Lemke (2015), writing against the literature on new materialism, suggests that Foucault's "government of things" presages this move to object-oriented ontology. He argues that the government of things is much more flexible than many contend precisely because it does not fix the boundaries between subject and object. Instead, there is an openness to "the specificity and the relationality of politics" (Lemke 2015, 16) where all the actors aren't human. Chris Philo (2012, 498) agrees, asserting that discourse is situated in bodies, which, for Foucault, "have always been more material, fleshy-and-bloody, rebellious and even mysterious than they have commonly been depicted."

Following these insights, there has been a raft of scholarship that considers the relationship between biopolitics and the animal. As Dinesh Wadiwel (2015, 66) suggests, "the species context of Foucault's definition of biopolitics provides many avenues for understanding biopolitics as precisely concerning the relation between human and animal." A number of studies have made this assertion more concrete, from lab animals (Kirk 2016) to presidential pets (Skoglund and Redmalm 2017). However, the factory farm may have become the most emblematic site to read the biopolitical into human-animal relations, where "practices of maximizing control over life and death, of "making live," in Foucault's words, through eugenics, artificial insemination and selective breeding, pharmaceutical enhancement, inoculation, and the like are on display" (C. Wolfe 2012, 46). Animals, these authors contend, are constitutive to the modern operation of biopower.

Much of this reflection is rooted in Agamben's (2004) *The Open: Man and Animal*. Agamben suggests, contra Foucault, that the sovereign has always been an agent of biopower, and one of its central roles is boundary making between human and nonhuman. According to Sinclair (2011), "at the heart of sovereign power lies anthropocentrism – the network of onto-political grammars that ceaselessly produce and exclude 'animal life' from the political"; this is the work of Agamben's "anthropological machine." The kind of bare life experienced by the cow on a factory farm, for instance, renders it into "life that occupies the space that is vulnerable to the exceptional violence of the sovereign" (Wadiwel 2015, 73); the cow, outside *bios*, can be, in the words of Agamben, killed but not sacrificed. For Shukin (2009), it is this process of rendering that matters, where biopower exercises itself in ways in which animals are both discursively assembled and materially disassembled through the circuits of capital. In this reading, animals are often found in the realm of *zoe*, exceptions to the rule of law. This has certainly been the case with reference to how systems of power interact with specific kinds of animals: livestock, pets, captive creatures, and animals used in scientific research.

Fewer scholars have applied biopolitics to free living creatures; those who have, often look at the politics and practice of conservation (see, for example, Lorimer 2015; Hodgetts 2017). In this vein, Krithika Srinivasan's (2014) scholarship has been particularly instructive for showing how the biopolitical practices of making live and letting die render free living animals into sometimes problematic, sometimes prized populations that require intervention and management. As Srinivasan notes in her work on a turtle sanctuary in Odisha, India, conservation is not necessarily only about saving animals from harm. It can be about "win-win governmentalities" (Srinivasan 2014, 505) that reduce rather than eliminate that which harms individual animals while allowing extractive and industrial practices to continue relatively unfettered. Crucially, Srinivasan contends that it is the collective that comes to matter in this conservation politics, underwriting the sacrifice of some for the lives of others: "Under biopolitical regimes the population is much more than the sum of the individuals constituting it; it forms a distinct aspect of social reality in itself. Individuals diminish in ethical and political significance and can be shaped, and even sacrificed for collective well-being" (Srinivasan 2014, 507). Collectives are also key to Rosemary-Claire Collard's (2012) understanding of human-cougar encounters on Vancouver Island, where individual cougars are rendered into biosecurity threats to people, livestock, and pets. The presence of cougars in landscapes thought to be safe generates a range of biopolitical, and expressly spatial, responses from people, where cougars are fenced out, caught, and killed. But, Collard notes, cougars continually unmake these efforts at safety and certainty, enacting their own spatial practices on the lands that some humans have claimed as their own. As such, if we seek to understand the asymmetrical biopolitics of human-cougar interactions, we need to reconfigure them not simply as encounters but also as "entanglements," where "space and power unfold in networks" that are "not preexisting and stable" (Collard 2012, 39).

Following these threads, this book seeks to understand how wild animals such as wolves are also subject to – and resist – rationalities, discourses, and practices. In this way, I seek to contribute to the analytical frame of more-than-human biopolitics, offering a history of one collectivity. I use wolves in Canada to elaborate on the operation of biopower in three main registers: the coercive, the pastoral, and the affirmative. I begin by examining settler understandings of the wolf as an invading presence that necessitates a purge. Here, wolves can only ever be a threat to white settlers who wished to make what became Canada a calculable space of commerce and who viewed the nomadism of the wolf as a menace not only to livestock but also to the pastoral lives they wished to build. This rendering of wolves into bare life is made manifest through the bounty, where wolves were killed so humans and other more-desirable animals could thrive. Next, I turn to recuperation of the wolf in Canada that emerged through a variety of outlets, from Ernest Thompson Seton to Douglas Pimlott, from Farley Mowat to Ian McTaggart-Cowan. I think about how each of these authorities advocated for the wolf in a different way, seeking to reimagine the apparatus or dispositif around lupine politics in this country. In so doing, they inscribed a whole new set of practices, romantic and scientific, that offered new, yet no less biopolitical, assemblages for wolves to join. Finally, I turn to an affirmative biopolitics where I explore the possibilities of coming to know wolves on more even terms, where the subjectivity – the "creaturely sentience" (Asdal, Druglitrø, and Hinchliffe 2017) – of animal life is taken as a starting point. In this section of the book, I examine the potential for biopolitics to open up spaces of precarious apprehension, where new forms of attachment can be made on the basis of an often tenuous and incomplete mutual recognition.

Affective Engagements and Emotional Attachments

As a quick look at the contents page reveals, biopolitics isn't the only analytical scaffolding deployed in this book. The chapters are organized along the lines of affective registers such as fear, disgust, and desire. While the overriding frame is a biopolitical one, this book also takes aim at the relationships among biopower, affect, and animals, historically and in the present. In my understanding, affect is fundamentally embodied, referring to the expression of intensity that exceeds meaning making but is not separate from it. It hinges, as many have remarked, on the capacity to affect and be affected. Moving away from solely discursive and representational readings of the world, affect theory invites an attention to embodiment and relationality. In this way, humans and other animals are alike in their mutual experience of the world – what Cary Wolfe (2008, 8) calls our "shared embodiment, mortality, and finitude." Donovan O. Schaefer (2017, 18) expands on the way that affect dwells in the corporeal and non-discursive: "Affect theory is exceptionally useful in diagramming the depth dimensions of vibrant, animated human and animal lifeworlds. What the affective perspective offers is a window onto the way that bodies operate prior to and in excess of language."

The relationship between affect and emotion has been a contested terrain with sometimes sharp lines drawn between an understanding of affect as only ever pre-individual versus the idea that it can't be separated from how it is felt. Like Schaefer (2017, 19) (drawing on Sara Ahmed), my interpretation of affect settles on the latter interpretation, contending that it is "thickly, if fluidly, entangled with emotion." Margaret Wetherell (2014, 145) agrees, noting that to sever affect from emotion not only understands people (and animals?) as the sum of hormonal and bodily impulses but also renders affect a "black box" that is impossible to account for methodologically. She asserts that affect is best understood as a "highly dynamic, interacting composite or assemblage of autonomic bodily responses (e.g. sweating, trembling, blushing), other body actions (approaching or avoiding), subjective feelings and other *qualia*, cognitive processing (e.g. perception, attention, memory, decision-making), the firing and projecting of neural circuits (e.g. from the thalamus to the cortex and the amygdala), verbal reports (from exclamations to narratives) and communicative signals such as facial expressions. An emotional episode, such as a burst of affect like rage or grief, integrates and brings together all of these things in the same general moment" (Wetherell 2012, 62). Drawing on Ahmed, Wetherell (2014, 158) contends that affect is "an in-between, relational phenomenon," neither just individual nor predetermined by structure. And so, affect, emotion, discourse, and representation are inextricably tied together. Ben Anderson (2016, 14) makes this clear: "Attention to affect does not preclude an attention to representation and affect is not somehow the non-representational 'object' *per se*. Instead, we must pay attention to how representations function affectively and how affective life is imbued with representations."

Neera M. Singh's work on affective ecologies is particularly instructive as a means to connect affect and the more-than-human. In a special issue of *Conservation & Society* on the topic, Singh (2018, 1) notes that affect helps us understand the world as one of entanglement and sees "agency not as a property of individuals but as emergent in relationships and provides a starting point to recognise the profound interconnections that exist everywhere." In the introduction to their edited volume *Affect, Space and Animals*, Jopi Nyman and Nora Schuurman (2016) make a similar argument, suggesting an attention to affect refuses the assumed "human orderings or otherings" and instead invites curiosity about the ways in which interspecies engagements are always constituted relationally. As I have argued elsewhere (Rutherford 2016), paying attention to affect can work to disrupt the taken-for-granted human exceptionalism that has characterized not only Western encounters with animals since Aristotle but also some studies that use a biopolitical lens to envision animal lives and capacities. It invites an understanding of agency as multiple, contextually situated, and not rooted to arbitrary definitions of reason. By decentring cognition and language, an attention to affect allows for the possibility that nonhumans also possess the capacity to affect instead of simply being passive objects to be affected.

This book is interested in the ways in which affect and biopower intersect and makes the argument that they can be stitched together in multiple ways. As Ben Anderson (2016, 8) notes, "forms of power work through affective life." Drawing on Foucault's notion of the apparatus, he contends that affects "are known and become both objects and mediums for forms of intervention that aim to produce and reshape life" (B. Anderson, *Encountering Affect*, 2016, 19). Anderson offers a range of examples to show how "affect becomes an object-target for different forms of power" (ibid.). However, he is careful to emphasize the continued indeterminacy of affect. Power may seek to shape and harness affective life, but it always exceeds efforts at calculation and regulation. The wolves of this book show us that.

I argue that an emphasis on the connections between affect and bio-politics is crucial when thinking about animals. Relational encounters between humans and animals can produce a range of "good" and "bad" affects, from love to rage. These affects are worked in and through biopolitical registers to produce a range of effects. For instance, if we return to Srinivasan's (2014) work on turtle conservation, those who engage in biopolitical practices of care, even when focused at the level of the population, are inevitably affected by the loss they witness. By contrast, registers like fear can inspire and inform strategies of biopolitical release, where the killing of an animal, for instance, might suture an affective wound. This might, in part, explain the violence of the bounty as a form of affective and biopolitical intervention. Affirmative biopolitical endeavours around making live can also be tied to affective (and perhaps biophilic) impulses to encourage some animal life to flourish; here we might think about biologists' efforts to come to know wolves in a fulsome way or Farley Mowat's efforts to become wolf. And there is the making of some animals into affective labourers, where their value is derived through the registers they illicit: love, wonder, and joy. All these assertions are explored more fully in the chapters that follow. If power is conditioned in part through the senses, then examining how a range of affects has authorized – and in some cases demanded – specific forms of intervention into animal life is a matter of concern.

Wolves are what Sara Ahmed (2004) would call "sticky" subjects, to which a range of affective registers attach. The visceral and embodied responses white settlers have had to wolves – the same animal invoking at different times terror, loathing, aggression, revulsion, desire, and longing – speaks to the entanglement of humans and wolves that have gone into the making of this place. The translation of these affective registers into policies and practices is a key concern of this book. And so, I would invite the reader to think about the relationships between wolves and people in Canada as what Jan Slaby (2019) calls an "affective arrangement," which "comprises an array of persons, things, artifacts, spaces, discourses, behaviors, expressions or other materials that coalesce into a coordinated formation of mutual affecting and being-affected. While its composite materials are heterogeneous, an affective arrangement is characteristically social." This understanding works well with the entanglements of the human and nonhuman, which are social, but never simply in human terms. As a result, this book seeks to unpack the intensities of co-living between wolves and humans in these shared lands over time.

The Nation

As a final conceptual consideration, I wish to bring together the affective dimensions of more-than-human biopolitics with a discussion of their role in shaping ideas about the nation. As Benedict Anderson (2006) and Homi Bhabha (1990) have shown, nations are made, rather than found, in and through iterative and unstable practices, myths, and narratives of power. Etienne Balibar (1990) showed that this making occurs via the naturalization of the nation form, rooted in mythic origin stories that offer comfortable narratives of the nation as always having already existed – obvious and unquestionable. Such a national imaginary suggests historical tendrils both reaching into the past and suturing over the instabilities that characterize its existence. For Balibar, this unity is formed through what he named "fictive ethnicity" (Balibar 1990, 349) that naturalizes specific kinds of belonging and offers the possibility of a coherent "universalistic represen-tation which attributes to each individual one – and only one – ethnic identity and which thus divides up the whole of humanity between different ethnic groups corresponding potentially to so many nations, national ideol-ogy does much more than justify the strategies employed by the state to control populations" (ibid.). The national narrative, then, is predicated on a history and unity that never existed.

In settler colonial countries like Canada and the United States, struggle with nonhuman nature is venerated as the vehicle through which national identity and this fictive ethnicity is born. Frederick Jackson Turner's (1893) articulation of the frontier as formative of American identity fits well within this frame, as do romantic tropes of the voyageurs seeking furs in the Canadian context. Such narratives are often used as a mechanism to legitimize both the taming and disciplining of landscapes and animals, as well as the incarceration and genocide of the people who first and still called these lands home. Eric Kaufmann (1998) contends that in Canada and the United States, the voyageurs or the frontier are part of a broader project of "naturalizing the nation," whereby wilderness is the vehicle through which national community is made. Kaufmann argues that in Canada, the wildness of the North became the ideological and affective glue that stitched together the disparate provinces of the newly emerging nation. Of course, this wildness – or wilderness – also had to be made rather than found. As William Cronon (1996, 69) has so insightfully remarked, wilderness "is quite profoundly a human creation – indeed, the creation of very particular human cultures at very particular moments in human history." Space had to be remade as wilderness – uninhabited, wild, and ready to be conquered – in an attempt to replace Indigenous nations with a settler colonial one. And so, in the "shared fiction" (Mackey 2000, 125) that came to be called Canada, nature and nation are sewn together in the imposition of colonial rule, then and now.

The nationing character of nature is writ large in sites celebrated as iconic. For example, Jocelyn Thorpe (2012) has shown that the national Canadian imaginary has been worked through n'Daki Menan (Temagami, Ontario), the territory of the Teme-Augama Anishnabai. In her analysis of the ways in which n'Daki Menan was claimed as national nature, she shows how these lands were reimagined as simultaneously a wilderness to be visited *and* a source of timber, but never a home. Instead, n'Daki Menan was transformed into Temagami (though this transformation was and remains contested by the Teme-Augama Anishnabai), racialized as a white space of Canadian nature, which served to naturalize it, and as national space, in terms of the imagined wilderness to which it belongs. In looking at the ways such imaginings have attempted to remake the territories of Indigenous nations into the cohesive, yet inherently unstable, Canadian nation, Thorpe (2012, 19) demonstrates that this claim to uncontested origins was always a fiction: "Canada's existence as French

and British colonies, then as a settler society, and later an imperial dominion before adopting official multiculturalism was and is neither a
phenomenon of ancient origin not a historical inevitability. Instead, Canada
is largely the result, to borrow Teme-Augama Anishnabai chief Gary Potts'
words, of a 'squabble between white men over land that doesn't belong
to them.'"

Catriona Sandilands's work on national parks has been similarly important in sketching out the ways that these venerated sites of national nature
have a pedagogical inflection and, indeed, have served as that origin that
authorizes the claim to nationhood. Sandilands (2009, 167) notes, "the
nation, despite its arbitrary beginnings and partial claims to the identity
of a given space, can appear solid, even destined, if it can stitch its recent
history to some 'deeper' time and meaning." In Canada, this temporal and
spatial depth is found in sites of national nature. In tracing the changing
role of national parks in Canada through time, Sandilands maintains they
always had this nationing impetus that encouraged a shared white settler
identity in a country founded on dispossession (not the least of which to
make the parks themselves) and characterized by regional difference
and tension.

While the landscapes of Canada have been seen as constitutive to the
imagination of white-settler identity, the animals – both wild and domesticated – that were so central to the making of Canada often haunt the
edges of historical work on nation making. However, the stories we tell
about animals, and the ways they support particular ideas about the nation
differently at different times, are an archive unto themselves, showing how
narratives of the nation are anything but static. Indeed, in the construction
of Balibar's fictive ethnicity to make the people of a nation, colonial genocide has often been justified through the language of animality, the rendering
of some people as nonhuman, in which "the human/animal distinction
served as a recurrent reference point for who was expendable and who
could flourish" (Burton and Mawani 2020, 1). With specific reference to
settler colonialism, Kate Gillespie and Yamini Narayanan (2020, 1) contend
nation making happens and is maintained through "violent erasure of both
human and animal nations already existing in place." It is critical, then, to
examine the ways in which animals have figured into nation building, both
rhetorically and materially. If we accept that nations, like all social forma-
tions, are fundamentally multispecies assemblages, then including animals
into understanding the forms of power that underpin settler colonialism
is an important endeavour. This book contends that while wolves have
been a highly flexible metaphor used to bolster particular narratives of

nationhood, their shifting meanings also demonstrate, as Homi Bhabha (1990) suggests, that the nation is historically contingent and characterized by instability.

CHAPTER SNAPSHOTS

The above is, of course, a too-brief précis on the relationship between these complex analytical frames. Therefore, each chapter in this book takes up these theoretical strings to think about how they weave together human-wolf relationships in Canada at specific moments in time. The chapters elaborate on and extend the theoretical preliminaries outlined here, making the argument that the wolf has always been implicated in the formation of Canada, first as a physical threat to explorers, traders, and settlers; next as an invader that stole land, livestock, and resources; and finally as a source of national pride, an exemplar of wilderness, and a subject of conservation measures to regulate its own well-being. A biopolitical frame that pays close attention to affect and emotional response affords an examination of populations (of wolves, of prey, of people), territories (nations, homelands, hinterlands, invasions), and security (of livestock, of agriculture, of the environment), thinking about the ways in which wolves move in and through different geographies, cultures, and contexts.

This book is divided into three parts. Part one offers two chapters that chart the relationship among colonial anxiety, wolf extermination, and nationhood. Chapter 1 focuses on how fear – or what often seems like outright terror – informed early provincial approaches to dealing with wolves in a consolidating nation. This chapter suggests that wolves were seen as wildness out of place, and as such, the only response to their brazen presence on the landscape was annihilation. I trace the ways in which wolves were figured as biopolitical threats to the emergence of the nation that white settlers were attempting to make. Chapter 2 thinks about how biopower was deployed in service of a different affective register: disgust. This chapter explores the bureaucracies of extermination that emerged to deal with an animal that, by the early 1900s, had been recast as vermin, a pest in need of management. It focuses on the bounty, the primary mechanism by which wolves were rendered manageable and killable, a source of revulsion rather than only fear. The bounty functioned as a biopolitical purge of the national body, rendering it livable for some and decidedly unlivable for others.

Part two examines the transformation that takes place in how we think about wolves in Canada. Chapter 3 suggests it is less of a radical break than a simultaneous and subjugated discourse. Focusing on the works of Ernest Thompson Seton, Charles G.D. Roberts, and Farley Mowat, I contend that, beginning at the turn of the twentieth century, there was a counter-narrative to the notion that wolves were always reviled. Authors like Seton and later Mowat see and lovingly craft wolves as subjects and agents in the world, and their writing is full of desire for wolves and for wolfishness. But this was revealed in ways that often reified race, nature, and nation. Chapter 4 turns from fiction to science, thinking about the scientific re-imagining of wolves that took place in Canada beginning in the 1940s. Biologists and zoologists such as Douglas Pimlott, Ian McTaggart-Cowan, and John Theberge allowed themselves to be curious about wolves in ways that operated outside the discourse of management. Indeed, their work opened up the possibility for Mowat to write *Never Cry Wolf* in 1963, setting the stage for understanding the wolf as central to rather than enemy of ecosystems. Chapter 5 thinks about the consequences of this recupera-tion, or at least how it has been taken up in some quarters. It traces two vignettes in the modern devotion to wolves in Canada. I look at the rise of the Public Wolf Howl in Algonquin Provincial Park in Ontario, mentioned earlier, as a tool of nature interpretation and science communication that also works on the affective registers of wonder and longing. I also explore the market in dogs that have been hybridized with wolves – wolf dogs – which has emerged in recent years. With an emphasis on the quality and quantity of DNA, these dogs have become a somewhat problematic status symbol for people who wish to curl up with a measure of wilderness.

Part three emphasizes what the politics of human-wolf kinship could look like on these lands. The first five chapters focused on misrecognition of the wolf: part one, at how this misrecognition and the anxiety it induces is assuaged through violence; part two, at how benevolent approaches can still operate as a form of misrecognition. And both are biopolitical endeavours. But what might it mean to seek to know a wolf on its own terms? Is that even possible? And how would it change the nation if it were? Chapter 6 thinks about what wolf-human relationships might look like if we begin from the place of multispecies assemblage. Here, the coywolf – the polluted and hybrid kin of wolf, coyote, and dog – is our guide. This chapter explores how ambivalence is central to our reaction to this animal, which so recently came to share our landscapes as a direct result of the bounty that led wolves to consider coyotes as mates. It also points to the ways that the coywolf's very indeterminacy might open space for new ways of encountering canids. Chapter 7 focuses on a radically different way than in previous chapters of hailing the wolf. Indigenous intellectual traditions and teachings have a very different (though not monolithic) understanding of the relationship between humans and wolves. For the Anishinaabeg, a key piece of their cosmology is the story of Ma'iingan, the wolf that taught us how to be human. This section thinks about how we might learn from Indigenous ontologies that allow both human and nonhuman to flourish while holding open space for a generative conversation about the ways in which our lives are always interspecies collaborations.

While these teachings have been shared among Anishinaabeg on these lands since time immemorial, I turn to it last, which might seem like a strange choice. A story about wolves – or really anything in Canada – is incomplete if it only focuses on settler colonialism. As Jocelyn Thorpe has reminded me, that would be like starting a story in the middle. It misses the lived experience of generations of people for whom these territories have always been home, who continue to have lifeways that are different from and resistant to settler narratives of nature and nation. Of course, the idea that history began with the advent of settler colonialism is a powerful myth of coloniality, one that has done and continues to do violence to the people whose lands are occupied. And so, while I was interested in finding out why white settlers in Canada seemed so obsessed with wolves – first by persecuting them, then by saving them from their own depredations – by focusing only on those stories, I risked reifying them as the only ones worth telling. This chapter comes at the end because, while the stories are old, the insights they offer are new, at least to settler ears. How might listening for and giving weight to these ways of knowing seriously advance an alternative life course for wolves and, at the same time, offer different possibilities for nationhood? This question not only animates this chapter but also offers the ethical purpose of the book.

I close with a brief epilogue, which considers the case of Kenton Carnegie, a young student presumed to have been killed by wolves in northern Saskatchewan. Reading the various elements of this book through this specific case, the epilogue suggests that rather than fear being eclipsed by wonder, wolves still evoke a range of affective registers that we must consider if we seek better and more sustaining relationships with them.

In the end, I hope this book contributes to generative theoretical conversations about human-nonhuman relations in both historical and contemporary frames. But I also hope it does something more. One of my most favourite quotations, credited to philosopher and public intellectual Dr Cornel West, is: "never forget that justice is what love looks like in public." What, then, do love and justice look like for wolves? This book seeks to answer this question.

PART ONE

Villains and Vermin

1

Fear

Settler Encounters with Wildness
Out of Place

On 17 April 1922, the *Calgary Daily Herald* reported that a trapper in Manitoba named Ben Cochrane was "torn to shreds" by a pack of at least twelve timber wolves (*Calgary Daily Herald* 1922). The article described the scene north of Lake Winnipeg, in which only bones were found: that of eleven wolves and one trapper. It appears that Cochrane was cornered by the large wolf pack and was able to shoot many of them before his rifle broke. The remaining wolves killed and ate Cochrane.

This is not an uncommon story. There are many such blood-soaked tales of people disappearing as they traversed the wild woods in different parts of Canada. For instance, a nearly identical story from 1914 features an Indigenous trapper near Thunder Bay, Ontario, whose "bones [were] picked clean" by a large pack of wolves, nine of whom he killed. The remaining animals killed and ate him, and then, in a gruesome twist, also cannibalized some of their own dead kin (*Globe* 1914, 1). However, trappers weren't the only victims. In other cases, the people starring in these tales of wolf depredation tended to be the vulnerable: a boy in Saskatchewan killed while playing just outside his father's cabin (*Globe* 1908), and two girls attacked on a Saskatoon street by a marauding wolf (kept as a pet by "a local Chinese") (*Globe* 1923, 1). Sensational, violent, and gory, the stories of wolf attack from the late 1800s to the early 1950s, and on occasion beyond, show the precarity of the so-called civilization white settlers were trying to craft. It seems that, despite the efforts of the settlers and of the governments that supported them, Canada was still a wild and dangerous place.

White settlers seemed convulsed by a fear of being consumed, engulfed, and swallowed whole – that wolves would eat them alive. I contend that this terror was both deeper and broader: settler stories of being stalked by wolves spoke of fear not only for their physical well-being but also, perhaps more importantly, for their economic health and psychic certainty. The multiple registers of anxiety that wolves produced worked to generate a particular approach to dealing with them, one that often involved an exaggerated violence that reasserted settler control over the land. Wolves were seen by many settlers in Canada as wildness out of place in two important ways. First, wolves were a reminder that the land remained resolutely untamed, something underscored by their howls heard across the landscape. Second, the physical, economic, and affective threats posed by wolves meant that they could render the ultimate predator – white settlers – into prey. Their extermination, with prejudice, was often the approach taken by those who sought to restore calm to the ambivalent space of a newly minted nation. Drawing on a range of historical sources, this chapter traces these anxieties to understand how fear, terror, and anxiety generated particular biopolitical responses to an animal construed solely as a threat to the physical and national body.

SETTLER ANXIETIES

I use the term "settler" or "white settler" throughout in this book; as a result, it requires some explanation. My starting place is with Patrick Wolfe (2013, 1), who reminds us that "settlers are not born. They are made in the dispossessing." What Wolfe's description points to is that settler is a relational subjectivity made in and through power (see also Vowel 2016). It emphasizes that which Canadian national identity often obscures: the long-term effects of colonial violence in this country. But the term also points to the fact that colonialism is not a thing of the past; it is a reminder of contemporary realities of ongoing systems of oppression that have come to define how Indigenous Peoples experience life in Canada, from residential schools and the Sixties Scoop to blood quantum and continued land appropriation (Lowman and Barker 2015). Moreover, it lends some specificity to conversations about "Canadians," the totalizing identity – and, indeed, Balibar's fictive ethnicity – which is often taken to mean white people of European descent.

Early white settlers, it seems, were a pretty anxious bunch. Lorenzo Veracini (2008) describes the settler orientation as paranoid. For many scholars in this field, the anxiety and ambivalence stems from a problematic bifurcation – or what Patrick Wolfe (2013, 8) calls an "affective double bind" – in the way they view the lands they are trying to make their own. On one hand, settlers view Indigenous Peoples as obstacles to progress, their cultures and practices in need of elimination to give rise to the emerging nation they imagine. On the other hand, Indigenous Peoples were of this land in ways that settlers could never be; as Hamish Dalley (2018, 31) notes, this results in a "constitutive anxiety about the past – about origins." This double bind is deepened by the fact that settler colonial countries like Canada were made (and sustained) through violence, but this violence is iteratively disavowed (Veracini 2008). This disavowal serves two aims: first, to (unsuccessfully) assuage guilt and anxiety over dispossession and, second, to delegitimize Indigenous claims to the land (ibid.). These dissonances in the settler mind, Wolfe (2013) says, can in some ways explain (though not justify, of course) the brutality with which settlers treated the Indigenous Peoples whose land they stole.

So, as Wolfe (2006, 388) has noted, settler colonialism "destroys to replace," proceeding via both nullifying and productive "logics of elimination" through a hydra-like series of practices, from residential schools to Indian status regulations to outright murder. These same rationalities of extermination, I argue, were also applied to the wild animals in lands being colonized. Billy-Ray Belcourt (2015) has been particularly convincing in his analysis of how our relationships with animals are structured through colonial practices of dispossession and replacement of Indigenous Peoples in service of settler colonialism. He argues that anthropocentrism is at the heart of the colonial project, where "speciesism intersects with the logic of genocide to secure a capitalist project of animal agriculture that requires the disappearance of Indigenous bodies from the land" (Belcourt 2015, 5). I suggest these sorts of structures were often at work when settlers thought about both wolves and Indigenous Peoples in terms of an animality that needed to be controlled. To be clear, I am not conflating Indigenous Peoples with animals, a move that would reinforce colonial ideology that hinged on both dehumanization and animalization (see, for example, K. Anderson 2000; Belcourt 2015; and Kim 2015). However, I suggest that settlers viewed Indigenous Peoples and wild animals – and particularly predatory animals like wolves – as improperly placed, both temporally and spatially. Temporally, both Indigenous Peoples and wolves were seen as out of time, anachronistic to the nation-building project. This applied spatially too, where the physical presence of both Indigenous Peoples and wolves on the landscape – their persistence in spite of the violences of the colonial project – required containment, displacement, and elimination. As Mary Douglas (1966, 35) has famously asserted, "matter out of place" is a threat because it subverts the dominant order.[1] In this case, both Indigenous Peoples and wolves troubled the project of settler colonialism in what were seen as unacceptable ways.

The primary strategy that early settlers – from ranchers and farmers to trappers and loggers – employed to suture this fearful sensation about wolves was a form of animal necropolitics. Achille Mbembé (2003) coined the term "necropolitics" to describe the way in which colonial authorities exercised power over life and death, engaging in practices of subjugation and control that, the author contends, had not been adequately captured in Foucault's original articulation of biopower. Instead, Mbembé (2003, 39) puts forward the notion of necropower not as the capacity to make live and let die (the hallmark of biopower under Foucault) but rather as sovereign efforts at the "subjugation of life to the power of death." Drawing on Giorgio Agamben's state of exception, Mbembé (2003, 27) suggests that necropolitics is a practice of disavowal rather than mainly productive force, one that renders "the capacity to define who matters and who does not, who is disposable and who is not."

Dinesh Wadiwel's scholarship has been particularly instructive in applying necropolitics to animal lives. He argues, following Mbembé, that biopolitics "cannot merely be considered as a beneficent power designed to 'foster life,' but as a politics that seeks to produce both life and death, simultaneously" (Wadiwel 2015, 87). For Wadiwel, then, animals almost always exist in Agamben's bare life, subject to continuous states of exception. Indeed, Mackintosh (2017) contends that animal bodies were central to the rise of biopower in the eighteenth and nineteenth centuries, where animals' lives offered a proving ground upon which new forms of power were tried, tested, and refined. The massive scale of animal death in service of human life has been most clearly articulated as it relates to livestock: cows, pigs, chickens, and sheep are brought into being, kept in conditions that approximate living death, and killed in the billions so that humans may thrive on a steady diet of meat. As Asdal, Druglitrø, and Hinchliffe (2017) point out, these acts of life and death sit in simultaneous tension with the extinction crisis of animals in the wild, where intentional and unintentional acts of anthropogenically induced habitat destruction, introduced species, climate change, and pollution render the lives of these animals disposable too.

In the case of wolves, this "war against animals" (Wadiwel 2015) has been well under way for hundreds of years. Wolves have often been conceived as an invading presence on the landscape. In early settler interactions with wolves, the animals were victim to the mentality of the purge. If, following Esposito (2008), we conceive of the national body as an organism – a community – then wolves represented that which needs to be immunized, contained, and expelled: wild animals were remade into a threat to the health and well-being of the emerging nation, especially because they were liminal creatures that upended both certainty and security in a variety of ways. The nation could not be made out of the colonial imaginary if wildness remained. As Andrea Smalley (2017, 6) points out in *Wild by Nature*, colonization "required a reinvention of the landscape," which the presence and actions of wild animals rendered challenging. This was particularly the case for wolves, which "symbolized the primitive state of the region, a condition that had to fall before the advance of civilization" (K.R. Jones, *Wolf Mountains*, 2003, 104). As a result, the relationship between humans and wolves in Canada – the co-shaping of landscapes, the anxieties they induced, the competition for food, and the policies enacted to deal with them – moulded a particular approach to dealing with them, one that for a long time meant that for Canada to progress on settler terms, wolves had to be exterminated.

However, there were always other ways of relating to the nonhuman – animals, land, and waters – than white-settler articulations allowed for. In fact, the idea of wilderness itself is a white-coded one that presents itself as the universal way of encountering nature (Cronon 1996; Finney 2014). The claim of wilderness's naturalness works to hide its cultural production, as well as the practice of power baked into its elaboration. But other ways of knowing the land were here before and operated simultaneous to the narratives of white settlers. For instance, as Carolyn Finney (2014, xiii, 9) has noted in the United States, while an attachment to nature is often represented as a "white thing," a powerful and rich "black environmental imaginary" exists that ties African Americans to land in different ways than the exclusionary logic of wilderness affords. Philip Dwight Morgan (2019) offers a similar reflection as a Black man accessing wilderness in Canada, the myth of which (and the nation on which it is founded) never quite seem his own.

Wolves, of course, were not the only animals driven off the land. A powerful example of the relationships that pre-existed white-settler accounts of the wilderness can be found in the buffalo treaties of the plains in the United States and Canada. They also offer an example of how the slaughter of animals was used as a tool of colonization. Nick Estes's (2019) book on the Oceti Sakowin's (Sioux) centuries-old resistance to colonial incursion and dispossession, culminating in the 2016 months-long action against the Dakota Access Pipeline that runs through their territory, traces the nation's origin to a buffalo treaty in which human and nonhuman were bound in mutual obligation. For the Oceti Sakowin, the Pte Oyate (buffalo nation) was kin and "the future of the Oceti Sakowin was bound to the future of the Pte Oyate" (Estes 2019, 110). Similarly, Tasha Hubbard describes the intimate connections between people and animal on what is now the Canadian plains. Citing John Lame Deer, Hubbard (2009, 68) elaborates that "the buffalo was part of us, his flesh and blood being absorbed by us until it became our own flesh and blood. Our clothing, our tipis, everything we needed for life came from the buffalo's body. It was hard to say where the animal ended and the man began." Both Estes and Hubbard note that a central part of the colonial project to "clear" the plains was to sever these treaty relations. Settlers embarked on a vast project of annihilation that saw millions of buffalo killed on the plains between the 1860s and 1880s, in what Estes (2019, 110) names a genocide not only for the buffalo but also for the Indigenous Peoples they were in treaty with: "For its part, the military began to take seriously this vital connection with the buffalo as sustaining continued Indigenous resistance. The frontier army's operations turned toward exterminating Oceti Sakowin kin – the Pte Oyate – as defeating highly mobile Plains nations in conventional battles was near impossible. From 1865 to 1883, the frontier army sanctioned the mass slaughter of buffalo to shatter the will to resist by eliminating a primary food supply and a close relative." These stories of kinship between human and nonhuman are not of the past; they remain important original instructions today. We turn to these instructions as they relate to the wolf in chapter 7. But the history of wolf vilification and abuse, as well as glorification and obsession, is very much a settler story.

HAUNTING THE LANDSCAPE

Rebecca Weaver-Hightower's book *Frontier Fictions* (2018) asserts that stories about animals in colonial contexts are important because they narrated how settlers saw themselves in the places they sought to make home. Such stories often serve as a vehicle to manage anxieties around the legitimacy of claims to the land and the use of violence to subdue people, animals, and nature. The stories found in newspaper articles and in the pages of magazines like the *Beaver* and *Rod and Gun* bear out Weaver-Hightower's assertion. A range of wolf stories from the late 1800s to the early 1900s demonstrates how such anxieties bled onto the page and were often worked out in the process of writing. Recall Dorothy Patrick Dyar's (1910) account from the introduction: it contains many of the themes found across examples of this type of writing. Perhaps most notable is the affective impact of the aural soundscapes that wolves produce. Put another way: their howling scared the crap out of settlers. In innumerable stories, the howling of wolves takes centre stage. In earlier writings, such as *Roughing it in the Bush* ([1852] 2003), Susanna Moodie recounts the dread induced by wolves howling in the Cavan Swamp, now a wildlife area some twenty-five kilometres from where I write this chapter at Trent University on Michi Saagiig land, in what settlers called Upper Canada.[2] A reluctant "pioneering" wife, Moodie ([1852] 2003, 295) writes of her own sense of isolation, a silence broken only by the doleful cry of a wolf: "my mind was haunted with visions of wolves and bears; but beyond the long, wild howl of a solitary wolf, no other sound awoke the sepulchral silence of that dismal-looking wood." In another part of the book, one unmistakably similar to Dorothy Dyar's account, she notes that it is one thing to hear wolves while in company; it is entirely another experience to hear them when one is alone with five children and waiting for the return of your husband. She convinces herself that her husband, John Moodie, has been attacked and killed in his search for a cow missing in the woods. She spends "the saddest and longest night [she] ever remember[s]" ([1852] 2003, 202) tormented by the howling of wolves as she awaits news of her (surely) dead husband. Like Dyar's story, the wolves plague Moodie, feeding and amplifying her fear, until the morning when, unable to hide in the shadows, they simply disappear: "Just as the day broke, my friends the wolves set up a parting benediction, so loud, and wild, and near to the house, that I was afraid lest they should break through the frail window, or come down the low wide chimney, and rob me of my child. But their detestable howls died away in the distance, and the bright sun rose up and dispersed the wild horrors of the night, and I looked once more timidly around me" ([1852] 2003, 203). She leaves the house and finds that her fears were unfounded. Her anxieties – while acute in the night – have been allayed, and the potential usurpers that would take her husband, her children, and her life have caused no lasting damage. They are impermanent, fleeting, remembrances of a past now fading. The return of her husband means this land, however reluctantly, is theirs.

Samuel Thompson, also in Upper Canada though separated from Moodie by thirty years, narrates similar stories of how wolves were heard. Although Thompson spent the majority of his life as a newspaper reporter and editor in Toronto, *Reminiscences of a Canadian Pioneer* ([1884] 2011) explores the three or four years he spent trying to make a farm out of the wilds of what is now central Ontario. Part of what made this place wild with nature for Thompson was the howling of wolves. At various points in his book, he describes being disturbed by the "hideous howlings" of wolves (S. Thompson [1884] 2011, 56). He recounts an incident where his dog chases and fights one of these howling wolves – a grisly tale of lupine blood lust and ferocity: "Next morning we followed the track further, and found at no great distance another similar spot, where the wolf had devoured its victim so utterly, that not a hair, bone, nor anything else was left, save the poor animal's heart, which had been flung away to a little distance in the snow. Beyond this were no signs of blood" (ibid.). Why a wolf would leave the heart – offal high in nutrition – while eating bones, hair, and snow stained with blood seems a function of myth rather than fact. But either way, the sound of wolves signalled death.

The terror generated by the howling of wolves persisted into the 1950s, likely because people continued to live in closer proximity to such communications than they do today. In a variety of texts, readers are treated to descriptions of lupine cries piercing the air. As J.E. Orr (1911), frequent writer for *Rod and Gun* tells us, it was a sound that every pioneer knew. And it was a sound, or rather the dread elicited by it, that necessitated action. This sentiment was summed up in a 1907 article entitled "A Life and Death Struggle": "The howls of the wolves were so persistent, and they grew so bold, that it was felt an effort must be made to clear them out" (*Rod and Gun* 1907, 878). Howling could only be read as an indication that the landscape had not been made productive, or at least not fully so. What Rath (2003, 147) suggests in the American context resonates in Canada as well: the "waste and howling wilderness" was perceived as nothing less than the intent to destroy the settler way of life. This was further compounded by the wolf's elusiveness; they were heard but rarely seen, an invisible presence haunting the landscape. For that reason, wolves – standing in for a broader and nefarious wilderness that refused taming – had to be destroyed, their death a clear indication of the completion of colonialism's mission of "civilizing" the landscape. Wolf presence on the land signalled a deeper and problematic issue: an unsettling sound in a place that ached for settledness. As Coates (2005, 646) contends, "the silencing of the wolf epitomized the taming of the frontier."

Of course, the lessons white settlers read into howling were misapprehensions: wolves don't howl to scare us; they don't howl for us *at all*. Rather, they are communicating with one another. The tones and resonances in howls – from low and sonorous to higher-pitched and nasal – while incomprehensible to us, are messages in the lupine world. A defence of territory, a warning for interlopers, an attempt to locate a lost packmate, an expression of happiness in pack reunion, or a conversation about prey (Harrington and Asa 2003): these often-misunderstood polyphonic choruses are the hallmark of a species that creates lifelong social bonds. Settlers narrated themselves into the middle of a story that had absolutely nothing to do with them.

Yet, clearly, the howling of wolves was able to affect even those who were not its intended audience. For settlers, the howl signified a deeper fear: the sonic precursor to stalking and attack. It rendered settlers into prey instead of predator (Coleman 2004). This theme of being hunted is found across the archival record during this period. For instance, James E. Orr shows this inversion in a literal way. He recounts a hunting trip in which he becomes separated from his partner. Alone and vulnerable, he is hunted by a wolf: "I saw coming towards me a big shaggy swamp wolf. I fired at the animal and missed and immediately the hunter became the hunted. Over bush and logs I ran with the wolf a close second. Soon I dropped my rifle and scrambled up a small tree. I was anything but comfortable as the wolf, growling and snapping reached the place and made several endeavours to reach me. To add to my discomfort I found myself too heavy for the small maple up which I had shied and it began to bend with my weight. The wolf saw what was happening and jumped straight upwards at me" (J.E. Orr 1908, 552). Unable to escape, Orr yells so loud he is able to alert his hunting partner of his predicament. His compatriot comes to his aid and kills the wolf.

Orr (1910b, 705) tells a very similar story in 1910, where a hunting camp is beset by a "discordant chorus" of wolves "running hither and thither over the snow, their numbers increasing until the whole forest seemed like a moving panorama." Helpless, the hunters can only wait out the wolves, using torches from the fire to keep them at bay. Although they had guns, Orr explains they didn't dare use them "for fear of rousing an uncontrollable thirst for blood in the rest of the pack" (ibid.). He continues: "No one can put into words the terrors of that fight for life which was never for a moment relaxed. The wolves had cornered a supper and were determined to have it, but the supper said 'No' and stuck to it, and so achieved victory" (ibid.).

These kinds of stories are written again and again, almost as if there was a cultural template for them. In northern Quebec, E.S. Shrapnel (1907) tells the story of getting lost in the woods. He decides it is better to camp out and wait until morning. He is awakened but the howling of wolves, but what comes next is even worse: "Suddenly, there was silence; they had evidently approached within view of the fire. A minute or so passed, when a low growl from my dog told me plainly they were at hand, and only prevented from rushing in on my dog by the nearness of the fire. I could plainly see their eyes by the firelight, but could not distinguish their forms as they slunk in a wide circle of intense gloom" (Shrapnel 1907, 851). Bitter cold and the fear of frostbite drive Shrapnel to leave the fire; following a trail, he finds an abandoned hunting cabin where he becomes trapped, and the wolves begin making their "hellish noises" at the door (ibid.). The hunter musters his courage and ends up killing two of the wolves; the rest, as cowards do, run away. Shrapnel's experience becomes something of a theme. In a similar story, two other hunters are also penned in a cabin, like livestock in a kill chute: "From time to time they looked out and saw the wolves circling the cabin. The beast kept howling almost continuously. As dawn broke, the howling stopped and the wolves slipped away" (*Globe and Mail* 1947, 8). Barager (1944, 6) tells a similar story of getting lost in the woods and hearing "the full-throated hunting cry of the timber wolf." And while not a hunter, a snowshoer in Algonquin Park also tells of being stalked (Jervis 1906, 550).

Some of the fear expressed in these stories is about being literally consumed, and given the tenor of popular reporting of the time, not an unreasonable fear to harbour. For example, Dr Emily Chambers, according to the author, "a woman ... to whom prosaic life was irksome," was apparently eaten by wolves when she journeyed alone to the Northwest Territories (*Globe* 1906, 13). In 1911, a trapper named Homer Wilson was eaten by wolves, leaving his recent bride to almost freeze to death as she awaited him in the hunting cabin with wolves howling for her blood every night (*Globe* 1911). In 1912, it was reported that a mail carrier was eaten by wolves, with only his hand and shin bone found (*Globe* 1912). And in Port Arthur, Ontario, a truly tragic series of events occurred in 1922. A man went to pick up his mail in town just before Christmas. Discovering it hasn't arrived yet, he promises to return the next day. When he doesn't, the authorities send two Indigenous trackers to find him; what they find are bones. A search party is organized, but the trackers go back first to claim the bounty for themselves. The search party then finds the bodies of the trackers as well as sixteen dead wolves from a pack they estimated at forty wolves (*Globe* 1922). It's no wonder people feared being eaten: it was a big part of the narrative they both encountered and helped construct about this place that was wild with nature.

As the case in Port Arthur illustrates, settlers also believed they were confronting huge packs of wolves. In both Ontario and Quebec, stories advise that there are so many wolves in the early 1900s, that it is best not to leave home without a weapon (*Rod and Gun* 1909a). It is no surprise, then, that settlers imagined wolves slinking around the wilderness in mighty numbers. In just a brief survey, I found the following: twelve wolves in a pack in Lake Manitoba (*Globe* 1904); fifteen to eighteen wolves that force the sacrifice of hunting dogs in Quebec (*Globe* 1926b); between fifteen and fifty wolves that trap miners in northern Ontario (*Globe* 1927b); and sixteen wolves that cornered lumberman (*Globe* 1927a). And in many cases, the size of these packs meant that they were emboldened to kill. As a hunter recounts to Susanna Moodie in *Roughing it in the Bush*, "I never felt the least fear of wolves until that night; but when they meet in large bands, like cowardly dogs, they trust to their numbers, and grow fierce. If you meet with one wolf, you may be certain that the whole pack are at no great distance" ([1852] 2003, 373). As wolf biologists will tell you, these numbers strain credulity. The more wolves you have in a pack, the more often that pack would need to hunt. Given that their hunts are unsuccessful between 80 and 85 per cent of the time, it seems unlikely that wolves would congregate in packs of more than twenty members. They are much more likely to be found in groups of between two and eight (International Wolf Center, n.d.a). But the exaggeration, I think, speaks to more than just the telling of a tall tale. It also signals the fear of a marauding and uncontrollable wilderness, one that will overwhelm and consume without remorse.

While fear and sometimes sheer panic is the through line of these stories, there is something else at work too. As much as these stories present wolves as haunting the borders of civilization, revealing the fiction of complete colonial conquest, many of these stories end in ways that ensure everyone knows who is at the top of the food chain. More specifically, the human protagonists of these stories often end up killing the wolves that have terrified them. They find their courage and prevail. This is certainly the case for Cowan (1904), Dobbyn (Moorhouse 1906), Orr (1908), Whittaker (1911), and Barager (1944), to name only a few. In each of these examples, human mastery is reasserted, and the wolf incursion into settler society – as well as the inversion of settler supremacy such an incursion implies – is restored. I would contend that these stories are not just warnings, though they certainly are that. They also act as pedagogies, narrating and reiterating settler control over a sometimes-unruly nation.

THE NATURE OF A WOLF

The cruel fangs gleamed as close he crouched
  Beside a fallen pine;
His muscles tensed, while in his eyes
  I saw the bloodlust shine.

Closer his unsuspecting victim came,
   A soft-eyed fawn, alone
Browsing amid the tender shrubs,
   Where lurked the foe unknown.

With hair erect and frothing mouth
   The wolf prepares to spring;
Too late, a rifle speaks hard by
   And loud the echoes ring.

The shaggy brute sins with a groan
   A bullet through his heart
For man, a mortal enemy,
   Had seen and played "his" part.
(A. Douglas 1910, 1186)

Douglas's poem illustrates how many settlers understood the nature of the wolf: cunning, savage, cowardly, and unsportsmanlike. The story of the wolf, animated and compelled by cruel sanguinity, setting upon a defenceless victim who then, miraculously, finds a champion at the end of a person's rifle echoes the same ground as some of the stories above.

But wolves often emerge as complex and contradictory figures in nineteenth- and twentieth-century Canada. One of the most confounding characteristics of wolves for settlers was their sly elusiveness. Heard but not seen, prowling at night, leaving only paw prints, bones, and blood as evidence of the depredations, wolves presented a spectral presence that unnerved settlers. They were far too clever and slippery. As early as the eighteenth century, trappers complained of the wiliness of their lupine enemy. George Cartwright, who wrote about trapping and living in what became Labrador, noted that wolves were more cunning than other species: "No beast, that I am acquainted with, is so suspicious of a trap as a Wolf, and one who has already been caught in, and lamed by one, is ten times more so; and, consequently, very difficult to catch: but yet he will frequent a trap-walk; eat out every animal which is caught, and rob the traps of their bait" (Cartwright and Stopp 2016, 285). The fact that wolves were opportunists made this supposed characteristic even worse. Over and over, wolves are bold and vicious when a person is alone, lost, and vulnerable. Again and again, they only attack if they have strength in numbers. Rather than seeing this as a wise hunting strategy, settlers read cunning and cowardice into the evolutionary behaviours that helped wolves become apex predators.

This craftiness was compounded by the animal's so-called cruelty. Wolves not only killed but also, according to many settlers, enjoyed it. For instance, E.J. McVeigh, a frequent contributor to *Rod and Gun*, writes of a conversation between a hunting party and a trapper in which wolves are both unpredictable and brutish. The trapper tells the hunters he is scared of wolves precisely because they are so hard to pin down: "Oh yes, damn wolves, I am afraid of wolves. Never know what they will do, and never know where they are. Maybe close to you, maybe ten, twenty miles away" (McVeigh 1910, 790). When the hunters ask how many deer the wolves kill, the trapper asserts their cruelty: "Don't know how many they kill, but they kill all they want to, not all they want to eat you know, but all they want to kill. They kill them just for fun – yes you bet they do" (ibid., 791). For this trapper, wolves don't kill to eat; they kill to satisfy some primal blood lust. And in at least one account, they seem irredeemable in their cruelty. A short note in "Our Medicine Bag" in *Rod and Gun* tells the story of a Saskatchewan trapper who tamed wolves to drive his sled. One day he works them for the whole day without food. As they return home, the trapper's three-year-old daughter runs out to greet the animals she knows as pets, and they rip her apart. Enraged, the trapper kills five of them with his axe. It is striking that wolves were seen as barbarous when, in fact, it was settlers who perfected cruelty.

Perhaps what sums up the depravity that settlers ascribed to wolves was the description of them as cannibals. Cannibalism as a shorthand for monstrousness has a long history in Western thought (Avramescu 2009), one that has often been used to define proper moral behaviour. In the case of wolves, their indifference to the species of the meat they eat renders them suspect. The fact that wolves cannibalize their kin catapults them to a whole new level of degradation and irredeemability. In one example of many such passages, Orr (1913) narrates the uncontrollable savagery that impels wolves to kill and eat each other's flesh. The basic grooves of the story are well worn. On the way home from a trip to the mill, a settler tarries too long and is forced to travel at night in the woods near his home. Under cover of darkness, the wolves appear, eager to take down the oxen pulling his sleigh. But as the settler slices the first of the wolves with his axe, the rest turn on their fellow instead of the draft animals: "At the smell of blood the other wolves tore their wounded mate to pieces and ate him. This was repeated five or six times on that eventful night and as the wild savages stopped to eat the wounded the oxen got a little start on the pack" (Orr 1913, 1090). It seems strange that settlers had so many feelings about wolves eating each other. Surely it was an expedient method of their control? But for settlers, wolves' capacity to eat one another only signalled the depths of their moral decay and offered yet another reason for their elimination.

Tied to their savagery was another, sometime-discordant story – that of wolf cowardice. It is an interesting narrative in part because it can actually work against tropes of savagery and cruelty, which, if nothing else, can speak to a boldness that pusillanimity would belie. In 1856, Catharine Parr Traill, sister of Susanna Moodie, picks up on this idea in *Lady Mary and Her Nurse, or, a Peep into the Canadian Forest*. Presented as a conversation between a child and her nanny, the book offers moral and practical instruction on living an upper-class life in "the colonies." In "A Story of a Wolf," one of the first in the book, the nurse tells the worried girl the truth about wolves: "No, my lady; the Canadian wolf is a great coward. I have heard hunters say, that they never attack any one, unless there is a great flock together and the man is alone and unarmed" (Traill 1856, 9–10). She continues: "All animals are afraid of brave men" (ibid., 11). Many agreed with Traill's assertion. For instance, Abel Johnson (1902) asserts that wolves are so frightened of humans they will avoid any kind of settlement. A similar view is expressed in 1904 in a letter to *Rod and Gun* wherein an unnamed author decried the tall tales of wolves attacking people as "fabricated out of whole cloth" (*Rod and Gun* 1904, 517). Instead, the letter writer suggests that a wolf is "such an arrant coward that he will not attack a deer while it remains in the shade of the bush" (ibid.), nor, Misner (1907) contends in a different article, will wolves "walk on glare ice." Wolves, it seems, can occupy the positions of wickedly barbarous, uncommonly savage, and skulkingly spineless at the same time.

The combination of these supposed character flaws certifies the wolf as, in the words of the writers examined here, unsportsmanlike. It's an interesting turn of phrase for an animal, and one that, like other descriptions of wolves, says much more about the people doing the describing. But for many settlers, wolves didn't play by the rules. This applied to their encounters with people, with livestock, and with other wild animals. But the suggestion that wolves were unsportsmanlike to other wild animals bears exploration. As Douglas's poem suggests, wild animals such as deer, moose, bears, wolves, and cougars were assigned their roles as either victim or aggressor, helpless prey or vicious fiend. For example, Brian the Still Hunter from *Roughing it in the Bush* tells of the tragedy of wolves hunting a deer:

> Presently a noble deer rushed past me, and fast upon his trail – I see them now, like so many black devils – swept by a pack of ten or fifteen large, fierce wolves, with fiery eyes and bristling hair, and paws

that seemed hardly to touch the ground in their eager haste. I thought
not of danger, for, with their prey in view, I was safe; but I felt every
nerve within me tremble for the fate of the poor deer. The wolves
gained upon him at every bound. A close thicket intercepted his
path, and, rendered desperate, he turned at bay. His nostrils were
dilated, and his eyes seemed to send forth long streams of light.
It was wonderful to witness the courage of the beast. How bravely
he repelled the attacks of his deadly enemies, how gallantly he tossed
them to the right and left, and spurned them from beneath his hoofs;
yet all his struggles were useless, and he was quickly overcome and
torn to pieces by his ravenous foes. At that moment he seemed more
unfortunate than even myself, for I could not see in what manner
he had deserved his fate. (Moodie [1852] 2003, 197)

A number of articles were so apoplectic about these wasters of game
that they found another justification for the bounty: that deer would go
extinct if wolves weren't controlled. The author of "Guardians of Game"
(1903), McVeigh (1911), MacLean (1926), and Eadie (1926) all worry that
wolves will leave the wilderness bereft of deer and moose, animals that are
both an economic resource and a source of pleasure for the sportsman. In
this story, the menace that wolves pose to "the most beautiful and harmless
of all our Canadian game" had to be put down (Eadie 1926, 782). With
their unfair natural advantages, wolves win against noble game every time,
at least in this version of events. Even in 1947 – after being subject to
decades of the bounty – the wolf remained a threat to game: a pack viciously
took more than they could use by slaughtering fifty-seven caribou in one
night (*Rod and Gun* 1947). Wolves were profligate wasters of game, unworthy of the hunting advantages unfairly bestowed upon them, and certainly
not up to the standard of the sportsman's code.
    If that description sounds familiar, it's because it was sometimes applied
to Indigenous people as well. Indeed, wolves and Indigenous people were
often conflated in settler colonial narratives. With regard to hunting, both
were seen as lazy wasters of game who were improvident and prone to
gluttony. Throughout the pages of *Rod and Gun*, authors complain about
the murder of deer, by both Indigenous people and predatory animals.
For instance, an article on hunting in Petawawa from 1911 includes an
image of a dead deer, captioned, "Deer murdered by wolves" (Lemieux
1911, 647). How the photographer had determined the species of the
murderer and why these same wolves hadn't consumed the deer is anyone's
guess. But the same language of murder, slaughter, and impropriety is also

used about Indigenous hunting of deer. In 1902, a letter complains about the "Indians of Nootka Sound, Vancouver Island, [who] seem to have been murdering deer in a wholesale manner" (*Rod and Gun* 1902, 127). Similarly, a year later, Gibbs (1903, 298) points the finger at the Tŝilhqot'in in central British Columbia, whom he accuses of "the wholesale slaughter of game." In a 1906 article, the same trope is deployed, where Indigenous Peoples are defined as unable to control themselves in the face of readily available wildlife. Here the hunting practices of the "Stoney Indians" (Îyâhé Nakoda) in the foothills of the Rocky Mountains in Alberta are used as an example of why Indigenous Peoples should be assimilated into white Canada: "Each year the Government attempts further restrictions, and have [*sic*] prohibited the sale of sheep and goat heads. The rule is a good one, but it does no good so long as the Indians are left uncontrolled. The animals are slaughtered just the same, but the heads instead of giving work to the taxidermist are left rotting on the mountain sides. A large proportion of the meat goes to waste as the Indians are the least provident of mankind ... If agriculture is spreading to the Stoneys [Îyâhé Nakoda] then the Reserve should be moved to a farming district away from the mountains. The present location is merely a temptation to the Indians to fish and hunt whenever they feel inclined, and in defiance of the laws or the seasons" (*Rod and Gun* 1906b, 227). The "Swampy Cree" (Omaškêkowak) are also indicted as wasters of game, this time of moose rather than deer. Roy North (1913, 695) makes this clear: "If these hunters would restrict themselves to the number of moose required for food, things would not be so bad; but their insatiable appetite for killing never fails to get the better of them whenever opportunity occurs, quite regardless of the shameful waste involved." But he also makes this metaphorical association between wolves and Indigenous Peoples literal by suggesting that their profligacy and laziness around hauling the full carcass back to camp actually feeds wolves who feast on the meat left behind (ibid.). For North, the indolence of one group encourages it in another.

At the root of this outrage was a fear that improvidence would spoil the nation. And it was often accompanied by a demand that some branch of government *do* something about it. Thus, both Gibbs and North assert that Indigenous hunting practices must be regulated as part of the white colonial project. For North, if this does not happen, the uncivilized character of wild Canada will persist; he writes: "so surely as the Indian is out of reach of the law, he will give rein to his inherent savagery and lust for blood" (North 1913, 696). If not managed, Canada will lose its wild character, where wildness is measured by the presence of game they wished to hunt. A strange article by Robert Owen presses this claim. Asserting that Canada's strength lies in its abundant nature (in contrast to the United States, and then more unusually to Asia), it is imperative to ensure it is maintained to avoid the decadence and decay of urban space. In this story, nature and nation were imbricated in the building of Canadian identity, not through the fact of Indigenous dispossession but rather because the Canadian nation was meant for white people, even before they arrived: "the primeval conditions of nature, Canada, the future country of the world, peopled with a vigorous northern race, offers herself, disdainful of competition" (R. Owen 1903, 379). The kind of racially informed environmental determinism espoused by Owen – that the Indigenous Peoples who called these lands home were not, in fact, suited to its climate – was part of the effort by settlers to claim the land and naturalize it as their birthright (Berger 1966; Mackey 2002). It disavowed any historical contingency and instead rendered the lands that would become Canada already available for their taking. In so doing, the colonial project could be understood not as a story of genocidal displacement but as one of reclaiming that which white settlers did not even know was already theirs. Settler anxieties around their role in colonial violence could be mollified.

However, this assertion of national identity could only take place if parts of Canada remained wild. Owen (1903, 379) makes this point clear: "But while in America, the advance of civilization has been extremely injurious to almost every species of game, Canada still remains the mistress of the world in this respect, standing unrivalled as the greatest game and sport producing country of the age. Her game flourishes in abundance, and almost every province of the Dominion offers advantages to the sportsman." In Canada, civilization and wildness could exist in tandem. Indeed, their coincidence in one nation made Canada strong and glorious. And so, the wasting of game – by both wolves and Indigenous Peoples – was a threat not only to the game itself but also, more importantly to the nation.

For many settlers, both wolves and Indigenous Peoples were anachronistic features of a former – and best forgotten – time. Tied together in assertions of profligacy and unsportsmanlike practice, both stood in the way of the nation that settlers were trying to build. But the two were bound in another way too. In the effort to replace one form of nationhood with another, made manifest in the establishment of residential schools among other technologies of colonization, attitudes toward wolves were occasionally invoked as part of the "civilizing mission." For instance, a 1935 letter written by the acting secretary of the Department of Indian Affairs to the principal of the Anglican Indian Residential School in Aklavik, Northwest Territories, asked that nuns embark on a "campaign of education" to convince students they should "destroy wolves" and end the Indigenous "superstition" against wolf extermination. The principal replied that the school would "make every effort to eradicate the superstition from the native mind" (Dept. of Indian Affairs correspondence 1935). In the kind of nation imagined by the Department of Indian Affairs, neither the wolf nor Indigenous nations' understandings of it as more than a beast to be eliminated could survive.

THESE VIOLENT DELIGHTS

For many settlers, the literal and metaphorical trespasses of the wolf could not be allowed to persist. The power of the wolf needed to be subdued for one layer of colonial anxiety to be assuaged. As seen in many of the stories presented above, the lupine threat is often met with the reassertion of settler control; more often than not, the wolf dies, even as it frightens or wounds people and more benign game. But it is how wolves die that says something about the apprehension they induced. The risk posed by wolves – to settler lives and livestock, to a sense of ownership, to colonial ideas about the improvement of land and its role in nation building – is countered with an overabundance of violence in the ways settlers dispatched their foe. And for many, the killing of wolves was as much about fun as necessity.

Alex Mackintosh (2017) has written about the role of spectacle in animal sports like dog fighting and bear baiting, noting that they hinge on many of the same signs and systems of power as Foucault's spectacle of the scaffold. He contends that a practice like bear baiting is not only about sovereign power "but also the God-given sovereignty of humans over other species" (Mackintosh 2017, 163). While not animal sport per se, the descriptions of wolf hunts can be read through similar kinds of logics. Indeed, such performances served to re-establish control, demonstrating that settlers had the right to dispose of the land and its inhabitants – both human and nonhuman – in any way they saw fit. As such, they served a pedagogical function, teaching right relations in an uncertain time. To look upon the battered and slaughtered bodies of wolves rendered the wolves' incapacity to stop the colonial project visible. They could be punished for their sins, often in public and retributive ways.

Take, for instance, the frequent references to wolf hunts in the pages of *Rod and Gun*. Here I refer not to three or four men going into the bush to kill wolves (and presumably other animals too), but rather to community wolf hunts, where men gathered in large groups to put down their foes. In

1906, "Our Medicine Bag" tells of a wolf hunt near Lake Superior, necessary to avoid deer extinction. Hunters came from all around to participate. One clever hunter decided to sound a cow bell to scare all the animals, including a female wolf that was fingered as the deer killer, into moving out of the woods in the same direction. The author notes: "It was near dusk when one of the men wounded the wolf by putting a rifle ball through its mouth, and the dripping blood made an easy trail" (*Rod and Gun* 1906c, 1238). The wolf is killed, and the deer are safe from her depredations.

L.O. Armstrong (1907b) describes the common encirclement method, where between five hundred and one thousand men form a tight noose by moving ever inward until the animals captured within have nowhere to go. The same method was also used in the United States. For example, Jon Coleman (2004) describes an 1803 wolf hunt in Vermont precipitated by the near-death of a boy who had been walking home in the woods at dusk. Between four and five hundred hunters gathered, surrounded the woods, closed the circle, and trapped both wolves and foxes in the centre. They skin the wolves and, with the money from the bounty, purchase rum for the hunters. In the "Great Hinkley Hunt" in Ohio in 1818, the same method ensnared "three hundred deer, twenty-one bear, and seventeen wolves, as well as an assortment of racoons, turkeys, and foxes" (ibid., 123). One can imagine similar results from wolf hunts in Canada. Animal life – even deer – could be laid waste to take down wolves.

For Coleman, the ritual of the circle hunt represents a version of Richard Slotkin's regeneration through violence, a means of subduing a wilderness that was out of control. Coleman (2004, 122) notes: "When wolves hunted humans in the lost-travelers stories, they violated the natural order so egregiously that only the harshest retaliation could repair the breach." Fear begat violence. But often, at least in Canada, wolf hunts were less grand, involving perhaps ten rather than one hundred hunters. Their aims were also polyvalent and perhaps a little muddier than the context Coleman describes. For instance, wolf hunts could also be a commercial enterprise. The Canadian Pacific Railway wolf hunt is emblematic in this regard. A series of promotional and instructional articles from 1907 and 1908 tell the story of the CPR wolf hunt and function as part travelogue and part advertisement, enticing tourists to participate in the masculine pursuit of killing wolves. Such excursions, often for American businessmen, were certainly about catching wolves. Indeed, part of the way they were sold was via a specific appeal to masculinity; L.O. Armstrong (1908, 675) notes that "the marvellous improvement that took place in the physique of the participants last year was a revelation even to me." This masculinity could only be achieved in the wild and only through the purchase of products that festooned these articles, from rifles and sleeping bags to snowshoes and ammunition. An article from 1906 details the list of equipment these sportsmen from New York, Chicago, Boston, and Milwaukee will have to secure before they can hunt in the wilds of Canada – all of which are advertised in *Rod and Gun* (Armstrong 1907c).

It matters, of course, that L.O. Armstrong was a colonization agent for the CPR. As the physical infrastructure intended to unite the distant lands that were to make up a confederated Canada, the railway cut through the wild to connect the west to the rest of the country. The CPR opened up the west for mass immigration, working in tandem with the government's policy of "pacification" of Indigenous Peoples across the southern prairies (Daschuk 2019). The role of the colonization agent, then, was to encourage settlement along the route. The CPR actively recruited across Europe to achieve this end. But how could lands be settled if they were teeming with wolves? And so, these wolf hunts were a project of colonizing the landscape, removing not just Indigenous Peoples but also animals like wolves who called the plains home.

Wolves' bodies were also claimed and displayed in ways that asserted settler authority. A good example of this is J.E. Orr's story entitled "Old Time Reminiscences in Old Ontario." He tells of trappers going to check what they've caught – which includes lots of wolves that they kill and skin. One in particular catches their attention: "a beautiful specimen of a swamp wolf" (Orr 1911, 809). The trappers decided that instead of killing this wolf right away, "for fun and excitement" (ibid.), they would tie the wolf's legs to a pole so it hung upside down and carry the animal into town, showing it at every settler house they passed. After serving its purpose of thrilling the townsfolk, "when all the settlement had seen him the wolf was despatched and made one less in the numbers that went barking and galloping through the swamps and forests of York County" (ibid.). The wolf was a curiosity, its body useful insofar as it could titillate, exhilarate, and amuse, but once the novelty passed, so too did the wolf's life.

AMBIVALENCE AND ANXIETY

Wolf hunts did not die with the settling of the country. They continued in a variety of forms through the twentieth century and into the twenty-first. For instance, in 2012, a group of local businesses in Fort St John, British Columbia, organized a wolf hunting contest. The reason would be familiar to settlers from more than a century before: huge packs of wolves were decimating local game. The North Peace Rod and Gun Club spearheaded a contest to run from November 2012 to March 2013, which ranged across wolf mating periods. Prizes were offered for the biggest wolves (cash winnings from between CA$250 and CA$1,000) with a $100 booby prize for the smallest wolf caught (Pynn 2012). For participants, the hunt balanced the scales upset by conservation. For wolf lovers, it amounted to wholesale slaughter of an unfairly maligned animal.

Such wolf hunts are not an uncommon event in BC's interior, but this one caught the public's attention. Articles in the *Vancouver Sun, Ottawa Citizen, National Post, Montreal Gazette,* and *Winnipeg Free Press* amplified the debate, making a local issue in rural BC into a national conversation. Its proponents called it fundamental to maintaining wildlife populations. The North Peace Rod and Gun Club stated very clearly that the goal was not wolf extirpation. And yet, the wolf hunting contest was publicized through the well-worn visual narrative of an aggressive and fearsome wolf, teeth bared and ready to consume people and animals alike (Gage 2012). For some, this revealed the true purpose of the event. Dr Paul Paquet, noted wolf researcher at the University of Victoria, suggested that rather than protecting game from wolves, the contest was motivated by a more primal affect: "It's hunting from a motivation of hate" (cited in Pynn 2012).

Although this particular hunt garnered a lot of press, such wolf – or predator – contests have continued, with rod and gun clubs sponsoring events across the province into 2019. In an open letter addressed to BC Minister of Forests, Lands and Natural Resources Doug Donaldson, fifty-four environmental and animal advocacy groups called for a halt to these contests (Wildlife Protection Coalition 2019). These groups compared the contests to other "blood lust" sports like dog fighting – the kind of spectacles Mackintosh (2017) describes. The Creston Valley Rod & Gun Club disagrees. They name the contest the Caribou and Young Ungulate Survival Project, harkening back to the early wolf hunts that sought to save these animals from murdering wolves. In a YouTube video entitled "I Killed 200 Wolves," released in response to the outcry, a representative of the group Howtohunt.com states that they actually perform a public service in contrast to the "cruel, ruthless" environmentalists who are a peril to ungulate species: "we are now experiencing populations of ungulates being absolutely annihilated beyond being able to repair and come back. They've become annihilated all because of you. Nobody else, 100 percent because if you" (Howtohunt.com 2019). The "you" here – punctuated by finger pointing – seem to be effete urban environmentalists, non-hunters, and people like David Suzuki and Charlotte Dawe (of the Wilderness Committee), both pictured in the video. So, while things have changed – wolves now have defenders – much of the narrative remains the same.

And maybe that's the point. In the end, the wolf has always been a flexible metaphor for settlers. It acts as an ambivalent cipher for colonial anxiety, but the words used to describe it have changed. Sometimes called cowards or villains, weak or bold, cunning or craven, wolves could be used to describe a variety of ills facing settlers. However, the approach to managing this anxiety was not ambivalent; wolf howling and depredation required a purge to cleanse the national body of its impure wildness. What we see on the part of settlers is a biopolitical effort at extermination and fear born out of anxiety – about their place in this new nation, the character of the lands they had come to settle, the legitimacy of their claim, and, more viscerally, whether or not they would be eaten. In chapter 2, we see how that fear is channelled into a new affective register as Canada becomes more settled and wolves become an animal that, while still reviled, presents a threat more to economic than physical health. The wolf still provokes white settlers, but in ways that move from fear to disgust.

2

Disgust

Bounties and Bureaucracies
of Extermination

On 22 October 1926, no less a pillar of the community than Reverend Father Harrington of Mount St Patrick, Ontario, pronounced wolves as vermin in need of extermination. Reported in the *Globe and Mail*, Harrington suggested that "the economic life of many farmers is being threatened by the menace of wolves" in this town near the Quebec-Ontario border (*Globe and Mail* 1926, 5). The priest described the dire circumstance: in twelve months, "the pests" ate sheep valued at more than $1,500 (ibid.). According to Harrington, this assault by wolves was even worse than the threat they posed in "the pioneer days of Ontario" (ibid.). Their depredations were so complete, according to Harrington, that sheep farmers were divesting of their flock. The answer? A government-devised plan of extermination.

Rev. Father Harrington's delineation of wolves as pests is quite different from the narratives explored in chapter 1. By the early to mid-twentieth century, ravening wolves slavering at the door, eager to frighten women and eat children, featured less in talk about wolves. By this time, the threat posed by wolves was both more and less straightforward. Adding to its menace of ripping apart and consuming humans, which animated the discussion in chapter 1, the wolf from the early to mid-1900s is reinvented as a trash animal – Harrington's pest – whose inversion of the natural order of things, often through a pronounced threat to economic practice, needed to be stopped. This new way of looking at wolves did not supplant fear but operated alongside it, signalling a different time, when we are less likely to imagine that we will be eaten. This shift in value, at least on the part of settler Canadians, did not necessarily mark a radically different approach to their encounters with wolves. Put simply: a good wolf was still a dead wolf. It did mean, though, that settlers began to regard wolves not only with fear but also contempt and disgust.

This need for erasure gave life to forms of governmentality that worked, first, through mechanisms like the bounty and, later, through efforts to bureaucratize wolf killing via the employ of experts like park wardens and predator control officers, often through the use of poison. In either iteration, these were biopolitical mechanisms bent on the efficient annihilation of a population deemed vermin. This chapter suggests that when fear turns into disgust, new forms of biopolitical practice are rendered possible to ensure the well-being of the community. It demanded a campaign of purification: wolves became evidence of impurity of the national body, and fear of the contamination they signalled meant they needed to be wiped out before the impurity could spread across the social body.

This purge of wolves in Canada can be set within the broader context of the settler assault on the wilderness. As environmental historian William Cronon (1996) has now famously shown, wilderness is a concept imbued with a surprising amount of culture. In the case of wolves in Canada, this wilderness howled with uncertainty. As explored in chapter 1, this meant that wolf presence (along with that of other predators) marked the surprising liveliness of the landscapes that settlers meant to bend to economic and ideological dictates of the nation. Andrea Smalley (2017) has charted the role that wild animals like beaver, wolves, and buffalo played in colonization in the United States. More specifically, she notes that the processes and practices involved in remaking the land in the settler image – from Indigenous dispossession to claiming the land as private property – ran up against the lifeways of these animals such that "wild animals complicated every part of that reinvention" (Smalley 2017, 6). The same can be said of the Canadian context, where, as George Colpitts (2002, 69) remarks, "obdurate wilderness conditions" needed to be stamped out. Writing specifically about the role that wolves played in this story, Colpitts suggests that this species "seemed to perfectly embody the troubles that newcomers encountered while improving wilderness areas" (ibid.). As this chapter shows, this obduracy – the very tenaciousness of wolves in their intention to remain on the land – fostered a range of biopolitical mechanisms aimed at their removal that were informed by disgust at their continued presence.

THE CULTURAL POLITICS OF DISGUST

"Disgust" is a word that feels almost onomatopoeic. It is evocative of a specific set of sensations and responses: crawling skin, cringing, nausea, a wrinkled nose. One might even recall particular things one finds revolting, like blood or feces, or imagine particular practices, like incest or bestiality. It is a universal response in the presence of the revolting, where the "characteristic facial expression, recoil, and nausea arise automatically, seeming to denote an object so intolerable that the body itself rises in protest against it" (Haynes 2013, 33).

But as William Ian Miller (1998) suggests, it is not just a physiological response to a repulsive stimulus. Disgust has a kind of politics; it is, he argues, "a moral and social sentiment" (Miller 1998, 2; see also Kelly 2011). In his full-length treatise on the subject, Miller submits that what is really at work with disgust is an attachment to purity and the concomitant fear of defilement and pollution. Writing both with and beyond Mary Douglas (1966), Miller agrees that disgust is precipitated by matter out of place – as Douglas would have it – but also suggests that something more is at work than Douglas's brand of structuralism can allow for. Miller uses a messy eater as an example: "The soup on the beard reveals the man as already contaminated by a character defect, a moral failure in keeping himself presentable in accordance with the righteously presented demand that he maintain his public purity and cleanliness of person and not endanger us by his incompetence" (Miller 1998, 4). So, for Miller, it is not just that which is physically gross – vomit, blood, feces, slime, dead bodies – that engenders disgust, though of course, those do. It is also the possibility of pollution by association that structures what we consider to be repulsive and how we respond to it. Porosity – of physical, social, and moral boundaries – is a problem.

Crucially, then, disgust orders, ranks, and stratifies. At the root of disgust for Miller is that capacity (and capaciousness) of disgust to set and police boundaries. Disgust's political dimensions can establish and buttress hierarchical forms, the violation of which is, in itself, disgusting. And so, in Ahmed's (2014, 88) view, "disgust is crucial to power relations." For Miller, it is those humans and nonhumans that are found at the bottom of said hierarchies that sicken: "As a general matter it is the low, the contemptible, that are contaminating; it is inferiority itself that tends to disgust no matter whether it be the inferior position in a classification system of plants or animals or in our own social and moral hierarchies" (Miller 1998, 43). Similarly, Ngai (2005) asserts this fear of contamination compels expulsion; the violation is insupportable.

It is within this register that I suggest settlers in the early to mid-1900s were disgusted by wolves, which motivated all manner of responses to deal with them as vermin in addition to villains. This might seem counterintuitive; disgust would seem more easily provoked by contact with specific kinds of animals, perhaps snakes, cockroaches, or rats, which are more traditionally defined as vermin. However, I maintain that wolves came to be defined as pests, an irritation in the economic stakes of the nation. They came to be thought of as a form of pollution, their depredations seen as endangering the economic safety and productivity of the nation. And their boundary crossing was defined not only through the horrors described in chapter 1 but also as the acts of vermin that required systematic annihilation. As Kelsi Nagy and Phillip David Johnson III (2013, 2) write in the introduction of their edited volume *Trash Animals*, these creatures "carry the myths, symbolism, stories, and violence of human history, because they have historically resisted domestication, because they transgress the boundary of domestic and wild, or because they have been a hindrance to larger human efforts to reorganize the landscape. Some trash animals thrive on the coattails of human colonization and imperialism; some continue to thrive in spite of human resource management and ongoing efforts to eradicate them." And so, during this period, the wolf – once terrifying and later idolized – joined the ranks of foxes, coyotes, cougars, and other animals that, because of their propensity to eat livestock and interfere with human life, became intolerable. And they were thought of as pests, a marker that signals killability in a variety of new ways, a disgust framed through and amplified by the economic costs that settlers were forced to endure. We see wolves labelled as "cruel, cowardly, crafty" and "sneaking" (Armstrong 1907a, 863), as "arrant cowards" (Hope 1907, 990), as "sneaking, thieving" killers of livestock (Orr 1909, 749), as "dangerous and useless pests" (Orr 1910a, 1050), as "varmints" (Williams 1915, 551), and as overly fecund (Motley 1928, 543). In one telling passage, the wolf is figured as without any value at all: "Now for Mr Wolf – what good is he? Insofar as I know, he has no value in or out of our forests. His main ambition is to destroy our game and domestic animals, not only for food, but quite often merely for the sport of killing" (*Rod and Gun* 1950, 42). Wolves were the quintessential discommodity, of no use to settlers and, indeed, a hindrance to them. It is this characteristic – their lack of use and economic value – more than their ferociousness that marked them for wholesale and sustained efforts at eradication.

JACK MINER

Perhaps no one in Canada found wolves more disgusting than their most inveterate hater, Jack Miner (1865–1944). Miner did not loathe wildlife indiscriminately; indeed, he held great admiration for some animals. As an early conservationist and a lover of birds, Miner established Canada's first migratory bird sanctuary in 1904 (The Jack Miner Migratory Bird Foundation, n.d.). But Miner had no love for the predatory animals he termed murderers. In what Tina Loo (2006, 74) calls his "folk taxonomy," Miner classified animals as good or bad based on his own moral assessment. Good animals were those that provided some benefit to people or modelled appropriate social behaviour, from parenting to monogamy. Bad animals were those that did not. Miner reserved his strongest objections for predators, whom he described as "degraded brutes, motivated by their base appetites" (cited in Loo 2006, 81). He also personified and anthropomorphized animals – naming and assigning them characteristics – in an effort to drive home the moral character of his taxonomy (Linton and Moore 1984). Moreover, Miner's mythology had a national imperative: "what's good for the goose in Jack Miner's sanctuary is good for Canada" (Loo 2006, 64).

And the wolf was no good for Canada. In Miner's taxonomy, it was only ever a despicable and disgusting beast. Over the course of many years, he wrote at length about the pernicious character of wolves and how their elimination was paramount. For instance, in 1908, 1909, 1911, 1912, and 1929, he wrote or was quoted in articles in *Rod and Gun* that suggested the wolf was the enemy of the deer, and for this reason should be slaughtered. A few examples from these articles demonstrate his vitriol. In an article entitled "The Big Game in Northern Ontario," Miner (1909, 1051) decried the "immunity" that benefited wolves, making them "big and fierce and emboldened." The fact that wolves continued to exist made them the enemy of the gentle and good deer, whom they hunted with impunity. Miner asserted this again in 1912, when he wrote, "the most deadly enemy of our native deer is the pesky timber wolf, that one wolf can destroy more deer in the course of a year than any Game Warden was ever able to protect. To the experienced deer hunter it is clear that the wolf is the greatest hindrance to the propagation of the deer" (J. Miner 1912, 1360). He echoed these assertions in 1929, when he claimed that between 90 and 95 per cent of deer born in Ontario were killed by these "howling murderers" (J. Miner 1929, 612). In each case, wolves and deer were at opposite ends of Miner's taxonomy, and one should be allowed to thrive while the other should be poisoned, shot, or trapped out of existence (J. Miner 1912).

Miner's delineation of good and bad animals was rooted in his ideas about man's dominion over nature. As both Tina Loo (2006) and Max Foran (2018) recount, Miner was no preservationist. Instead, he felt that humans were duty-bound to control nature – to turn it to their own ends. In this view of the world, deer were animals that were of use to humans as food, clothing, and other goods. Wolves were of no use at all; in fact, by eating deer, they harmed human interests. He notes: "If we could only get rid of the wolves there would be good shooting all over the northern portion of the Province in less than ten years, as I veritably believe there is no part of that wild country where deer cannot thrive and do well (J. Miner 1909, 1051–2). His son, Manly Miner, amplified and extended this sentiment: "We feel that when man came to North America, and took over, the deer should have been preserved for man's food and use, and not for the sport of a horde of rapacious wild beasts, the wolves, bent on killing purely out of lust (M. Miner cited in K.R. Jones, *Wolf Mountains*, 2003, 125). As Karen R. Jones (2003) points out, the fact that wolves also killed for food and that humans often killed for sport was lost on Manly Miner, or conveniently elided. So too, perhaps, was the fact that many Indigenous Peoples, who were here before "[white?] man … took over," had an entirely different perspective on the lupine presence. For many Indigenous nations and particularly those in the various wolf clans, rather than pests, wolves were kin or, at the very least, hunters to be emulated. But in the Miners' view, wolves could only ever be vermin, an impediment to man's control and stewardship of the wild.

For Jack Miner, there was no dispute that wolves didn't merit life. But how to get rid of these wolves was a different question. It is interesting that in Jack Miner's discussion on the matter, he did not support the increased bureaucratization of wolf killing. This was discordant with the wildlife politics of the time, which was increasingly state centred (Loo 2006). In direct reference to wolves, Miner makes this point clear: "The last few years I have received a number of letters requesting that I advocate salary-paid wolf hunters to kill the wolves in Ontario. So far I have refrained from answering such requests, but now, when the Superintendent of our largest Provincial park comes right out and calls our rising generations of Canadian-born manhood "Howling Calamity" this removes the barrier and breaks the chains from my conscience and gives me perfect liberty to say that the total failure to control the wolves in Algonquin Park by hiring men by day, week or month or year system speaks for itself" (J. Miner 1929, 614). Instead, Miner was an early and effective advocate for an expanded bounty, which he thought should be increased to incentivize hunters to "never give up the chase" (cited in *Rod and Gun* 1906a, 137). This preference for the bounty can perhaps be explained through his own lack of formal education and his insistence that experiential knowledge of the wild was the best teacher. For Miner, wildlife conservation officials, with their newly minted degrees, lacked the practical skills – and perhaps sport hunting experience – necessary to make proper decisions about management (Linton and Moore 1984). Linton and Moore (1984, 154) describe Miner's "growing disagreement with and animosity toward scientifically oriented and academically trained wildlife officials," whom he felt put ideas like natural balance and the role of predators in ecosystems above common sense. The bounty, then, was a vehicle to bolster rural knowledge against the onslaught of professionalism. It seems that the enmity between Miner and professionally trained wildlife managers was mutual; Fred Bodsworth, naturalist and novelist, noted that "among the scientists most qualified to judge him Miner was regarded as a naive, but well-meaning crackpot, a dabbler in the scientific field of wildlife management with no understanding of the scientific fundamentals involved" (cited in Linton and Moore 1984, 156).

This debate between those who felt the bounty was the appropriate method of wolf control versus those who emphasized the need for a professionalized system was most clearly articulated by Jack Miner but was not limited to him. However, even the bounty was bureaucratization, at least of a kind. As I explore in subsequent sections, unlike the United States that fully bureaucratized predator control, Canadian provinces relied on a patchwork of bounties, predator control units, and programs implemented by park wardens to control, and hopefully exterminate, wolves in Canada.

RED IN TOOTH AND CLAW

In October 1886, so the story goes, George Lane, foreman and later part-owner of the Bar U Ranch in southern Alberta, was attacked by a pack of wolves. Established in 1882 as a cattle and horse ranch, Bar U became something of an iconic place in the Canadian West, one that has been made into a national historic site recognizing the role of ranching in early Canada. Part of the mythology of this place relies on the story of George Lane and the wolf attack. According to legend, he had been visiting his wife and new child in hospital in Calgary. On his return trip home, he came upon six wolves eating one of the Bar U cows they had just killed. The wolves, perhaps emboldened by blood lust, attacked Lane and his horse. Lane shot five of them and lived to tell the tale. It was memorialized first by the painter Charles M. Russell in 1914, and later by Rich Roenisch's interpretation of the painting in a sculpture called "A Question of Survival" (figure 2.1). In this depiction, Lane, grim-faced with a downturned mouth perhaps signalling disgust, aims his gun at the wolf that is attempting to take down his horse from the front. Another wolf bites the horse's

2.1 Famous sculpture entitled "A Question of Survival" depicting the legend of George Lane fighting with a pack of wolves at Bar U Ranch. Now memorialized as part of a national historic site in Longview, Alberta.

hindquarters, and a third runs alongside, tongue lolling and ferocious. As Michael D. Wise (2016, 32) asserts, this story became emblematic for the experience of wolves on the range: "The tall tale, never entirely dispelled, grew into foundational myth for the stock industry in southern Alberta." In Wise's interpretation, the story and the sculpture that depicts it cleansed the rancher of the violence inherent in the cattle industry, while casting Lane (and all other ranchers) in the role of protector of innocent livestock. In this story that became a legend, the threat that wolves posed was not only economic but also moral. In addition, as the title of the sculpture suggests, it was a battle cast in terms of man versus animal. The wolf survives or the rancher does, but the two cannot co-exist.

It is true that wolf attacks on livestock aren't pretty. As a friend of mine who raises sheep will tell you, in her experience, wolves will take a sheep down at the haunches and then eat it from the spine out. Similarly, wolf predation on cattle starts by ripping out the hindquarters, rectum, or vulva.

The wolves then wait for the animal to bleed out as it stumbles around in shock (Lay, n.d.). Or wolves will disembowel a cow or calf, ripping away its stomach until its innards fall to the ground (ibid.). So, beyond their economic losses, ranchers and farmers had to contend with the viscerality of wolf attacks. For instance, at a cattle kill, ranchers may have found blood, hair, bones, and a partially consumed corpse strewn across the area (Agricultural Environmental Partnership Initiative 2005). It is no surprise, then, that this engendered disgust. Co-existence with predators is not an easy business, particularly if one doesn't take loss as inevitable.

Yet according to Stanley Young (1946), such attacks were both expected and endured until the late 1800s. This might be in part because wolves were common creatures on the landscape and the rangelands were far from settled. Citing John McDougall, a hunter who pursued the last of the buffalo on the Great Plains in the 1860s, wolves were everywhere: "I have never seen gray wolves so numerous as now. When we are skinning and cutting up the buffalo they form a circle around us and wait impatiently until we load the meat into the Red River carts. Then as we move away, they rush in to fight over the offal. Many wild fights are witnessed but ammunition is scarce and we refrain from shooting" (cited in Young 1946, 116). Similar stories were recounted by Isaac Cowie (1913), who wrote that wolves would follow them as they hunted buffalo, taking advantage of the trails they forged and sitting always outside the range of their guns. They remained numerous in the Canadian West, even as ranching took a foothold in the region; as natural prey was extirpated, wolves turned to livestock as a new source of food: "In the year 1885 they [wolves] were still quite common, their raids on stock at the ranches west of Calgary being frequently noted in the newspapers. By this time, however, the creatures were outlawed and a bounty offered for their destruction. A full-grown wolf was considered capable of killing horses and cattle to the value of about one thousand dollars annually. A female wolf, with a litter of half-grown pups was even more of a scourge to the stockman. She dragged down and killed many colts and calves, not for food alone but also to give her young a lesson in making a kill" (Dan McGowan cited in Young 1946, 116–17). Wolves ate the "lively commodities" (Collard and Dempsey 2013) that farmers and ranchers sought to structure their economic futures around. Sheep, horses, cattle, pigs, and poultry were on the wolves' menu, especially as some of them replaced wild ungulates. As the letters of William Wallace to his sister Maggie attest, the canid threat to rancher lifestyles emerged coincident with the colonization of Canada and the decimation of local wildlife. For instance, in July 1883, Wallace writes: "On Tuesday

I surprised a large timber wolf feasting his eyes on our calf. They are big fierce brutes. The calf is better looked after now" (Wallace, Coates, and Morrison 2015, 173). Wallace writes throughout letters to his "Dear Maggie" that wolves were numerous, seen and heard across the plains they were trying to settle. His letters often worry about the fate of cows left in pasture (ibid., 75) and joke about the "parliamentary meetings" in the form of howls that wolves hold on neighbouring farms (ibid., 186). Similarly, a *Rod and Gun* series appearing in 1910 but recalling life in "pioneer days" notes that sheep were the most imperilled from these pests of rural Canada:

> These wolves proved very destructive to the sheep which were kept by most of the early settlers for the sake of the wool they furnished. An eye had to be kept on the sheep in the daytime and at night they had to be well secured if they were to be safeguarded. One night the wolves broke into our sheepfold and, having full swing with the defenceless sheep, killed twelve of them. On another occasion one of the sheep would be neither coaxed nor driven into the fold. Finally with the remark that "there'd be a dead sheep in the morning," the men had to leave it and dead sure enough it was when found next morning.
>
> One fall afternoon the sheep came towards the barn at a gallop. They were bleating most piteously, and when we ran to find out the cause we saw a big, swampy wolf, of a grizzly, grayish color, closely following the sheep and barking at them most savagely. He never ran after sheep again, for a rifle ball soon caused him to turn up his toes. With a bounty on their scalps and the fright and injury caused the people, wolves were shot and trapped upon every occasion. Soon they became scarce and with a great increase in population these dangerous and useless pests became extinct in Western Ontario. (Orr 1910a, 1050)

Similarly, a writer from Magrath, Alberta, notes that wolves were "making serious inroads on the cattle and old timers declared that never in their recollections had they seen coyotes as ferocious as they were this year" (*Rod and Gun* 1913, 1130). According to some, this violation was biblical. In a 1902 article in the *Globe*, which compared the sometimes-divergent interests of farmers and ranchers in the Canadian West, the author notes that "since the time of the old Hebrew patriarchs" the "man of flocks and herds has put his faith in the natural increase of his stock" (*Globe* 1902). Wolves threatened this natural increase, and it was left to the Stock Grower's Association "to send the wolf after the buffalo" (ibid.).

The problem of wolves eating livestock was not confined to the Prairie provinces, nor to the late 1800s and early 1900s. Accounts from Ontario stress that wolves were an ever-increasing impediment to the raising of livestock – especially sheep – such that many farmers considered abandoning the enterprise, as noted in the introduction to this chapter. For instance, in a 1924 article documenting the loss of six sheep to predation in two days in Sault Ste Marie, the author makes the broader argument that unless wolves are killed, sheep raisers will go out of business. In order to maintain sheep raising in the province, the "pests must be eradicated" (*Globe* 1924, 6). A similar refrain is found in articles throughout this period in Haliburton (Morrison 1928), Manitoulin (*Globe* 1928; Hambleton 1929), Tyendinaga (*Globe* 1934), Kinloss (*Globe and Mail* 1938), Renfrew (*Globe* 1927c), and Parry Sound (*Globe* 1936). Because of wolves, in the words of Clifford McLeod, once-lucrative "sheep raising is precariously conducted" (*Globe* 1929, 22). And the precarity was increasing rather than decreasing; it seems, commonsensically, that as agricultural settlement pushed up against the edges of the wild, it provoked more and more conflict with predatory animals. Indeed, one article in the *Globe* (1926a) suggested that "these four-footed pests" – wolves, bears, and cougar – were migrating southward and have "cleaned out the flocks which a few years ago were considered among the most vigorous in the Province."

It is not difficult to understand why the wolf rankled. The theft of livestock was not only an economic loss but also a loss of certainty. Michael Wise (2016) contends that wolves revealed the fiction upon which settlers built their lives: that humans were in control of the landscape and the animals that inhabited it. Attacks on livestock showed a different power at work, one that they tried to understand within their existing frameworks. The gruesome remains of their once lively property showed settlers that, despite their understanding of the land as their own, there were always other stories at work. Andrea Smalley (2017, 81–2) puts this eloquently: "When wolves attacked domestic pigs, calves, and sheep, they simultaneously hamstrung the developing ideologies of improvement and possessive individualism on which Anglo-American claims to legitimate occupation and possession rested." I would add to the analysis of both Wise and Smalley that this violation prompted feelings of disgust about a pest who served no useful end. Figuring out how to dispose of them thus became an animating conversation between 1900 and the 1950s.

"ONE WOLF IS A LOT OF WOLF"[1]

The question was: how to eradicate the wolves? Two coincident, though sometimes oppositional, tactics were designed to deal with this pestilential menace. The first relied on individual citizens – often hunters, trappers, ranchers, and farmers – to keep wolf populations in check via the bounty. The second was a more systematized approach to killing, usually carried out by provincial employees. These mechanisms of extermination were not mutually exclusive, though they were sometimes in tension with one another. They operated simultaneously as spikes on the same biopolitical mace intended to bash wolves out of existence. But there were key differences. The bounty was more haphazard and, Michael D. Wise (2016, 23) contends, was mostly practised by "the poor, the unemployed, or the colonized." It was also harder for government officials, whether county or provincial, to budget for bounty payouts; some years saw record claims and others very few. Furthermore, the practice was subject to fraud: people presented pelts and ears in multiple jurisdictions or claimed bounties on wolves caught in other provinces or townships. In contrast, the bureaucratic approach offered more regulatory and budgetary certainty. It also moved the practices of wildlife management into the realm of expertise rather than backcountry know-how, further entrenching the notion that the Crown was the rightful sovereign of the Canadian wilds (Loo 2006). However, more bureaucratized killing also had the potential to amplify and crystallize the critique directed toward authorities, who often were accused of not doing enough to keep the wolf menace in check; indeed, as we will see, game managers were sometimes accused of acting as protectors of the animals they were charged with killing. Nevertheless, the bounty and provincial programs of predator management served the same aim in different ways: to protect settlers' economic interests against the scourge of vermin wolves.

Making a Business Out of Death

The bounty on wolves was not new in the late-nineteenth and twentieth centuries. The first wolf bounties were established in 1793 in Upper and Lower Canada. However, the bounty as a mechanism of predator control gained new resonance during this time period. This was especially the case at the beginning of the twentieth century as a new conversation emerged about the best way to rid Canada of the menace of wolves. And it was a matter of heated debate. On the one side were those who felt the bounty was the correct method to keep wolf populations in check. Indeed, bounties served a dual aim as both a mechanism for predator control and a supplement to rural incomes (Loo 2006). An economy arose around the bounty that benefited many of those struggling to live off the land while rendering what was once a discommodity into a commodity. Wise (2016) makes this argument about the bounty in Montana, but it resonates in Canada too: the bounty transformed wolves into economic objects.

However, the problem was that since the bounty had been in place in many regions in Canada for such a long time, it should have already done its job. That it hadn't, according to bounty supporters, had less to do with the fact that wolves will increase breeding to make up for decreasing numbers (Fuller, Mech, and Cochrane 2003) and more to do with their pelts being insufficiently incentivized. Jack Miner, one of the most vociferous champions of the bounty system, felt it would be the most successful means to kill wolves; its failures were linked to the government not paying hunters enough to track down their foe. What was required was an increase in the payment for proof of a dead wolf: "The bounty is not large enough to induce a wholesale slaughter of these marauders. In my opinion it should be doubled. This would be some encouragement to hunters to destroy these pests" (J. Miner 1912, 1360). In Miner's view, the $15 bounty in Ontario (at the time of his writing) made sense when pelts for other fur-bearers were low. But while the price paid for otter or mink increased, the wolf bounty remained the same (M.F. Miner 1972). As such, at least according to Jack Miner, hunters and trappers aiming to maximize earnings would focus on those animals that would bring them bigger gains. Miner was not the only commentator who felt this way. Many suggested that the reason the bounty was ineffective in wolf control was that the amount paid was too low. J.A. Reid (1920, 328) made this exact point: "I have been in·the woods myself, a man would be foolish to go to all kinds of trouble to trap a wolf that will give him the small price of twenty dollars, when he can trap a poor innocent animal that will give him as far as one hundred dollars, and all the time the wolf is doing his share and destroying the deer as fast as he can." Reid recommended a bounty of $50 per animal to incentivize wolf killing. W.A. Eadie (1926) suggested that the problem was variation in bounty amounts; his solution was a harmonization across the provinces. In 1928, the Ontario Hunters' annual meeting discussed the bounty and felt an increase to $40 was necessary to protect deer (*Rod and Gun* 1928). W.J. Moody (1929) reported that Ontario hunters were very disappointed when this increase did not come to pass. The pages of *Rod and Gun* were filled with entreaties to increase the bounty on wolves so that this "most cunning of animals" (Ontario Game and Fisheries Commission 1912, 215) could finally meet its end.

One theme that emerged in arguments around the bounty's effectiveness with regard to wolf control was its racialized and classed undertones. In a short article entitled "Wolves in British Columbia," the author ends with the following: "Couldn't the Government be stirred up into giving a bigger bounty so that it would pay a white man to make a business of hunting wolves" (*Rod and Gun* 1909b, 611)? This emphasis on the whiteness of the proposed hunters served two aims. First, it seems that Indigenous people often had to be convinced and coerced to hunt and trap wolves. In 1908, L.O. Armstrong makes this explicit in his article on the Canadian Pacific Railway wolf hunt:

The Indian is not a wolf hunter. There are three chief reasons for this:

1 – His Indian religion has left within him a superstitious fear of killing a wolf.
2 – He has a horror of handling poison, which might be explained by the possibly infrequent washing of the hands. There are clean Indians who wash frequently, however.
3 – Wolf hunting does not pay as well as hunting the fox, mink, otter, marten, fisher etc., etc., with trap and poison and therefore the trap hunter will not bother with wolf hunting. (Armstrong 1908, 960)

The Ontario Game and Fisheries Commission Report, 1909–11, employed similar racist narratives. Here the authors relied on the trope of the "lazy Indian," who could not be relied upon to control predators: "Consequently, although many Indians in these regions will at times undertake some form of labour, such as guiding or the moving of merchandise, for which they receive good pay, and will, also, sell the results of their trapping operations which not infrequently net them considerable sums, in general they are loath to undertake prolonged or steady work, and what money they make disappears with astonishing rapidity, so that during a great portion of the year food is with them a question of no little moment" (Ontario Game and Fisheries Commission 1912, 199).

The second thrust to this idea that white men should be incentivized to hunt wolves was also a story of the nation. If white men sought to legitimize their claim to the land and make it safe for the profound reshaping of the landscape that was agriculture and ranching, then they needed to be at the vanguard of the wolf's destruction. But this was a classed argument too. Michael D. Wise (2016), in his analysis of wolfers in the late nineteenth century, notes that they came to be seen as subhuman, as disgusting as that which they trapped. According to Wise, these hunters had to emulate their quarry, thus they shared the stain of guilt by association. Wolfers were seen as degenerate expressly because they were so effective at finding their prey: "The mimetic ability to 'live like a wolf' was crucial to effectively killing wolves, but it was also a major obstacle to wolfers' abilities to claim their labor as legitimate" (Wise 2016, 26). Wise argues that this was particularly the case with wolfers who baited and poisoned wolves since they had to track and stalk them, spending countless days in the wild. Thus, the exhortation to encourage white men to hunt wolves for the bounty pointed to a different cultural politics of predator control, one that did not require the hunter to become wolf – with its racialized and classed connotations. Instead, it "transformed wolves into money" (Wise 2016, 37) and, in so doing, made their pursuit the purview of both wealth and whiteness. The effort to clear the plains of wolves for settlers had to be white man's work if they aimed to keep the land for themselves.

Interestingly, one of Canada's most well-known wolfers hunted them before the bounty. John George "Kootenai" Brown was a white wolfer who later became the first superintendent of Waterton Lakes National Park in southern Alberta. Leading somewhat of a storied life, Brown is said to have been a prospector, trapper, trader, and subject of "hoary myth" (G.A. MacDonald 1995). In his biography of Brown, excerpts of which were published in *Rod and Gun,* William McDougall Tait describes Brown's brief career as a wolfer emerging at the time of near exhaustion of the buffalo on the plains in the late nineteenth century. He notes that while there was no bounty at the time, Brown could easily fetch $2 per pelt and his pack of fellow hunters could take close to 1,000 wolves in a single winter (McDougall Tait 1921). This volume of death was accomplished through poison. He describes how these buffalo hunters turned wolf hunt-ers always poisoned their quarry, usually by baiting a buffalo carcass: "It was a common thing to get twenty wolves dead the first morning after the poison has been put out. Instances have been known where fifty to eighty have been poisoned and old Bill Martin who was my partner in the Sweet Grass Hills one winter tells that he once got one hundred and twenty-five wolves in one week within two hundred yards of a big bull buffalo bait" (McDougall Tait 1921, 1019).[2] Wise (2016, 27) explains the practice in detail: "After procuring a bait animal, wolfers rolled it onto its back and disembowelled it, slicing open the belly in a wide oval. With the organs and digestive tract removed, wolfers dumped strychnine granules into the

bait animal's body cavity, called the 'tub,' where they slathered poison
with the animal's blood and chunks of its heart, liver, and other tissues.
Then they scattered the blood and toxic morsels all around the body, killed
another bait animal, and repeated the process." In his exploration of the
entanglements of settler colonialism with buffalo skins, wolf pelts, and
whisky that made up the "Whoop-Up Country's" economy that ran across
the Alberta-Montana borderlands, Wise charts an ecological cascade,
where the mass slaughter of buffalo, both for profit and to force the
Niitsitapi onto reserves, allowed wolves to multiply and gave rise to wolfing
as a practice.

Buffalo and wolf deaths were stitched together in a necropolitical effort
to clear the plains. While bison might have initially been the primary target
and the means to cut the connections between Indigenous Peoples and
their nonhuman kin, their deaths could serve two ends. Baiting their
carcasses – which settler hunters often left to rot, taking only the hide
(Estes 2019) – offered these bison cum wolf hunters opportunity for a
second kill, maximizing their profit. Discommodity was transformed into
commodity. So, while never an explicit strategy of colonization like the
extermination of the buffalo, wolfing turned an economically disgusting
beast into something valuable in settler colonial terms. Wolves and buffalo
were connected in another way too: as the buffalo was decimated,
Indigenous Plains nations found themselves having to eat the skinned wolf
carcasses left by these hunters or face starvation (Daschuk 2019).

That Kootenai Brown hunted these wolves before the bounty was
established in Alberta should probably come as no surprise. The bounty
system was not monolithic; it would be more appropriate to speak of a
patchwork of bounty systems administered unevenly across the provinces
and territories. For instance, in Atlantic Canada, wolves were mostly missing from the landscape by the time the bounty debate was heating up
elsewhere (Hillwood, n.d.). In Quebec, the bounty was in effect from the
late eighteenth century but operated and was understood differently because
of their seigneurial land system (D. Ingram 2013). Bounties were established
in Manitoba in 1878, in Saskatchewan and Alberta in 1899, and in British
Columbia in 1900 (Proulx and Rodtka 2015) but operated through different procedures and authorities. Some bounties were paid by the province,
supplemented by additional payments from the county or municipality (as
in Ontario); others were established and fronted by stock growers' associa-
tions (as in Alberta), rod and gun clubs, or farmers' groups. Indeed, some
of the private bounties were much more lucrative. In 1915, the Western
Stock Growers' Association made payments of $100 per dead wolf in

2.2 "Fox and Wolf Skins Near Fort McMurray, Alta, 1936."

southern Alberta, which, Wise (2016) points out, was sometimes more than what ranchers would fetch for their cattle or horses. A kind of moral panic had set in across the plains because wolf predation made settler life on the range even more precarious. The high bounty, then, performed ideological as well as economic work. As Colpitts (2002, 68) recounts, killing wolves was not enough: their bodies were made into an example of triumph over the wild, "appearing as trophies in shop windows in High River."

In the Yukon, a wolf bounty was established in the 1920s and mostly employed strychnine as its technology of elimination (Yukon Wolf Management Planning Team 1992). The Northwest Territories sometimes had state-sponsored predator control programs and sometimes partnered with private concerns (Wise 2016). Different places and times also had different objectives behind the bounty: the prevention of livestock damage and death, rabies control, and the defence of wild game like the caribou, moose, or deer were all deployed as justifications.

Among these differences was a common goal: to establish and maintain necropolitical practices that informed the attempted elimination of one animal for the benefit of others. The various bounties served both economic and affective ends, creating populations of animals to be managed. Like Jack Miner's articulation of good and bad animals, wolves were vermin – pests in need of extermination – and livestock, as well as wild animals like caribou, moose, and deer, were valuable commodities in need of conservation. And so, as I have argued elsewhere, the bounty was politics by other means (Rutherford 2019). Bounties sought to alleviate anxiety and reassert human control over an unmanaged wild, whether this "wild" took the form of attacks on livestock or ungulates. As such, it was a biopolitical reordering of the landscape at the behest of colonial ends. The Ontario Game and Fisheries Commission Report of 1912 made this evident:

> In a country developing in civilization and increasing in population the pioneer settler still performs a service to the public which it is hard to estimate at its intrinsic value. New country is broken up, prepared and improved, to the increase of the public wealth and to the ultimate benefit of posterity, at the cost to the settler and his family of an existence below the general standard of comfort and prosperity of the community. It would seem unreasonable, therefore, to begrudge some little advantage to these pioneers over the rest of the community in the matter of game privileges. On the other hand game is undoubtedly a public asset, which, after its primary function has in large measure disappeared, none the less continues to be of equal, if not increasing, value in its general effect on the moral and material welfare of the population, and it is evident that as the game areas and game diminish before the advance of civilization, those living on the land under conditions of average comfort, or with reasonable facilities to do so if they choose at their disposal, can no longer expect to be privileged above the general community in the matter of game, but must rest content to submit to the regulations and restrictions which are imposed on the public in the interests of the common weal.
> (Ontario Game and Fisheries Commission 1912, 192–3)

Was the bounty effective? It probably depends on how you define effectiveness. In terms of sheer numbers, many thousands of wolves were killed across Canada during the bounty period. Take Ontario as an example. The bounty paid on wolf pelts or ears in the province steadily increased at the urging of both farmers and hunters (with some hiccups) across the late nineteenth and early twentieth centuries. It was $10 in 1892, $15 in 1900, $20 in 1918, $40 in 1920, then back to $15 in 1924 (but claimants could retain and sell their pelts). In 1930, the bounty was raised again, to $25, then reduced in 1933 to $15, and increased in 1941 to $25 (Omand 1950, 426). The annual administrative payments for the wolf bounty increased accordingly, with the provincial government paying just $5,406 in 1905 to a high of $91,297.27 in 1928. That means that in 1928 over 6,000 wolves, wolf pups, and coyotes were killed and their pelts presented

2.3 Trapline Management Officer John Macfie with two large wolf pelts submitted by Indians in the Patricia District for bounty payment ($25 each).

for bounty payments (Omand 1950, 429), compared to approximately 360 animals in 1905. But even if we ignore this one exceptional year, between 1925 and 1948, on average 2,500 wolves were killed per year in Ontario. By any measure, that's a massive number of dead wolves.

Yet in spite of the bounty, wolves persisted, their decimation more fully realized through the bureaucratized means of control discussed below.

However, if we think about the bounty as a biopolitical mechanism rather than simply a tool for extermination, the way we judge its efficacy changes. From this perspective, the bounty did not only regulate wolves and coyotes; it also regulated the humans who were framed within its domain. The ranchers, Indigenous nations, hunters, trappers, government employees, wolves, deer, sheep, and cows caught up in this regime of regulation were part of a larger project to fundamentally alter human-nonhuman relations in the lands we now call Canada. The bounty, then, was more than a wildlife management strategy: it was a tool of nation building. Put differently, it became an incentive to reify specific claims to the land – for ranching, farming, hunting, and settlement – which secured an understanding of wolves only ever as problematic vermin in need of elimination rather than a more generous or even complicated understanding of them as predators. Wolves went from frightening to disgusting because, more and more, the land occupied by settlers looked less and less wild; once wolves were thought to be controlled by settlers, terror was not the primary response. But the wolves' continued presence on the land also revealed the slipperiness of the nation-building project.

These are the reasons why the bounty persisted in the face of evidence that it did not achieve its intended aim of wolf extermination. And indeed, there were rumblings about its efficacy almost from its inception. For instance, in 1902, James Dickson suggested that the real culprit for the decline of deer in Ontario was human hunters. In a sardonic turn, he noted: "We have spent many an hour listening to harrowing tales by poor settlers, of the havoc committed amongst the deer by wolves, but have never met one who admitted that either he or his mongrel dogs killed any by other than lawful means, or at improper seasons, or any other variety of game, although evidence to the contrary was palpable in all their surroundings. That Mr Wolf is correctly held responsible for a great slaughter of game can be no doubt, but withal he is blamed for many black crimes of which he is entirely innocent and were he a human biped who could take advantage of the law of libel, what rare chances there would be of him securing heavy damages" (Dickson 1902, 8). While Dickson was strident in explaining the deficiencies of the bounty, not many joined his cause until the 1930s and 1940s. But by then, the floodgates had opened. In 1944, Adolph Murie published his now-classic text *The Wolves of Mount McKinley*, which showed that the bounty worked only to trim rather than eliminate wolf numbers; wolves simply bred up to the gaps in their population (A. Murie 1944). In an undated memorandum, Harrison F. Lewis, the first director of the Canadian Wildlife Service, wrote that the bounty was a failure:

For three centuries guns, traps, poison, and bounties have been used against wolves in North America. During that time wolves, which were once numerous in the region east of the Mississippi, as well as west of that river, have disappeared from a large part of their former range. This extirpation of wolves over a large part of the continent was not brought about by guns, traps, poison, and bounties alone. Wolves maintained themselves against these agencies in the east for a long time. New York State was not cleared of wolves until the close of the nineteenth century. It was the white man's alteration, on a large scale, of the environment, and the building up of a large human population, that made regional eradication of the wolf possible. As long as the Northwest Territories and the Yukon Territory contain a scanty human population and large tracts of territory in a natural state, wolves will maintain themselves there and payment of bounties will have little effect on their numbers. (Lewis 1930–55, 2)

By 1950, Omand similarly declared that the bounty "has little effect" and "that the greatest number of bounty claims originate in those areas in Ontario where deer are thriving, according to available reports" (Omand 1950, 434). And Douglas Pimlott, who would undertake the first sustained scientific research on wolves in Ontario, described the bounty "a crime cloaked under the misnomer of 'conservation'" (cited in Loo 2006, 166).

Taking Manitoba as an example, it is clear how the case against the bounty was increasingly informed by the kind of scientific evidence that Jack Miner and others abhorred. For instance, the Premier's Office Files from 1954 to 1957 contain a digest of remarks from Stanley P. Young and Edward A. Goldman's *The Wolves of North America*, which was published in 1944. The passages excerpted for the premier's consideration included the argument that the bounty system was "honeycombed with fraud" and worked against its own interests by only catching those wolves who were not smart enough to avoid the traps, leaving a wily and wizened population to thrive (Premier's Office Files 1954–57). Found too among these excerpts was the argument that the bounty was at the same time ineffective and more expensive. The authors advocated for the "more orderly and scientific control that can be applied through the employment of trained hunters and trappers whenever wildlife conditions warrant" (ibid.). The notion that bounty seekers were being paid to do labour that they would likely do for free (Parks Canada fonds 1947) compounded by accusations of rampant fraud made the bounty less and less attractive. Instead, more formalized and systematic efforts at predator control – staffed by provincial or federal employees, and sometimes those seconded temporarily to official roles – overtook the bounty as the preferred means of vermin management. But for a while, both systems existed simultaneously, as did the arguments for and against each approach.

Professionalizing Wolf Killing

In the early part of the twentieth century, in tandem with demands for an increased wolf bounty came a call to professionalize the slaughter of this vermin species. Those who supported a continuation of – and increase in – bounty payments suggested that the intimate knowledge of predators that hunters and trappers accrued over their lifetime in the woods would win out in the war against wolves. This was borne out in various articles in *Rod and Gun* (see, for example, Thiessen 1914; Hutton 1916) as well as by conservation authorities such as Jack Miner. As Tina Loo (2006) has remarked, the attachment to the bounty had much to do with attempts to shore up "backcountry" knowledge against the perceived onslaught of professionalism and, later, scientific authority. But calls for professionalizing the killing of wolves were also present. In large part, this was because professionalization was the path followed in the United States, where the members of the Bureau of Biological Survey were employed to hunt and kill predatory wildlife. It was a system much admired in Canada, especially because of the results: as Jon Coleman (2004, 192) puts it, "from 1900 to 1950 American wolf hunters cleared the animals from every region in the temperate United States in which a human could grow a marketable plant or animal." This systematic approach to killing wolves was never fully embraced in Canada – but we did have professionalization of a kind.

For some, the government's role was obvious: it was the duty of the provinces (or the federal government in national parks) to remove the wolf menace. Speaking directly to the debate between the bounty and more professionalized approaches, E.C. Cross (1930, 746) noted: "The popular demand is for a higher bounty and it has been so insistent that sportsmen have lost sight to some extent of the other remedy – the employment of professional wolf hunters." Like many around the same time, Cross suggested that Canada should take up the American model. Another commentator noted that wolves should be killed by professionals because the bounty system was too inconsistent; in some years, the take was high but in others, far too low to be effective (Raoul 1928). One trapper employed by the US Bureau of Biological Survey, G.E. Gillam, addressed this issue in *Rod and Gun*. He argued that the bounty had been an abject failure in the United States, especially because fraudulent claims were rampant. Writing against the mythologizing of wolf hunters, Gillam (1929, 693) had this to say: "There is no mysterious fetish connected with wolf trapping. The public conception that one must be closely allied with Houdini, Sir Conan Doyle and Daniel Boone to catch wolves, is all bosh. Man has a brain with the power of reasoning far superior to that of an animal. He has the benefit of the experience of others. The poor wolf really has no chance against him when he makes an honest effort to exterminate him."

A more active and prescriptive role for the government was also being considered by bodies like the Ontario Game and Fisheries Commission (later the Department of Game and Fisheries). As early at their 1912 report, the commission recognized the importance of professionalization for wildlife management and that they should employ skilled officers at good wages to do this work (Ontario Game and Fisheries Commission 1912). The emphasis was even more obvious with the release of the *Report of the Special Committee on the Game Situation* in 1933 (Ontario Special Committee on Game Situation 1933). This report, authored by W.D. Black and commissioned by Charles McCrea, minister in charge of the Department of Game and Fisheries, aimed to provide recommendations as to how game resources might be improved in the province. At the beginning of the report, the committee describes three periods of game protection in Ontario, which point to the increasing bureaucratizing and professionalization of wildlife management. The period before 1890 was characterized by something of a vacuum, which the report only notes was "Before Game and Fish Commission" (Black; Ontario Special Committee on Game Situation 1933, 10). Next comes the establishment of the Game and Fisheries Commission, which lasts until 1906. In the third period management became subsumed under the more formalized Department of Game and Fisheries. As the report describes: "The third period has witnessed the development of game law enforcement on a more adequate scale, the division of the Province into districts and reduction in the quantity of game that may be taken under license" (Black; Ontario Special Committee on Game Situation 1933, 10). Beginning in 1906, then, the department undertakes projects of regulation and rationalization that were unthought of previously.

Of course, management was keenly focused on the animals that looked upon game as prey. In discussing what to do with "The Menace of the Wolf" (Black; Ontario Special Committee on Game Situation 1933, 22), the report suggests that the American model of establishing a corps of hunters might also be possible in Ontario. But in the end, the report concludes that until such plans can be made, both the bounty should remain in effect (and harmonized with that of Quebec and Manitoba) and permits for the poisoning of wolves should be issued to "experienced and responsible persons" (Black; Ontario Special Committee on Game Situation 1933, 91–2). As such, neither the success of the American model nor the suggestion that the bounty was not doing its job could fully extinguish the importance of the latter to rural communities, both economically and affectively. As Douglas Pimlott (1961a) notes, there was a period of about ten years in most western provinces when bounties and government-led control systems overlapped, before the bounty was abolished altogether. So, they were not mutually exclusive mechanisms of control but rather co-existed – in something of an uneasy relationship and informed by different ideologies of wildlife management – until the cost and evidence of the bounty's ineffectiveness made it insupportable.

While discussed for some time, the move toward the systematization of predator control really took root in the 1950s, especially, as Pimlott (1961a) notes, after the Canadian Predator Control Conference advocated for the repeal of provincial bounty systems in 1954. In his article entitled "Wolf Control in Canada," Pimlott charts the history of this shift. The western provinces were at the forefront of this change, with British Columbia establishing the first and most robust unit with their Predator Control Division in 1947. Other western provinces followed suit, but their programs were not nearly as strong: for instance, in Saskatchewan, there was a wolf program with no dedicated employees; in Manitoba, there was only one employee (Pimlott 1961a). It took Ontario until the 1960s to heed this call. A 1963 *Weekly News Release* of the Department of Lands and Forests announced plans to hire predator control officers "whose main job it will be to assess reports of predator damage, conduct thorough investigations and select the best method for eliminating the problem" (Ontario Department of Lands and Forests 1963, 2). Loo (2006) notes that Quebec was also resistant to the shift; while provincial employees were involved in predator control, the efforts were never as systematized as they were in the west (see also D. Ingram 2013).

These early predator control officers most often dealt with noxious animals through poisoning, using either strychnine or sodium monofluoroacetate, commonly known as Compound 1080. A typical approach was to set out a number of poisoned baits and return a number of weeks later to collect the bodies of animals that had been poisoned (see, for example, Lemieux 1912, 52). This was the approach taken in an experimental area of some 600 square kilometres in northern Manitoba in 1949. It proved so successful that Saskatchewan adopted the protocol, and Manitoba's director of game and fisheries, G.W. Malaher (1952), remarked that "there are not enough wolves left this year to warrant the expense of continued control" in the experimental area.

But there were concerns about the use of poison. Strychnine had long been used to kill vermin in Canada and the United States, but Compound 1080 was more recent, developed in the Second World War as a rodenticide (Addison 2019). Poisoning vermin was always a fraught endeavour, with some arguing it was the most efficient way to kill larger numbers of wolves (*Rod and Gun* 1912b) while others suggested the potential for collateral damage, understood as the death of beneficial species that might also eat baited carcasses, was too great (*Rod and Gun* 1912a). These concerns remained in place throughout the 1900s. At least one Cree community in Fort Chipewyan near Wood Buffalo National Park in Alberta objected to the use of strychnine because of its impact on other animals (Department of Indian Affairs, n.d.). The response from the administration of the Northwest Territories, it seems, was to dismiss their complaint since poisoning was "a most satisfactory means of reducing the number of these predators" (ibid.). Despite poisoning's blanket efficacy, concerns remained. As such, experimental wolf poisoning programs were established to test their success. One such program was enacted in Kenora, Ontario, in 1955–56 to determine not only the best techniques of poisoning but also whether other – more valuable – fur-bearers were being poisoned through this practice (Linklater, n.d.). The results of this experiment were inconclusive as it seems, in something of a telling turn, the pilot paid to spot the dead wolves cut off their heads for the bounty.

Concern amplified when Compound 1080 became the predominantly used poison. As Cluff and Murray (1995) point out, the BC government favoured Compound 1080 over strychnine, and it was in regular use, with baited meat dropped aerially, through much of the 1950s. The authors note that although the bait was dropped from airplanes, it was rarely checked; the cost of return trips over the baited areas proved prohibitive. Thus, these baits remained on the land for long periods of time, when other animals could come into contact with them, and carried a significant possibility of killing wildlife other than canids. Also problematic for many were the ways in which both target and non-target animals that came into contact with Compound 1080 died: "when misplaced, 1080's effects are particularly affecting because of the slow and painful death it inflicts: herbivores suffer heart failure, carnivores nervous system failure and suffocation"

(Addison 2019). As Cluff and Murray (1995, 498) note, while 1080's effectiveness as agent of canid death was not in dispute, this "nonselective"
approach "helped initiate antipoisoning campaigns in North America."

Perhaps the most obvious example of this necropolitical practice of wolf
killing through poison is found in Alberta's efforts to eliminate canids
during the rabies scare between 1952 and 1956. Rabies became a concern
in the early 1950s when rabid red fox populations moved into the Prairies
from the Northwest Territories. In response to what Karen R. Jones (2003,
179) calls a "rabies hysteria," the province, through the Pest Control
Program of the Department of Agriculture, embarked upon a systematic
and widespread campaign to ensure that Alberta was wolf and coyote free.
In practice, this meant massive amounts of poison and huge numbers of
traps were deployed against this threat. As Douglas Pimlott (1961a, 147)
catalogued, from 1951 to 1956, "39,960 cyanide guns, 106,000 cartridges,
and 628,000 strychnine pellets" were distributed in the effort to eliminate
wild canids. In addition, in 1953 and 1954 alone, "170 trappers were hired
to ring the settled area of the province with 5,000 miles of traplines and
poison stations" and poison was given to landowners as well (ibid.). In
addition, thousands of bait stations were installed across Alberta and
British Columbia (K.R. Jones, *Wolf Mountains*, 2003). These provinces were
literally blanketed in poison. The results of this systematic program
were astonishing: the wolf population in Alberta went from a stable
5,000 animals in 1950 to between 500 and 1,000 by the late 1950s
(Gunson 1992). An estimated 246,800 coyotes were killed in the same
period (Pimlott 1961a). Perhaps even more astonishing is that in the entire
campaign only one wolf was found to have rabies (Theberge 1973).

These efforts at efficient and rational control of predators were not
limited to the agricultural or settled areas of the various provinces. National
and provincial parks became both flashpoints for concern about wolves and
sites for their regulation. This might seem surprising to us today since the
park system is seen as an assemblage of sites of ostensible wildlife protection. But as environmental historian Alan MacEachern (1995) has shown,
from inception, the managers of the national park system subscribed to
Jack Miner's taxonomy of good and bad animals. In practice, this meant
one of the central roles that park wardens took on was the killing of wolves.
And until 1928, they were incentivized to do so: they could establish
traplines and sell the pelts of the animals they trapped, wolves or otherwise.
Tina Loo (2006) estimates that this work added between 10 to 50 per cent
to their salaries. In the words of James Harkin, the first commissioner of
the Dominion Parks Branch, this led to a situation where the agency was

"in the winter time virtually paying them a salary to carry on a general trapping business" (cited in MacEachern 1995, 202). Once wardens were prevented from selling pelts, Harkin established a quota system to ensure they continued to kill predators (MacEachern 1995). MacEachern tells us that the Parks Branch approach to predatory wildlife began to change, informed at least in part by scientific assertions of their role in ecosystems. However, he also notes that "the staff's deference to science made it ever easier to rationalize the sacrifice of a few predators" (MacEachern 1995, 206), like wolves and coyotes. Karen R. Jones's (2003, 129) work regarding Banff bears out this assertion: whereas the stated policy was to let ecosystem dynamics play out, it remained highly interventionist "to determine the 'correct' faunal complement." By the 1940s and 1950s, it seems that wolves could exist in the parks system, but never in large numbers and certainly not if they extended their territory beyond the boundaries of the parks. For instance, J. Smart (1945), the controller of the National Parks Bureau from 1941 to 1953, noted in correspondence to the editor of *Game Trails* that "the wolves in the National Parks are controlled by the park wardens, under instructions, and are not permitted to become too numerous. In spite of the relatively low population of wolves in Jasper Park as a whole, we have considered it prudent to reduce their numbers in certain areas of the park and, in accordance with that policy, the wardens have shot and killed or seriously wounded 18 wolves in the past three years."

Similarly, although scientific studies such as those of Ian McTaggart-Cowan, a professor at the University of British Columbia who was engaged to ascertain the population of wolves in the western parks, were mentioned along with discussion of the general rarity of wolves in these parks, justifications for their killing persisted. In the "Summary of Discussion on Wolves and Wolf Control at the 10th Conference of the Provincial and Dominion Wildlife Officials, Ottawa, February 23, 1945," this was made explicit in comments attributed to McTaggart-Cowan: "The occasional random killing of wolves by park wardens is not justified from the standpoint of conservation of game animals, but there are sound *psychological* reasons for permitting it to continue until we have evidence that indicates that it should be modified, one way or another" (Parks Canada fonds, n.d., 3, emphasis added). And if they presented a threat to life or livelihood – as wolves did in the rabies scare in Alberta – they would be targeted anew: "The Canadian Parks Service may have dismissed calls to eradicate wolves during the 1940s as irrational, but in 1953, principles of factual analysis were lost amidst pressures for control" (K.R. Jones, *Wolf Mountains*, 2003, 134). Indeed, in 1955, park wardens were trained in predator control, which included demonstrations around poisons (strychnine and 1080), snares, and traps (Sime 1955). So, there were sharp limits to this ecological turn, especially as the parks came to be seen as a safe haven for a predatory and potentially infected foe.

Similar narratives played out in Algonquin Provincial Park in Ontario, now home to the famous wolf howl. The idea that this park was a sanctuary for wolves – and that rangers and scientists like Pimlott were actively breeding them – became part of the anti-wolf narrative. Much like the national parks, Algonquin's official policy in the early 1900s was wolf extermination, exemplified in a *Rod and Gun* article that champions park rangers in the "war against the wolves":

> In fall and winter the rangers put in their best work. They are waging a war against the wolves, and to encourage them in their efforts the Government leaves them to purchase their own poisons. They all agree that the wolves are too numerous in the park and that they have made great havoc with the deer. The rangers receive bounty for every wolf killed, and this is the only addition to their pay that they obtain. So far they have not had as much success as they would have liked, but they are constantly learning something of the ways of these crafty animals and devising means to overcome them. Without doubt they poison more wolves than they find, and the ceaseless warfare carried on appears likely to achieve its great object, viz., the thinning out of the wolves. (AHS 1910, 793)

Edwin Godin (1931), an Algonquin Park ranger, wrote of his efforts to balance the ratio of deer to wolves in the park. He noted that although he was not a trained trapper, he was able to snare twenty with little trouble in one small part of Algonquin Park. Echoing the ideas of the time, Godin (1931, 575) suggested that the increasing number of wolves was best managed via rangers (rather than wolf hunters) and that they should continue to receive the wolf bounty in addition to their salary, so they could "control them and keep them from moving to the settled districts."

However, by the 1930s, there were some doubts about the rangers' intentions. Ontario rangers being paid their salary and the bounty on the wolves they killed was celebrated in the 1910 quote but derided by 1930. The *Report of the Special Committee on the Game Situation* specifically noted concerns that Algonquin "has become a *wolf farm* for the exclusive profit of rangers" (Black; Ontario Special Committee on the Game Situation 1933, 30, emphasis added). This idea that Algonquin was a "wolf retreat" (ibid.) was compounded by the wolf research that took place in the park from 1958 to 1965 under the direction of Douglas Pimlott: while in effect, it banned the killing of wolves in the park. It also ushered in a new conversation about wolves, one that was backed by the science of ecology. In some quarters, this was entirely unwelcome. Echoing the earlier concerns of trappers, hunters, farmers, and ranchers in other Canadian provinces, the Ontario Deer Preservation Committee worried that the protection of wolves in Algonquin would lead to the extinction of deer (Chapeskie 1973). But once it gained a foothold, it seems the shift toward expert knowledge was difficult to derail, even if it took a while to inform the guiding principles of the predator management, as Jones, Loo, and MacEachern attest. (This is the focus of chapter 4.) That said, it would be a mistake to suggest that the disgust that characterized settler feelings about wolves in this period has completely faded. One need only look at the wolf culls and sponsored hunts to see how the ideas of good and bad animals haunt the present.

BRITISH COLUMBIA'S WAR ON WOLVES

In 2015, the BC government launched a program aimed at saving the province's mountain caribou herds. Like caribou across Canada, the mountain caribou face steep population declines. Once said to be "like bugs on the land" (Habitat Conservation Trust Foundation 2020), woodland caribou, of which the mountain caribou are a unique population, were likely among the first mammals present in British Columbia after the last ice age nine thousand years ago (Morris 2002). The vast majority – 98 per cent – of the world's mountain caribou are found in BC (Ministry of Forests, Lands, Natural Resource Operations and Rural Development 2017); without action, their extinction is imminent. The southern mountain caribou are even more gravely endangered than their kin to the north; for instance, the South Selkirk herd, which straddles the US-Canada border, is now functionally extinct (Shore 2018), with only one penned female remaining in 2019.

It is widely acknowledged by scientists that the main factor driving mountain caribou to extinction is habitat loss and fragmentation related to logging, mining, and oil and gas operations (see, for example, Johnson, Ehlers, and Seip 2015; Hebblewhite 2017). This is particularly the case for the southern mountain, or deep-snow, caribou that thrive on the lichen in old growth forests, which are being consumed by these industries (Harding et al. 2020). Clearing out trees also makes the land more hospitable to deer and moose, primary food sources for wolves. At the same time, these operations establish logging roads and utility lines through once remote and impenetrable caribou habitat, packing down deep snow, which makes following the deer much easier for wolves (Harding et al. 2020; Proulx 2017). And so, we have a perfect storm for precipitous caribou decline: decades of industrial development and logging shrank critical caribou habitat while creating entry points for predators to pick off the remaining ungulates.

And yet, the BC government has chosen to target just one of the drivers of potential mountain caribou extinction: wolves. Taking their cue from what was hailed as a successful strategy for caribou recovery in Alberta (see, for example, Hervieux et al. 2014; Boutin 2017; Serrouya et al. 2019),[3] in 2015, the BC government established a wolf cull program focused on the South Selkirk, South Peace, and Columbia North herds. The Provincial Caribou Recovery Program (2019) notes that the wolf cull is the fastest and most efficient way to stabilize caribou populations, at least in the near term; it is not meant as a long-term recovery strategy though scientists suggest such culls would need to persist (Boutin in Pagé 2018). Managers of the program contend it works: "Wolf reduction has been used over the last five years in the Central Group of Southern Mountain Caribou, resulting in a shift from an average rate of decline of 15% per year to an average of 15% increase per year. Within the Kootenay Region, primary prey management supplemented with recent wolf reductions resulted in a 5% annual growth rate for the Columbia North herd, including an increase in calf recruitment. Multiple years of wolf reduction has resulted in a decrease of wolf recolonization rates in the area and adjacent areas" (Provincial Caribou Recovery Program 2019). Killing wolves, it seems, allows caribou a chance for life on a landscape they've inhabited for millennia. Why should a few thousand wolves stand in the way of that?

The Caribou Recovery Program does not invoke disgust when referring to wolves; it does not rehearse the hatred of Jack Miner or the antipathy of the Ontario Game and Fish Commission. Instead, it offers a dispassionate assessment of what needs to happen for caribou populations to stabilize: for one species to live, another must die. In this articulation, wolf slaughter is a regrettable but necessary result of the immediacy of mountain caribou extirpation. Wolves are not under threat in British Columbia (or in Canada for that matter), at least as defined through our endangered species legislation. The province is home to an estimated 8,500 wolves (Ministry of Forests, Lands, Natural Resource Operations and Rural Development 2017). However, while there is no contempt expressed for wolves, there is an implicit ranking and ordering in a way that asserts the relative value of different species. Mountain caribou are iconic, critically endangered, and increasingly threatened; wolves are characterized by fecundity, ubiquity, and the killing capacity to wipe out the remnants of a keystone species. As with Jack Miner, a hierarchy is established where some lives are worth more than others, but in this case, rather than invoking a moral judgment on predators, this killing is justified by the numbers – a caribou population under threat trumps the lives of individual wolves. Irus Braverman (2017, 134) notes in her work on endangered species lists, like the International Union for Conservation of Nature's Red List, that they are biopolitical efforts made in and through the "laborious calculations that go into ranking nonhuman species on a linear scale further from, or closer to, extinction." Braverman contends that such lists operate in part via comparability across species, where those that are threatened are ranked more highly than those which are not, an ordering that becomes both an unquestionable and authoritative mechanism enabling biopolitical regulation. She notes that the "listing of life is thus also a making of this life – it grants life" (ibid.) by making some species visible to policy-makers and conservation officials who would seek to enact regulations to save them. The same is true of the designations offered by Committee on the Status of Endangered Wildlife in Canada (COSEWIC), upon which the caribou management plan is based. In fact, the BC government suggests its hands are tied: it is forced to kill wolves because COSEWIC's determination of mountain caribou as threatened mandates a recovery plan under the Species at Risk Act. Lists such as these do not leave animal lives untouched. But in the act of naming caribou life as worth saving and, hence, regulating, wolves become part of the "listless lives that fall outside the realm of the threatened" (Braverman 2016, 7) – at least in the case of Canada, where they are under no threat. In this situation, conservation becomes the biopolitical sacrifice of one species for another: making life through death.

This sacrifice is not paltry, either in terms of wolves' lives or the cost of their extermination. In just one year – 2020 – the BC government authorized the killing of 463 wolves in ten regions at a cost of $2 million (Cox 2020b). As Sarah Cox (2020b) notes, this is approximately $4,300 per wolf, much higher than the bounties of decades before. Ironically, some of this cost is defrayed by the very industries that cause caribou habitat loss and fragmentation. For example, Coastal GasLink received approval for a liquefied natural gas pipeline through endangered caribou habitat conditional on the establishment of a $1.5-million monitoring and predation program, $171,000 of which went to the wolf cull (Cox 2020c). Of course, this might seem a small price to pay for the oil and gas industry, given that a more fulsome approach to caribou recovery might mean fewer project approvals. That the critical habitat for caribou is being lost or bisected by oil and gas pipelines presents a much thornier issue, one that is linked to systemic economic and political change and cannot be solved through what conservation scientist Chris Darimont calls "the blunt instrument of wolf culls" (cited in Imbler 2020). The responsibility for species management has, in this case, been outsourced to the very industries that benefit from blaming the wolf for damage they themselves have wrought. This is underwritten by provincial and federal governments through environmental assessment processes that emphasize economic development and "through fragmented environmental laws and processes that displace the fundamental problem of relentless growth on a finite planet" (Collard, Dempsey, and Holmberg 2020, 7).

More chillingly, what is proposed in the BC wolf cull is a necropolitical project with no clear end date. As the Caribou Recovery Program (2019) notes: "To reverse caribou population declines, high rates of wolf removal (greater than 80%) must be achieved." This figure is made more astonishing by the fact that these numbers must be killed every single year, for decades, to continue to stabilize caribou populations. Stan Boutin, a population biologist at the University of Alberta whose work has been important in testing whether wolf culls can save caribou from extinction, mentions this with regret in a CBC article: "The sad part of it all is that if we're going to do a wolf cull to keep caribou populations around, we're in this for the long haul. As soon as you stop the cull, wolf numbers come right back up to what they were before, and caribou populations decline again" (Pagé 2018). This strategy necessitates the kind of sustained slaughter that those who felt disgust for wolves could only have imagined. This enterprise of death is waged in the name of wildlife management.

One method to track down and kill enough wolves to meet this 80 per cent quota is through the making of a "Judas wolf" (Pacific Wild 2018). Judas wolves are those that are tranquilized and radio-collared by wildlife officers. Once released, they lead scientists back to their pack, and then all of them can be killed "to ensure sufficient rates of removal" (Provincial Caribou Recovery Program 2019). The manner of death is aerial shooting via helicopter, a practice that is difficult to accomplish humanely because of the near impossibility of a clean shot (Brook et al. 2015). Sadie Parr and Paul Paquet (2017) make these ethical stakes clear, noting that animals in labs are afforded more stringent protocols for humane death than these wild wolves. But in the biopolitical move that transforms individual lives into populations, there is only the delineation of ones that can (wolves) and cannot (caribou) "absorb mortality" (Brook et al. 2015, 76). The capacity for wolves to be killed again and again for decades remains the case though their sacrifice may not even work to halt mountain caribou extinction.

However, there is another story to tell about the wolf and caribou in British Columbia, one informed by connection to and intimate understanding of place on Treaty 8 lands. In this way of thinking, caribou are culturally as well as ecologically important. In 2020, the provincial government signed an agreement with the Saulteaux and West Moberly First Nations in the Peace River region of northeastern BC to manage the northern mountain caribou population through means that include but do not end with killing wolves (Cox 2020a). Caribou is an ancestral food source to these First Nations but one that many have not tasted since the 1960s when the elders advised community members that caribou numbers were declining so sharply that they needed to cease their hunt (Follett Hosgood 2020). By 2012, there were only sixteen caribou left in the Kilnse-Za herd (Askewbud and Napoleon 2019). The Saulteaux and West Moberly First Nations began their own program to recover caribou herds outside of the provincial efforts and indeed have sued the provincial government for approving development projects that violate their treaty rights by endangering the caribou. This program focused on three principles: establishing maternal pens, wolf management, and habitat restoration (Dre Anderson Photography 2019). As part of the Indigenous Guardian Program, members of the community patrol the caribou pen for predators and – in what one biologist poignantly called "conservation life-support" (Askewbud and Napoleon 2019) – volunteers "spend hours on hands and knees collecting the hundreds of bags of lichen needed to feed the animals during calving season" (Follett Hosgood 2020). This is a labour of love, one that sees deep connection between the lifeways of the caribou and the First Nations that care for them. And while wolves are killed to ensure calves can reach adulthood, the efforts at habitat restoration, which is the third pillar of this program, mean this practice will not have to continue indefinitely; caribou life does not hinge solely on wolf death. Their work has proved successful. The Klinse-Za herd has not only stabilized but is also recovering, growing by 15 per cent annually (Ministry of Forests, Lands, Natural Resource Operations and Rural Development 2020). In 2020, after a three-year negotiation, the provincial and federal governments reached an agreement to formally recognize the work of these nations and provide longer-term protection for the herds. Significantly, the agreement includes over 700,000 hectares of habitat protection (Ministry of Forests, Lands, Natural Resource Operations and Rural Development 2020).

These First Nations are not engaged in a biopolitical practice of making some lives killable while venerating others, even as they kill wolves to save caribou. As Carmen Richter, a biologist and Saulteaux band member, told *The Tyee*, this project restores the relationship to caribou, to the land, and to each other: "Restoration means more than just enjoying a park on the weekend for people here. It's protecting our grocery store, our pharmacy, our church, our way of life for our kids and our health for our kids. In order for our children to be healthy, they have to go back and know about our traditional way of life" (Follett Hosgood 2020). Rather than a biopolitical imperative, the recovery of the Klinse-Za herd is premised on connection, intimacy, and understanding of place. The First Nations' successes with the caribou points to a deeper truth: that Indigenous-led conservation, through land management and care for wildlife, may be the best way forward for our nonhuman kin: "Indigenous-led stewardship of all species, including those that are hunted for food, and of the places they inhabit provides in some ways a best-case example of what wildlife management can be: inspired by a close relationship to wildlife and their habitats, informed by knowledge and values borne of the deep history of that relationship, complemented by cutting-edge science, and led by people who not only live in the area but also shoulder the consequences of management directly – well aware that their decisions will determine the world that their children and their children's children will inherit" (Artelle 2019).

FROM TRASH ANIMALS TO THE LAST OF THE WILD

In this chapter, I contend that the story of wolves from around 1900 to the 1950s was primarily one of disgust. The tropes of justification and methods of death that were mobilized served to absent wolves from the landscape of the nation. Both the bounty and more systematic efforts at control were about purging the nation of something unclean, a being whose very presence and perceived transgressions marked it for death. Seeing wolves as contemptuous and disgusting creatures – contagions, if you will – accorded them the status of killable, outside of Agamben's *bios* and firmly in the category of *zoe*. Even when they are no longer considered disgusting, their deaths are still mandated, as we have seen in the case of the cull in BC. In their killability, as Irus Braverman (2015, 165) remarks in a different context, wolf deaths were already rendered "not grievable"; their lives "never counted in the first place." To kill a wolf was just a common-sense reaction to an animal that had no right to exist at all.

But it was something of a fascinating creature too. Pages and pages were devoted to its wanton destruction and depredations, its cunning and cravenness. Settlers were captivated by wolves even while seeking to obliterate them. And as William Ian Miller (1998, x) suggests, this makes sense: "Even as the disgusting repels, it rarely does so without also capturing our attention. It imposes itself upon us." It is this imposition that necessitated a biopolitical response.

However, it would be too neat a narrative to suggest that all settlers only ever feared or were disgusted by wolves. The next two chapters chart different affective registers: passion and curiosity. Then, as now, wolves provoked strong reactions; their capacity to affect us is one of the characteristics that guarantees their imbrication with human lives.

PART TWO

Recuperating the Wolf

3

Passion

Writing the Wolf in Canadian Literature

Never Cry Wolf has become iconic for many reasons, from its lovingly written portrayal of a wolf pack to the recipe for "souris a la crème." But the passage almost everyone remembers involves a literal pissing match. As part of his efforts to become wolf and make the pack acknowledge his presence, author Farley Mowat decides he will emulate their practice of marking their territory with urine. He drinks a huge amount of tea and spends the night peeing on rocks and grass every fifteen feet and right across one of the pathways the wolves used to navigate their territory. When one of the wolves comes across this insult, he pauses, then replicates in fifteen minutes what Mowat did over the course of twelve hours: "Briskly, and with an air of decision, he turned his attention away from me and began a systematic tour of his own. As he came to each boundary marker he sniffed it once or twice, then carefully placed his mark on the outside of each clump of grass or stone. As I watched I saw where I, in my ignorance, had erred. He made his mark with such economy that he was able to complete the entire circuit without having to reload once, or, to change the simile with one tank of fuel" ([1963] 2009, 84). It is this story, full of Mowat's characteristic wit and self-deprecation, that captured the hearts of Canadians – and, later, many more people when the Disney adaptation was released in 1983 – and worked to further a reconsideration of a much-maligned predator.

The wolf's recuperation in Canada might have been both brief and ill-fated if it were left only to ecologists and the burgeoning environmental movement. As scientists who work on climate change can attest, all the data in the world is sometimes not enough to move people. The evocation of affect – either positive or negative – rarely comes through information alone; engagement requires the senses. Literature offers a way into this realm and can spur sudden ruptures in ways of thinking that might otherwise have been difficult to produce. As Susan McHugh (2011, 3) suggests with specific regard to animals, "in certain historical and social moments, some literary and visual narrative forms become inseparable from shifts in the politics and science of species." For the purposes of this book, how wolves have been narrated through time has both shaped and been shaped by the political context in which these works are authored. And so, fiction – by telling lupine stories that rely on us seeing them as, at the very least, complex instead of simply wicked – has been important in offering a mechanism by which settlers could reimagine wolves in Canada.

In this chapter, I focus on three authors of Canadian wolf stories: Ernest Thompson Seton, Charles G.D. Roberts, and Farley Mowat. Writing at about the same time, Seton and Roberts developed the realistic animal story, offering a navigation point in the quagmire generated by Darwinian assertions of nature versus nurture. Mowat comes much later, but follows many of their traces, and because of the social and cultural context within which he both participated and advanced, he ushers in a renaissance for wolves in Canada. There were other authors I could have selected. For example, R.D. Lawrence had a prolific career in nature writing, often using the wolf as his muse. However, I wanted to focus on the authors whose work was seen as important to shifting conceptions of the wolf. R.D. Lawrence's work was much like Farley Mowat's, but without his broad appeal.

I contend that each of these authors demonstrates the ambivalent and complicated cultural context the wolf has inhabited across space and time, often relying on indigeneity, nature, and nation to elaborate their understanding of the wolf and its role in Canadian society. But I also suggest that their view was animated by the affective register of passion. Passion is an urgent affect, an intensity that can manifest via positive or negative attachments. In one of his very scant gestures to affect, Foucault elaborates this idea in a conversation with German film director Werner Schroeter. He contends that passion is "a state, something that falls on you out of the blue, that takes hold of you, that grips you for no reason, that has no origin. One doesn't know where it comes from. Passion arrives like that, a state that is always mobile, but never moves toward a given point. There are strong and weak moments, moments when it becomes incandescent. It floats, it evens out. It is a kind of unstable time that is pursued for obscure reasons, perhaps through inertia. In the extreme, it tries to maintain itself and to disappear. Passion gives itself all the conditions necessary to continue, and, at the same time, it destroys itself. In a state of Passion one is not blind. One is simply not oneself. To be oneself no longer makes sense"

(Foucault 1996, 313). It seems to me that the authors examined in this chapter demonstrate some kind passion for wolves; at turns, it is obsessive, nostalgic, and devouring. Also, as I explore below, this passion implicates a particular version of manhood that all three writers inhabit. Both Seton and Mowat were compelled by a passionate yearning: in Seton's case to know the wolf and in Mowat's to become it. Both abandon reason – and by some accounts, truth – in favour of a kind of sensuous engagement with the lives of wolves. Roberts also demonstrates passion, but of a different kind. He is animated by a passionate hatred for wolves as that which pervert the order of things. For all three, their passions for and about wolves moved between bodies, generating and shaping particular ways of understanding wolves in the time they wrote.

At the same time, I suggest that the stories of Seton, Roberts, and Mowat offered a starting point in western thought for animals as subjective beings thereby unsettling taken-for-granted truths about the divisions between human and nonhuman. Put differently, each of these authors, in different ways and to varying degrees of success, grappled with the question of whether and how animals can be subjects, the relationship between individual and species-level agency, and how we can come to know animal lives. Nevertheless, their gesture is both limited and circumscribed by particular ideas of nature and nation.

ANIMAL STORIES IN CANADA

Animals are so fundamental to our writing that it might indeed be said that our literature is founded on the bodies of animals – alive or dead; anthropomorphized or "realistic"; indigenous or exotic; sentimental, tragic, magical, and mythical.

Janice Fiamengo (2007, 5–6)

In her book *Survival* (1972), Margaret Atwood dedicates an entire chapter to animal stories, suggesting they are shot through with allegories about nation. Asserting that Canadians are an anxious bunch, whereas Americans are full of the blind confidence of conquerors, Atwood theorizes that animal bodies offer the surface upon which these identities are played out. She contends that animals in American literature are told from the point of view of the humans who hunt them and are undergirded by "the general imperialism of the American cast of mind" (Lutts 1998, 216). By contrast, Canadian literature writes from the animal's own perspective, "as felt emotionally from inside the fur and feathers" (ibid.). In the Canadian iteration, then, animals become the proxy by which national anxiety – fear of being subsumed by a colonizing American spirit – is made manifest. The bears, mountain lions, and wolves that appear in Canadian literature become part of a national menagerie of victimhood and loss in the face of inevitable cultural destruction; animal stories in Canada, according to Atwood, are fundamentally extinction narratives.

It was once a compelling story, and one that fits the period's focus on thematic analysis and nationalist angst. But in recent years, the idea of a national anxiety embedded across CanLit has been both complicated and refuted. Atwood assumes the nation as a coherent and stable entity rather than one made (and continuously remade) in and through power. Post-colonial work in Canada (cf. Moss 2003) and beyond (cf. Bhabha 1990) has demonstrated the fiction of this premise. More importantly, it would seem to erase those who lived first in these lands called Canada, for whom colonization was and is experienced and on whom it was indeed perpetrated by the very same people who Atwood suggests are animated by fear of such from the south. Such an account also ignores the now very clear articulation of a multiplicity of voices in CanLit – Black, Indigenous, people of colour, queer, feminist, and so on – which would unsettle the thrust of her narrative.

But even as it relates to writing about animals, Canada is not so distinct as Atwood asserts. Sandlos (2000) suggests that there are many more areas of commonality between nature writing in the United States and Canada than differences, with contemporaries like Jack London, William Long, Charles G.D. Roberts, and Ernest Thompson Seton often drawing from the same literary well. Part of their commonality was that each, in their own way, grappled with the fallout from the revolution of Darwinism. Darwin's work generated a series of debates and anxieties that reverberated through many sectors of society, including nature writing. According to MacDonald, animal stories offered a space to "attempt to impose a kind of order on the 'chaos' of Darwinism" (cited in Lutts 1998, 227). Evolutionary theory and the principle of natural selection threw into question all sorts of settler certainties about the nature of humans and non-humans, and the relationship between them. Humans were, without warning, demoted from divine creation to part of the animal kingdom. Moreover, the aim of reading morality into nature seemed doomed since the biophysical world appeared to be governed more by chance and a drive to reproduce than by teleological design. For Seton and Roberts, the animal story became, in part, a mechanism to sort out these existential debates, to refuse "Darwinian determinism" and play with the notion that animals (and by extension, humans) were not only driven by instinct but also could learn and change within the course of a life. Put differently, there could be "rational, ethical animals, who, as they rise above instinct, reach toward the spiritual" (R.H. MacDonald 1998, 225–6). In some ways, then, the works of Seton and Roberts can be seen as early progenitors of the biological discipline of ethology: the notion that "instinct and reason act in tandem in all organisms" (Sandlos 2000, 80), which is revisited later in Mowat. This has little to do with the myth of Canadian nationalism or settler colonial imagination of a Canada under threat. Instead, animal stories have the possibility of offering an opening – a literary and affective entry point – into the lifeworld of animals who are not us. This chapter suggests that stories about wolves were important to the idea of the Canadian nation, but perhaps not in the way that Atwood contends. Through some of Canada's most famous nature writers, I argue that wolves have been a highly flexible metaphor used to bolster particular narratives of Canadian nationhood. Their shifting meanings also demonstrate, as Bhabha suggests, that the nation is a historical contingent and characterized by instability.

ERNEST THOMPSON SETON: THE NOBLE WOLF

Ernest Thompson Seton was particularly interested in opening space to the more-than-human world. In the late 1800s and early 1900s, Seton became massively successful in writing amalgams of fictional short stories and ethological accounts that earned a wide readership, especially among children.[1] A master of self-promotion, Seton followed a model that had garnered him fame. He first published stories in a variety of magazines like *Scribner's*, *The Century*, and *Recreation*. The next year, he followed up with a collected volume of the most popular stories and then toured giving readings and lectures based on the stories (Keller 1984). In so doing, he created his lasting legacy as the progenitor of the "realistic animal story," although his work remained haunted by questions of just how "realistic" his writing was.

John Wadland's definitive biography, *Ernest Thompson Seton: Man in Nature and the Progressive Era 1880–1915* (1978), contends that Seton was a proto-ecologist who saw intelligence in nature (see also PBS Nature 2008). He emphasizes that "it was to the wild animal and its natural habitat that Seton owed an almost political allegiance" (Wadland 1978, 47). Wadland is not alone in these assertions. For example, Manina Jones (2008, 137) argues that Seton offers a kind of "resistant animal speech" where, in a sense, animals write back; through Seton, animals are able to convey the reality of their own lifeworlds. She further suggests that the animal track illustrations found in the margins in almost all of Seton's stories – wolf, bear, rabbit, dog, otter, and so on – operate as traces that demonstrate the manner in which humans have come late to the party. Referring specifically to *Wild Animals I Have Known* (E.T. Seton [1898] 2009), Manina Jones (2008, 137) asserts that these imprints "hint at an elusive storyline to which the narrator has only limited, indirect, and belated access." The way Seton writes about wolves offers a test case for the idea that the author allows animals to write for themselves.

Seton was particularly fond of wolves. He wrote a number of now-famous stories in which wolves figured, often as the protagonist. Indeed, Seton closely identified with wolves. In them he saw a misunderstood maverick akin to treatment he experienced throughout his life – from his father; from the Grand Salon in Paris, which rejected his technically proficient yet gruesome *Triumph of the Wolves* (also known as *Awaited in Vain*) (1892), a painting that depicted a hunter devoured by a vengeful wolf pack; from Theodore Roosevelt, who named him one of the "nature fakers"; and from the Boy Scouts of America, an organization that he helped found and that later ousted him (Wadland 1978). So deep was his sense of lupine connection that Seton took for himself the moniker "Black Wolf" and signed his name with a wolf paw print (figure 3.1). What is most interesting about his wolf narratives is that they were largely not of their time, which is to say that they often venerated rather than vilified things lupine.

Lobo and Other Tales

As our starting point for this discussion, let us take Seton's most famous wolf story: "Lobo, the King of Currumpaw" ([1898] 2009). Lobo, according to Seton, was a leader of a wolf pack that tormented ranchers in New Mexico between 1889 and 1894, until he was killed by Seton. Lobo was termed an "outlaw wolf" – those seemingly unkillable creatures that had survived wolfers' attempts at extermination. Part of the reason for Lobo's success was his exceptionality, both in size (approximately 150 pounds) and cunning. The pack Lobo assembled was equally remarkable: "Certain it is that Lobo had only five followers during the latter part of his reign. Each of these, however, was a wolf of renown, most of them were above the ordinary size, one in particular, the second in command, was a veritable giant, but even he was far below the leader in size and prowess" (E.T. Seton [1898] 2009, 10). The wolf managed to outwit all his pursuers, which is what brought Seton from Manitoba to New Mexico in 1893. He spends

3.1 Ernest Thompson Seton's wolf insignia.

months attempting to kill the pack, but they prove too canny to succumb
to his efforts. For example, Seton explains that the pack would only eat
what it had killed, thereby avoiding poisoned bait. They knew the smell
of steel, thus skirting traps. And when Seton attempts to lay traps for the
wolves, utilizing all precautions against detection, Lobo disdainfully
defecates on them. Seton is humiliated by the wolf and needs a different
tactic. He notices that Lobo always follows a particular wolf, the one to
which he is mated: Blanca. He decides to use the love he witnesses between
Lobo and Blanca as a weapon against the wolf. He makes a complicated
plan to fool both wolves, and it works – Blanca is captured. He and his
cowboys kill her by placing ropes around her neck and riding in opposite
directions. They then use her body as bait, dragging her across the 130 traps
he sets at each entrance to the canyon where he hopes to trap Lobo. By
relying on the subjectivity of Lobo – his apparent feelings of love and his
desire to find Blanca – Seton finally catches his prey. Yet after all this time,
the capture is bittersweet. Instead of killing the wolf, Seton brings it back
to his camp alive. But Lobo asserts his agency once more: "A lion shorn
of his strength, an eagle robbed of his freedom, or a dove bereft of his
mate, all die, it is said, of a broken heart; and who will aver that this grim
bandit could bear the three-fold brunt, heart-whole? This only I know, that
when the morning dawned, he was lying there still in his position of calm

repose, his body unwounded, but his spirit was gone – the old kingwolf was dead" (E.T. Seton [1898] 2009, 22). Chastened, sorrowful, Seton takes the wolf's body and lays it next to Blanca's, and the story closes.

What to make of this story, one that provokes fond attachment even among conservation luminaries like David Attenborough who acknowledge its more unrealistic elements[2] (Gooder 2008)? In my view, Seton writes the story on two distinct but related registers: transformation and lamentation. Much like Aldo Leopold would write years later in his now-famous essay "The Land Ethic" (1949), Seton has a moment of revelation in the act of brutally killing a wolf. He writes that the slaughter of Blanca and the death of Lobo "proved one of the turning points of my life" (cited in Wadland 1978, 209–10). In Lobo, Seton allows himself to see wolves not as vermin or killers of prey but as noble and loyal creatures whose deaths are to be mourned rather than celebrated. But tied up with this transformation is a concomitant emphasis on the evitability of this loss. Seton gives the reader an expression of grief in the form of anticipatory elegy: of course, the death of Lobo, extraordinary wolf hardened by the settler war waged upon it, is lamentable, but it is also a necessary tragedy. The death of Lobo – and Blanca – are a function of progress, of civilization, of the nation moving on. Seton writes lovingly of Lobo: "Grand old outlaw, hero of a thousand lawless raids, in a few minutes you will be but a great load of carrion. It cannot be otherwise" (E.T. Seton [1898] 2009, 21). As he suggests in his prelude to *Wild Animals I Have Known,* all wild animals have tragic ends. Lobo, then, is no different. While Seton dedicates his life to the study of natural history, to exploring their lifeworlds in what he asserted were on the animal's own terms, their individual lives cannot be saved. As a result, the transformation that Seton suggests is possible is only for humans: the biopolitical work offered by engagement with the wild only goes one way.

Seton's other wolf tales map similar terrain, emphasizing the stories of exceptional, singular creatures who, having survived the brutal and near-complete human onslaught, have arrived at the category of anachronism. Yet Seton did not write the same wolf story time and again (unlike Charles G.D. Roberts, in many ways), and so there are other broad themes that emerge through which Seton attempts to teach his readers about the wild. For example, in "Badlands Billy: The Wolf that Won," Seton tells the story of an orphaned wolf whose mother and siblings are killed by a trapper who skins them for the bounty. Billy escapes the trappers' depredations and is adopted by a new mother who teaches him how to avoid harm at the hands of humans: "Instinct is no doubt a Wolf's first and best guide, but gifted parents are a great start in life" (E.T. Seton 1905a, 140). However, predictably, given Lobo and Blanca's fate, the mother is finally caught in a trap: "Thenceforth he must face the world alone" (ibid.). The wolf forms his own pack and teaches them the perils of humans with their guns and traps. In passing on this knowledge, learned rather than inborn, the pack begins terrorizing ranchers. Seton enters the story at this point as he – and a wizened wolfer named King Ryder – begin to hunt the pack. This might seem odd in the face of his self-professed transformation, but I suspect it is the ending that matters here. Like Lobo, Badlands Billy is lured through his good nature: he attempts to help a packmate escape the hounds that have it cornered. But as the dogs – genetic co-travellers – take on their foe, he leads them up a narrow path on the side of a mountain and dispenses with them, one by one. Badlands Billy survives to see another day. So, in this story we see some of the same elements that made "Lobo" much beloved: a noble wolf demonstrating "moral" reasoning, a story that emphasizes human rather than animal cruelty, a testing of the boundaries between nature and nurture, and an exploration of the bonds animals can form with one another. The difference here, of course, is that Badlands Billy escapes this time. And yet, there is a weariness to Billy that suggests the escape, while lauded by both Seton and Ryder, will not last long: "A moment he waited to look for more to come. There were no more, the pack was dead; but waiting until he caught his breath, then raising his voice for the first time in that fatal scene he feebly gave a long yell of triumph" (E.T. Seton 1905a, 163–4). Badlands Billy, like Lobo, is the last of his kind.

Seton tells a different kind of narrative in "The Winnipeg Wolf," also found in *Animal Heroes*. In this tale, we are introduced to another astonishing wolf, who experienced the loss of his entire family at the hands of a trapper. He becomes an urban wolf, his nature perverted by both captivity by and proximity to humans. Similar to Tito, the imprisoned coyote that Seton describes in a different story (E.T. Seton 1901), this wolf leads a tortured life, chained outside a saloon where he is tormented by the town. His only kinship is with a boy – the tavern owner's son – who saves the wolf from death before himself dying from a fever. The wolf mourns the boy and, in his grief, seizes upon the possibility of escape, for he now has nothing to lose. But the wolf does not make for the wilderness; instead, he haunts the edges of the town, slaughtering the dogs that had been set upon him when he was chained outside the saloon. This is how Seton begins the story, when, from the window of a train, he sees the Winnipeg Wolf take on and best "a huge mob of dogs" (E.T. Seton 1905b, 291). Moreover, the wolf seeks its revenge on its original captor and kills him. Finally, the townspeople get serious about hunting this wolf, bringing not only dogs but also guns to the fight. The Winnipeg Wolf succumbs but, much like Lobo, on his own terms: "He had made his choice. His days were short and crammed with quick events. His tale of many peaceful years was spent in three days brunt … He chose to drink his cup at a single gulp, and break the glass" (E.T. Seton 1905b, 319–20). With that, the wolf is killed.

Seton's story entitled "Wosca and Her Valiant Cub" (1937) offers a different lens: a child caring for his aged mother. The backstory here is similar to the Winnipeg Wolf: the reader is witness to the barbarity not of animals but of people when a trapper kills all but one of the pups in a den to lure the mother, a prized white wolf. After an escape and recapture, the cub is purchased by the legendary Buffalo Bill, who takes his new pet to his ranch. It grows, like all of Seton's wolves, to be an extraordinary giant. Thinking that the wolf's association with humans has made him more dog-like, he is let off his chain with increasing frequency. One day, he doesn't return and, instead, seeks out and finds his mother. They haunt the badlands together for ten years, but eventually she grows frail. Their connection means that rather than abandoning her, he hunts and brings her food. This is where the wolfers in Seton's tale finally catch up to these two wolves: the mother, lame, confined to a cave, and the son bringing her food for survival. But even as they acknowledge the emotion and self-sacrifice in the wolf's actions, it matters little. As Seton contends, "they were not here for sentiment, they were here to kill that wolf" (1937, 21). To achieve their aim, they capture the aged mother and use her as bait. Like Lobo and the Winnipeg Wolf, these wolves are fated to die, but they do so on their own terms: "The rifles rang – and down they went together, riddled through, gripping the steel, gripping the dust, each with their last defiance. And two big animal souls – big, strong, heroic souls – had fled" (ibid., 25).

An interesting biopolitical thread runs through each of these stories. Lobo, Badlands Billy, the Winnipeg Wolf, and Wosca have all been made strong through the bounty. Rather than extermination, numbers have only thinned, and the wolves that remain are smarter, wiser, and more able, by turns, to avoid traps and torment lively property in the form of cows and sheep. In some ways, then, the bounty – a boundary-creating mechanism used to divide vermin from valued species, as explored in chapter 2 – works against itself. In short, the survival of an improved wolf was an unintended consequence of a necropolitical project (described in chapter 1) and points to the ways in which power, even the power to kill, is never total. Simultaneously, however, Seton suggests in each of these stories that even if wolves are exceptional creatures made even more so by their capacity to learn from loss, their time is at an end. The lamentation of Lobo inflects all of Seton's wolf stories. For Seton, the wolf's fate is tied to Indigenous Peoples, with both giving way to the relentless inevitability of colonialism. The myth of the "vanishing Indian" is writ large in Seton's works and finds both expression and conflation in his articulation of the last of the wild wolves: "There was a time when the American wolf was, above all things, a creature of valour and speed. By these he lived, and had no fear of any other creature, however great its speed and valour. But a mighty change came over the big buffalo wolves when the whiteman appeared on the scene, equipped with horses for speed and modern guns for destruction – a combination too strong for any beast, however valiant it might be" (E.T. Seton 1937, viii). As Brian Johnson suggests, drawing on Patrick Brantlinger and Alan Lawson, the imperialist nostalgia embedded in the trope of the vanishing Indian serves to justify the displacements of colonialism. It does so by naturalizing a hierarchy based on the entanglement of ideas of species and race ripped open by social Darwinism. In this way of thinking, the fact that it is regrettable does not make it any less inevitable. For Seton, this too is extended to wolves, similarly out of place and time. No matter their strength, "the life of a wild animal always has a tragic end" (E.T. Seton [1898] 2009, 4); these wolves, like the "easy" ones before them, will succumb to human will. Seton sees individual wolves as majestic and noble creatures, capable of loyalty, love, bravery, altruism, forethought, and planning as well as the capacity for revenge. But as a population, wolves can only ever be anachronistic. Their time has passed.

CHARLES G.D. ROBERTS: THE SAVAGE WOLF

Charles G.D. Roberts also began crafting his realistic animal stories at the turn of the twentieth century. He admired Seton's work and dedicated *The Watchers of the Trails* to "my fellow in the wild Ernest Thompson Seton" (1904c). But Roberts was interested in a different kind of wolf narrative, as much as he was interested in wolves at all. Indeed, wolves appear in only 10 per cent of Roberts's animal stories (Brazier-Tompkins 2010). This may be, in part, because when Roberts penned his stories, wolves were largely extirpated in the Maritimes, which is the setting for most of his work. While they do not appear as often as bears, they do operate as important vehicles for understanding Roberts's view about nature.

Roberts did not see wolves as noble, majestic, and loyal guardians of wilderness, in the way Seton did. Rather, Roberts's wolves tend toward viciousness and depravity, much like the stories found in *Rod and Gun.*

A common theme in Roberts's wolf narratives is the idea that they make sport out of stalking people. In at least four of his stories, wolves hunt humans, who often cannot believe what is happening. For example, in "On the Night Trail" (Roberts [1909] 1966), wolves hunt a woodsman who has captured a lynx alive with the goal of selling it to a menagerie. In "The Passing of the Black Whelps" (Roberts 1904b), a lumberman headed back to camp is hunted by a pack of wolves. Yet again, this time in "The Homeward Trail" (Roberts 1904a), wolves stalk human prey – a man and his son attempting to return home for a Christmas surprise – before they give up their chase. A section of his story "The Grey Master" (Roberts 1907) recounts how a wolf, escaped from a miner who brought it to New Brunswick from Alaska, follows a young boy who must cross the woods to seek medical attention for his ailing mother. In a final and intriguing example, Roberts tells the story of an Indigenous man protected against a ravening wolf pack by a supernatural wolf, the bond between the two forged at the moment of the man's birth (Roberts 1922). As mentioned, more often than not, the reaction to being stalked is disbelief. These wolves are out of place, attempting to reoccupy settler landscapes from which they have been long removed. As the trapper in "On the Night Trail" asserts, "Ther' ain't never been a wolf in New Brunswick!" but, "even as he spoke, the sinister cry arose again, nearer and yet nearer" (Roberts [1909] 1966, 226). In each case, people stubbornly resist the notion that wolves could have returned. They have to confront their assumptions about settled versus wild lands if they are to prevail.

In addition, Roberts uses his stories to explore the boundaries not only between wild and tame landscapes but also between animals. Two of Roberts's narratives speak to this assertion: "Mixed Breed" (1925) and "The Passing of the Black Whelps" (1904b). "Mixed Breed" is the story of Bran, a dog with "a strong strain of wolf close to the surface" (Roberts 1925, 103). Invoking both an anxiety around and disdain for hybridization, Roberts suggests that such admixtures lead almost necessarily to duelling natures: the self cannot be whole in this context. This is true of Bran, who begins to slip into his wolf nature while minding his master's sheep: "Stealthy, almost imperceptibly to himself, a savage impulse began to creep up, itching, into his brain. He felt presently a fierce craving to dash among the silly, comfortable flock, and scatter them – to see the fleeing in wild terror before him – to slash at their tender, woolly throats – to feel the gush of their hot sweet blood upon his tongue. Even so would that ancestral timber wolf have felt, watching, from behind a bush in the Yukon wilds, the approach of an unsuspecting little herd of caribou" (ibid.,

103–4). In the end, after a winding tale where Bran eventually follows his instinct and kills a sheep, regret forces him to cut himself off from humans. Yet Roberts asserts that he craves the mastery of men to soothe the wolf inside. In the end, he is adopted by a woodsman turned aspiring gold prospector who takes him to the Yukon in search of new adventures.

But this fear of miscegenation and the reassertion of human mastery and control – and the animal desire for it – is found not only in "Mixed Breed." Roberts dealt with the subject much earlier in "The Passing of the Black Whelps." In this narrative, a wolf, driven from its pack through injury, feeds off the edges of civilization where prey is much easier to find and slaughter. As a result, the wolf encounters a female dog whose owner has recently died, opening up the potential for corruption. Both wolf and dog seize on this and become mates, the dog giving herself over to the wolf side of her nature: "That night they hunted together. In joy of comradeship and emulation, prudence was scattered to the winds, and they held a riot of slaughter. When day broke a dozen or more sheep lay dead about the pastures. And the wolf, knowing that men and dogs would soon be noisy on their trail, led his new-found mate far back into the wilderness" (Roberts 1904b, 338). Eventually dog and wolf breed, having eight pups that appear to be more than the sum of their parents, both bigger and more fearsome; it seems, at least initially, that their hybridity makes them stronger. And yet, this strength is paired with a kind of unboundedness and an inability to know one's place: "the hybrid whelps, by some perversion of inherited instinct, hated man savagely, and had less dread of him than either of their parents" (ibid., 340). The pack sets upon a lumberjack headed back to camp (who, once again, is bewildered to discover there could be wolves in New Brunswick). He is surrounded, and likely done for, when he sees one of his pursuers is a dog rather than a wolf. Asserting his mastery over her nature, he commands the dog to cease her hunt. And then something interesting happens. The dog remembers it is a dog and the wolf remembers it is a wolf: that which had been upended returns to normalcy. For the dog, she suddenly hates her progeny and defends the lumberjack against their assault. The pups, blinded by blood lust and their own cruelty, attack their mother. The wolf responds by recognizing the pups now for what they have always been: freakish. "These unnatural whelps that attacked her – he suddenly saw them, not as wolves at all, but as dogs, and hated them with a deadly hate" (ibid., 346). In the end, the wolf helps the lumberjack kill the aberrant half-breeds, a strange human-animal unfolding of a biopolitical drama where the alien is purged and purity is once again restored.

Misao Dean (2013, 374) contends that Roberts's creatures are "(m) animals," or what she calls "simulacra of social subjects." If we take this as a reasonable proposition, Roberts is telling his readers something about living in the world. It is hard then not to see at least these two tales as a broader allegory against racial mixing. The taint of "savagery" found in the black whelps comes from their miscegenation. The admixture of dog and wolf is a perversion, not only of genetic boundaries but also of domesticated and wild. But this emphasis on the perils of racial mixing emerges from a broad conflation of wolves and Indigenous Peoples that was not limited to Roberts. However, its expression in Roberts hinges on the notion that both represent the kind of savagery that the white settler sought to displace – both native to the landscape, both supplanted by the civilizing forces of colonization. In Brian Johnson's (2007, 344) reading, Roberts's woodsmen "go native" but adhere to their whiteness as evidenced by the reassertion of control over wild nature (wolves) and the articulation of "the human hero's special kinship with the world of nature." The human protagonists of Roberts's wolf stories are knowledgeable about – but not of – the wilderness. They retain their whiteness even as they "play Indian," and in so doing, naturalize their claim to the land.

So Roberts's stories contain a racial anxiety, but one that is complicated by its relationship to masculinity. As Dean (2013) suggests, Roberts's stories echo late-nineteenth-century nativist fears that the racialized and feminized stain of the city was working to destabilize the social body. Patricia Jasen (1995, 105) has shown this desire to escape the degeneracy of the city as a key factor in the popularity of tourism and summer camps in Ontario, where visitors could slough off the "effects of overwork and 'overcivilization' on personal and racial health." With specific reference to Roberts, Jasen (1995, 110) notes that "Canada's 'serious' nature poets ... were also preoccupied with the menace of urban life to health, well-being, and the survival of the race itself. For them, real danger (real wildness, in the pre-romantic sense) lay in cities, not in forests." As such, a return to nature was seen as an antidote to such ills. But it was also an assertion of masculinity of a particular kind: a passionate manhood that required a recovery of the "primitive man" in nature to assuage the feminizing and overcivilizing effects of urban life (Rotundo 1993; see also Scharff 2003). It was a tempered rather than unbound masculinity, tied as it was to the performance of whiteness. So, "a return to nature" could not also include "a return to barbarism" (Dean 2013, 372). Roberts's stories reflect this tension most often through the assertion of a commanding masculinity, which heralds the inevitability of the white man's triumph over nature. This was clear in both "Mixed Breed" and "The Passing of the Black Whelps" explored above. However, it is a theme in other stories that feature wolves. For example, in "The Grey Master," Roberts (1907, 162) writes: "Of course, the result was inevitable, for no beast, not even such a one as the Grey Master, is a match, in the long run, for a man who is in earnest." In "The Lone Wolf" (1912) and "On the Night Trail" ([1909] 1966), animals are similarly cowed by the voice of a man. In both, the sound of a man's voice is enough to render inert the violence incipient in the bodies of wolves.

FARLEY MOWAT: THE ELEGIAC WOLF

Both Seton and Roberts storied the wolf in ways that sought to work out the gendered and colonial anxieties of white men, but through different approaches. For Seton, the wolf offered a chance to go native, his dissolution into the wilderness complete in his transformation into Black Wolf. For Roberts, wilderness was important as a means to reassert white masculinity – wolves (among other predators) became the foil through which this was made possible. Half a century later, Farley Mowat takes up the charge left by these early nature writers. Indeed, Lutts (1998) contends that the realistic animal story does not disappear but is transformed by an attention to environmental consciousness.

Farley Mowat is known as Canada's premier popular narrator of the natural world. Penning some forty-four books and selling 25 million copies of them, Mowat is perhaps most celebrated for *Never Cry Wolf* (McGoogan 2011). In the book, Mowat recounts his six-month love affair with a pack of wolves in Canada's Subarctic as part of his work with the Canadian Wildlife Service to determine the cause of caribou decline. Framing himself as an inept neophyte, in terms of both the nature of the North and the nature of intransigent bureaucracy, Mowat's journey is one of self-discovery: he comes to know himself as flawed and biased, yet eventually partially redeemed, through the gaze of a wolf. Through an attempt to "become wolf," Mowat discovers that rather than the ravening beasts he expected, wolves are social creatures that display kindness, affection, play, and parental skill. Mowat suggests that the Arctic wolves subsist almost entirely on mice, and when they do take a caribou, it is only the old and the sick. So non-aggressive are Mowat's wolves that when he crawls into one's den and comes face to face with mother and cubs, the wolf doesn't even growl. Hence, Mowat's task becomes the recuperation of the wolf in Canada, the recasting of this marauding villain in its true form: an environmental hero.

The genre that Mowat deploys to heal the wounded reputation of *Canis lupus* is creative non-fiction, through which he updated and expanded the realistic animal story. As a genre, creative non-fiction holds both possibilities and pitfalls in its attempts to build environmental consciousness. Put another way, there is a kind of margin-dwelling to the genre that can be both fruitful and dangerous. As Borich (2013) tells us, creative non-fiction inhabits the shadow between the novel and the documentary, and, as such, may be more a matter of feeling than fact. In this way, the emotive character of creative non-fiction – the use of real events layered over with subjective interpretation – can act as a powerful vehicle to encourage particular ways of encountering the world. Because the focus on these animal lives is an imaginative and perhaps intuitive act of putting oneself in the shoes of the animal, creative non-fiction offers the opportunity for identification with animals that an ethology of wolves could not – and does not – hope to accomplish. As such, the genre was useful in terms of generating sympathy and hence conservation action for a much-maligned predator.

That said, the "creative" part of creative non-fiction has been a source of some controversy similar to the realistic animal story. In some quarters, Farley Mowat is credited with "inventing the North" (as if it was a place that did not pre-exist his construction of it). However, for Inuit and other inhabitants of the Subarctic, as well as biologists and members of the Canadian Wildlife Service, Mowat is often hailed by the sardonic moniker "Hardly Know-it." A 1996 exposé in the now-defunct *Saturday Night* magazine emphasized the fiction in Mowat's work, suggesting that much of *Never Cry Wolf* was based on limited experience and exaggeration, and drew heavily on the work of "real" wolf biologists (Goddard 1996). For example, Goddard notes that rather than spending two years in the North, Mowat was only there for six months in total and only observed wolf dens for a month of that time. Similarly, Doug Pimlott (1966) suggests that Mowat committed the cardinal sin of crying wolf himself through his distortion of the facts of wolf biology. So, there are also risks associated with the adoption of this genre, both in the representation of people and animals and the impact of the book when it is discovered that it might be more fiction than reality. However, Mowat remained unmoved by this criticism. As he himself suggested, he did not feel bound by fidelity to actual events. He is quoted as saying, "Fuck the facts. The truth is what is important" (Mowat in Martin 2014). For Mowat, the ends justified playing fast and loose with some of the real details of the narrative; the goal of his exaggeration was to correct misconceptions that promoted wolf suffering and death, a noble pursuit to end misery.

"THE WOLF'S AT THE DOOR AND HE HAS SOME QUESTIONS ..."

3.2 "THE WOLF'S AT THE DOOR AND HE HAS SOME QUESTIONS ..."
Editorial cartoon drawn by Malcolm Mayes and published in the *Edmonton Journal*
that pokes fun at the veracity of Farley Mowat's claims.

Following the narrative conventions of early nature writing found in
Seton and Roberts, Mowat, as the noble and misanthropic hero, must suffer
to come to know nature in any meaningful way. Attempting to escape the
miseries he saw in the Second World War, Mowat encounters the North
already a wounded subject (Mowat [1952] 2004). While Mowat's spirit is
eventually salved by his relationship with the wolves, his physical and
emotional hardships magnify. For example, he recounts the swarms of
mosquitos that plague his movements (Mowat [1963] 2009, 43), the
difficulties in mimicking wolf napping (67), the challenges associated with
urinating like wolves to mark his territory (61), and the complications of
restricting himself to a diet of mice to see if he could model wolf behaviour
(84). Yet these physical indignities, though humorously told, pale in comparison to his emotional struggle. *Never Cry Wolf* is animated with the
task of Michel Foucault's (2001) parrhesia – the burden of truth-telling.
As Karen R. Jones notes, Mowat casts himself as the "valiant dissident"
(2003, 12), struggling against the bureaucratic incompetence and willful
blindness of the Canadian federal government committed to the position
that wolves were responsible for the decline in caribou herds (see, for

example, Mowat [1963] 2009, 7, 9–11, 13, 27, 133, 165). His job is to make them see what they would not, and he rails against the futility of the mission he has set himself. He suffers for a truth that no one wants to hear.

The root of much of Mowat's misery is found in the suffering felt by the wolves themselves, anachronistic moral subjects adrift in a world beset by the violence of modernity. Like Seton and Roberts, he relies on proleptic elegies of extinction to narrate his tale. And yet Mowat is central to this narrative as he charts his own implication in this assault. He lingers on feelings of terror at his first meeting with the wolf pack he comes to love (ibid., 40, 43) and his sense that he is nothing more than a prey species to these creatures. At a number of points, he notes that breaking his preconceived notions about wolves, even as he has experienced their true nature, remains elusive at best (ibid., 54, 56–7, 170–1, 180). Even in the book's conclusion, his raw fear of the wolves endures: he struggles to shed his own bias against the predator he has come to venerate. While the wolves suffer, they do so through Mowat's pain at their vilification.

Moreover, Mowat commits a kind of epistemic violence, erasing the very nonhuman he purports to champion through imaginative acts of anthropomorphism. While Mowat makes the wolves of his study – George, Angeline, Uncle Albert – apprehendable as individuals, he also renders them into "a menagerie of most lovable creatures" (K. Jones, *Never Cry Wolf*, 2003, 6) who seem more human than lupine. For example, he describes George as a good father, Angeline as passionate, and the two as a devoted pair (Mowat [1963] 2009, 68). Similarly, he remarks on George's well-developed sense of humour (ibid., 82), which saved the wolf's relationship with Mowat from an irrevocable break. The wolves in *Never Cry Wolf* are always virtuous in human terms: for instance, only killing weakened and sick caribou, always caring for their extended families, and sometimes taking in the pups from slain wolf packs. In this way, Mowat finds common cause with Seton rather than Roberts. Instead of encountering the wolf in all its complexity as an apex predator, we are presented with rather large and fluffy dogs whose primary purpose is to teach us how to be good humans (see also K. Jones, *Never Cry Wolf*, 2003). Mowat could have seized on the ambivalence and intuition inherent to the genre to tell a different kind of story, maybe one that stuck with the alterity of wolfiness, without resorting to anthropomorphizing. Or he could have invited his readers to think of wolves as individuals whose agency was not dependent on human interpretations of family life, affection, or play. He could have lingered much longer on the Inuit insistence of wolf as kin, as well as their ability to hear wolves talk to one another, as a much more interesting challenge to the kind of scientific pursuit he derides but cannot quite rid himself of. Rather, he remained firmly locked into a declensionist narrative of grief and loss culminating in the epilogue, where predator control units likely kill the wolves that Mowat grew to love.

These three layers of misery and grief, two foregrounded and one obscured, allow for a particular environmental subjectivity to unfold and be rendered legible in the Canadian context, a subjectivity that works through a kind of imperialist nostalgia – a lament for that which we ourselves have destroyed. And I would contend this is precisely why the book has been so popular, made more so by the 1980s Disney film version. Mowat's misery around the persecution of the wolves in the Subarctic succeeded because it was of its time: it was "attractive to a public alienated from technology and progress and eager to identify, at least vicariously, with nature … the glimpse of Eden lost" (Dunlap 1983, 63). The grooves of the story were already beginning to be well worn in environmental circles in the 1960s, and the disappearance of the wolf could be read alongside the "vanishing Indian" narrative Mowat espoused in *People of the Deer*: the uncorrupted yet hapless victims of modernity. Never mind that wolves endured 200 years of the bounty, adapting to their new conditions of possibility in a world asymmetrically aligned against them. Mowat's trope of extinction fit better with the environmentalism of the time, and it still wields power today.

The genre of creative non-fiction helped this along. Because Mowat seemed so truthful with his reflections based on scientific observation, people accepted *Never Cry Wolf* as truth, so much so that they wrote the Canadian Wildlife Service in the thousands to excoriate them about their efforts at wolf extermination, efforts that had long since ceased in the area (Goddard 1996). Because of *Never Cry Wolf*'s veneration of a literal underdog, victim to a faceless bureaucratic machine, to a scientific community that chose to vilify rather than understand, and to trappers who quite happily blamed wolves rather than admit their own profligate ways, it was hard not to sympathize with the creatures of Mowat's book, especially as they were so darn affable. In short, *Never Cry Wolf* became popular because it appeared to be a radical challenge – when it wasn't. Mowat seemed like he knew the wolf – when he didn't; really, he only knew himself.

STORIES OF NATURE AND NATION

In the 2003 Massey Lectures, novelist and academic Thomas King (2003, 2) asserted that "the truth about stories is that's all we are." King (2003, 9) contends that "stories are wonderous things. And they are dangerous."

Recounting the Anishinaabe teaching around the origin of Turtle Island and contrasting it to the Christian creation story found in Genesis, King shows that the content of the story and the manner of its telling have an impact to how we encounter the world far beyond the story itself. Emilie Cameron (2015, 12) echoes this sentiment about the power of stories, noting that their "relational and material ordering practices" do not simply reflect but also make up the world. In other words, stories carve and render, shape and relate worlding as they are told and retold.

The stories written by Seton, Roberts, and Mowat demonstrate how this has been the case for the wolf in Canada. The manner in which they have narrated wolves over time has shown not only that writers respond to the cultural currents they navigate but also how they create them, rendering words into matter. In their own way, each author both relied upon and curated visions of the wolf that have impacted how Canadians have come to see them, participating in a reimagining of the role of wolf in this country. In different ways, Seton, Roberts, and Mowat have used the wolf as a cipher to explore the complexities of indigeneity, gender, nature, and nation, even as they ostensibly sought to show their passion – positive and negative – for all things lupine.

The Vanishing Wild

Each of the authors examined in this chapter relies on a kind of anticipatory elegy for the wolves they write into existence. Put another way, each offers his own version of extinction narrative. For Seton, we hear the elegy as a lamentation, as sorrow at the inevitable loss of a remarkable foe. But Seton's expression of sorrow is for more than just wolves – it is for all the wildness he sees being supplanted by the perils of civilization. For this reason, he started the Woodcraft Indians in 1902, the precursor – and in some ways a beleaguered competitor – to the Boy Scouts of America. Through this organization, Seton sought to preserve and inculcate the practices that he felt secured his particular version of manhood. Through tracking, reading of animal signs, camping techniques, and nature appreciation, white upper-class boys could shed the veneer of civilization (laced as it was with feminine taint) and return to a primitive time, at least temporarily (Deloria 1998; see also Jasen 1995). Philip J. Deloria has shown that this supposed veneration of anti-modernism and a fixation with Indigenous virtue was, in fact, a reassertion of an improved modern identity. The summer camps conceived under the banner of the Woodcraft Indians worked to suture the positives of the anti-modern to white masculinity, to assuage the perils of a declensionist inauthenticity that turned boys into "flat chested cigarette smokers, with shaky nerves and doubtful vitality" (Seton in Deloria 1998, 107). Programs like the Woodcraft Indians were meant to "devise a better modern" (Deloria 1998, 102).

It makes sense, then, that Seton's assertion of the value of Indigenous knowledge of the wilderness for young white boys was predicated on the notion that the real Indian was vanishing; it could be no other way, otherwise Seton couldn't take their place. Seton saw his role in life as an interlocutor for a disappearing Indigenous knowledge. Julia Seton in *The Gospel of the Redman* recounts a mystic's admonition to her husband when they arrived in Los Angeles in 1905: "You are a Red Indian Chief, reincarnated to give the message of the Redman to the White race, so much in need of it. Why don't you get busy?" (Seton and Seton 1966, vi).

Taking on Indigenous identity – or "playing Indian" – was not and is not uncommon among settlers in colonial countries like the United States and Canada. In the United States, Deloria (1998) contends that the twin desires of appropriation and annihilation drove white men to masquerade as Indigenous and, in doing so, claim a sense of authentic identity in a land they stole from others. In Canada, white men like Archibald Belaney – a.k.a. Grey Owl – similarly walked the line between desire and dispossession, using what Erickson (2011) has called "Indian surrogacy" to preserve not only wilderness but also white entitlement to it. In both nations, it served to assuage a sense of "anxious unbelonging" (B. Johnson 2007, 338). Seton falls within this tradition of venerating the "noble savage," where, as Deloria (1998, 4) suggests, "pure and natural Indians serve to critique Western society," even as their own actions continued to dispossess these very same Indigenous People. Seton deployed pieces of Indigenous culture from different nations at different times (at least Sioux, Algonquin, and Haudenosaunee, according to Wadland 1978, 358) and sutured them into a patchwork that offered "an act of double appropriation of wildlife and Aboriginal discourses" (M. Jones 2008, 139). Seton recast both nature and Indigenous People as disappearing and elevated himself as the Black Wolf, able to speak for both. For Seton, "going wolf" also meant "going Native." His elegy was also an imaginative act of self-aggrandizement, while at the same time securing wilderness as a space for white Canada.

For Roberts, extinction was no less certain to happen, but contained fewer tears. The extermination of wolves was but one part of a longer evolution, which saw the transformation of the land from wild to domesticated. In Deloria's (1998) typology, Roberts falls more on the side of annihilation than veneration. If we take seriously Manina Jones's contention that Roberts's nonhuman characters are "manimals," then what does he offer us with his exploration of wolves? Johnson argues that Roberts's wolves are symbolic of a "threatening indigeneity" (B. Johnson 2007, 345) that requires suppression and elimination. This seems clear as one traces the wolves as they move through his stories, where they are always reimagined as radically out of place, so much so that the human characters have to be convinced repeatedly that they inhabit the same landscape. In Roberts's view, wolves have already been removed from the landscape, sometimes they just don't know they are dead.

While this narrative thread might initially seem to be complicated by the story "The White Wolf" (1922), closer examination reveals the way the tale actually shores it up. As briefly mentioned, this is the story of an Indigenous man named Wind-in-the-Night who, since birth, has a connection to, and is favoured by, a mythical white wolf. Wind-in-the-Night goes south to work as a guide for prospectors but hears about the harsh winter at his home and decides he must bring supplies. Unbeknownst to him, at the same time, his son is suffering from an illness and one of the community members offers to take him south for medicine (we find this out much later in the story). Wind-in-the-Night notices that he is being stalked by a pack of wolves. As he is about to succumb to their depredation, the white wolf saves him from the pack and then, later, from the cold. As one might expect, he crosses paths with his child as he heads north, and before he knows who it is, he recognizes that the pack is now following them. Presented with the difficult choice of helping them or pressing on to his community, he chooses the former. The white wolf tries to kill the boy's escort, but Wind-in-the-Night intervenes and kills the animal. The boy is already recovering, and they take the white wolf back with them to bury it like a chief. The people in this tale are not surprised to encounter wolves, but this is because they are Indigenous rather than white. Both Indigenous Peoples and wolves, then, can be rendered anachronistic, their lifeways interesting to document but also passing out of memory. In "The White Wolf," the village itself suffers from an inability to support itself, and its illness must be cured with medicines from the white man. And while Wind-in-the-Night has a connection to the wild that no white man could match, it is also unreliable, since the wolf turns on him in the end. As a parable, "The White Wolf" offers the sense that the wolf and Indigenous Peoples are the last of their kind.

Mowat's extinction narrative is perhaps more poignant than Seton's and certainly more so than Roberts's as the wolves he has come to love – not just as symbols but also as creatures with their own personalities – meet their dreadful end. He has genuine affection for and wonder at the wolves that he writes about. He seeks to know them by being one, casting aside human rationality for animal embodiment. Like Seton, he wishes to know the wolf from the inside out – and he goes much further in this aim than claiming a new moniker and shared persecution, as Seton did. One has the sense that in the death of Angeline, George, and Uncle Albert, there is a psychic death too for Farley Mowat.

Mowat also takes up Seton's mantle as the defender of Indigenous Peoples, seeking to indict Western disdain – as expressed through his exasperation for Canadian governmental bureaucracy – for both nature and Indigenous Peoples, even as he re-inscribes his whiteness through authorial appropriation. In Mowat, again as in Seton, there is a kind of conflation at work between lupine and indigene, with both possessing a deep land-based wisdom that Mowat covets but can never achieve. Brian Johnson (2007, 337) asserts that this conflation operates as technology of legitimation, "creating a veiled 'postcolonial' allegory that mitigates settler-invader guilt by legitimizing the displacement and dispossession of First Nations people." If Indigenous Peoples are the true advocates for the wild and their way of life is being destroyed, then it falls to soothsayers like Mowat to take up the mantle of saving nature. This ignores, of course, the fact that Indigenous Peoples did not disappear at all. They both actively resisted and, in some cases, steered settlers' representations of their cultures and knowledge. For that matter, neither did the wolves disappear, though their extinction was foretold again and again by authors like Seton, Roberts, and Mowat. There is no doubt that their life chances were fundamentally altered and made much more difficult. But erasure of wolves from the landscape has remained incomplete.

This narrative also ignores the way in which the writers themselves are implicated in the loss that they lament. Seton, Roberts, and Mowat present themselves as chroniclers of extinction rather than its agents; they are simply watchful bystanders in a world that is moving on, evolving from savage to civilized. In this articulation, they might be passionately nostalgic, but they are not responsible. And yet, these men did not stand outside the circumstances that brought the wolf close to extinction or that impacted and further threatened the lives and lifeways of Indigenous Peoples. As Emilie Cameron (2015) has argued in her discussion of Samuel Hearne's infamous account of the "Bloody Falls massacre" in the Arctic, this kind of witnessing was not neutral. Hearne's story, one that has survived in a number of iterations since the late 1700s, is a supposed first-hand account by a Hudson's Bay Company employee of the Dene slaughter of a sleeping

Inuit encampment. What Hearne's continual retelling of this story of uncertain provenance elided was that his role was not an act of witnessing but, at Cameron notes, one of constitution. What Hearne offered was "a subject position from which Qablunaat [non-Inuit people] can witness the suffering of northern Indigenous Peoples without feeling involved or implicated in that suffering" (Cameron 2015, 36); this view persists in today's "settler moves to innocence" (Tuck and Wang 2012), where colonialism exists in a regrettable past for which no one can be held responsible. Hearne also positioned the Dene guides – rendered into proxies for indigeneity – as irredeemably violent, while settlers were only ever the witnesses rather than the perpetrators of this kind of harm. Seton, Roberts, and Mowat all affect this witnessing stance, offering a defeatism that is both romantic and privileged.[3] Like Hearne, each claim innocence for that which threatens the lives of human and nonhuman others. They can comfortably mourn the changes that colonization wrought while continuing their own lives unimpeded and unaffected by this mourning.

THE LIMITS OF PASSION

The stories offered by Seton, Roberts, and Mowat have shored up, in different ways, the kind of separation between humans and animals (and humans and humans, for that matter) that has provided the scaffolding for much harm. In particular, Seton and Roberts buttressed colonial justifications for the dispossession of Indigenous Peoples and the ideological remaking of the lands now called Canada into white settler space. These stories were often about foreclosure, particularly for Indigenous Peoples, who actively resisted Seton, Roberts, and Mowat's temporal erasure.

What the stories advance in terms of settler relationship to wolves is somewhat more ambivalent. In some sense, each author offers an opening through which a reimagining of human-animal relationality became thinkable. But even this way in, slight as it may be, was hard won, with both Seton and Roberts taking a great deal of punishment for transgressing the conventions of their time around the human-animal divide. This was exemplified in the "nature fakers" controversy, in which luminaries like John Burroughs and Theodore Roosevelt wrote publicly to chastise Ernest Thompson Seton, Charles G.D. Roberts, William Long, and Jack London for sentimentality rather than scientific fact in their writings (Burroughs [1903] 1998; M. Jones 2008; Walsh 2015). John Burroughs took particular exception to Seton's *Wild Animals I Have Known* ([1898] 2009) and the vigour with which he pressed his argument is worth quoting at length:

Mr Thompson Seton says in capital letters that his stories are true, and it is this emphatic assertion that makes the judicious grieve. True as romance, true in their artistic effects, true in their power to entertain the young reader, they certainly are but true as natural history they as certainly are not. Are we to believe that Mr Thompson Seton, in his few years of roaming in the West, has penetrated farther into the secrets of animal life than all of the observers who have gone before him? There are no stories of animal intelligence and cunning on record, that I am aware of, that match his ... Such dogs, wolves, foxes, rabbits, mustangs, crows, as he has known, it is safe to say, no other person in the world has ever known. Fact and fiction are so deftly blended in his work that only a real woodsman can separate them. (Burroughs in Lutts [1903] 1998, 132)

Roosevelt entered the fray in 1907, lending the legitimacy of the office of the president to his contention that the nature fakers should be exposed and their work shunned. Roosevelt (1920, 261) suggested that knowledge drawn from Indigenous sources – and one might assert he was specifically targeting Seton here – was suspect, as "they live in a world of mysticism" and hence their truth cannot be trusted. More broadly, he went on to caustically and brutally assault the writings of Seton and company as "comic absurdities," cataloguing their various flaws (ibid.). With respect to wolves, Roosevelt's (1920, 262) derision is barely contained: "Certain of their wolves appear as gifted with all the philosophy, the self-restraint, and the keen intelligence of, say, Marcus Aurelius, together with the lofty philanthropy of a modern altruist."

What seems to grate here is the idea that these nature writers committed a kind of intellectual fraud – using their imaginative capacities to enter the lives of animals. Years later, this nature fakery would be put forward once again to also smear Mowat's work, as explored above. But the claims of Seton, Roberts, and later Mowat were more radical and hence unnerving than that. Each author had contended having deeper insights than naturalists, who had made a scientific study of the biophysical world. But they further asserted that because of their attentiveness, they recognized something that others had missed: that animals possess agency that cannot be reduced to instinct. This stood in contradiction to the Western ontological assumption that subjectivity and consciousness belonged only on one side of the human-animal divide. As Manina Jones (2008) attests, Darwin's subversion of the supremacy of humans had all sorts of effects, one being that Seton and the other nature fakers began to see the possibility that animals were not so different from humans after all. Perhaps even more broadly, each of these authors suggested that animals might have something to teach us about how to live.

This assertion of animals as individual and collective agents in the world remains radical in settler culture even today, though such assertions are not at all strange to Indigenous ontologies. All three authors, in different ways, allowed for the possibility that wolves could be other than what their historical and cultural contexts dictated. Lobo or the Black Whelps or Angeline could be more than we had imagined: they could be agents crafting their own way in the world and, in turn, shaping the landscape we encounter. They could be actors that moved us in particular ways, not only through fear and loathing but also love and joy. Wolves could arouse in humans a reflection of the permeability of species divides. All three authors gestured toward an embrace of the animal, not necessarily because it was always knowable but because it was worth the encounter. As something new in the realm of the wolf, the work of these authors offered a dramatic reshaping of the political and cultural landscapes that wolves inhabited in Canada.

However, it would be risky to suggest that Seton, Roberts, and Mowat upended – as opposed to simply twisted – some of the ontological assumptions of Western thought. For example, none of these writers allowed wolves to author their own stories (whatever that might mean) nor can they be considered co-authors, as Seton would suggest. Moreover, their simultaneous efforts at speaking for and erasing of Indigenous Peoples are both deplorable and yet all too familiar. There are sharp edges to the project each author undertakes in his veneration of wolfkind; his passion is limited. Manina Jones (2008, 137) contends that Seton trafficked in a kind of lusty and uncertain potential to disrupt "anthropocentric claims to difference, superiority, and dominance." That may be, but in my view, these stories cannot point us toward a reconfigured relation with the wild, even if they allow for animal individuality. They remain inescapably burdened by racial, classed, and gendered anxieties and passions that are then relieved through the crafting of an extinction narrative where that which disrupts human exceptionalism is destined to fade away. They show that passion for something or someone is not enough, especially if it is framed through a nostalgic obsession. If we want to save wolves, we need a different kind of politics, one that upends rather than provides cover for the settler colonial state (chapter 7). We also need to be curious about wolves' capacities to affect and be affected. This is the subject of the next chapter.

4

Curiosity

The Scientific Reimagining of a Predator

On 21 March 1995, "Operation Wolfstock" delivered creatures to Yellowstone National Park that had been absent for almost seventy years: grey wolves. The story is well known, for it generated both light and heat. The battle over wolf reintroduction in the park raged in the decades following passage of the US Endangered Species Act (1973), involving "120 acrimonious public hearings and over 160,000 comments, required executive directives from six presidents, prompted the attention of dozens of congressional committees, and elicited over $12 million for scientific analysis" (Wilson 1997, 453–4). Once in motion, it took thirteen years just to craft and have the wolf recovery plan approved (Fritts et al. 1992). But Matthew Wilson contends that this story was not about just this animal; rather, the wolf became a proxy for bigger cultural shifts. The wolf, Wilson (1997, 454) suggests, was a "biopolitical pawn" in a much more complex assemblage of ideas around federal power and overreach, the social marginalization of rancher culture, and assertions around how humans should relate to the natural world. Some of the stories are the same as those we have encountered in other chapters. Ranchers felt their way of life was under threat, and that they themselves were an "endangered species threatened by what one rancher called the 'hazardous waste' of wolves" (K. Jones, "Fighting Outlaws," 2002, 40). Environmentalists – informed by scientific principles around the importance of predators for ecosystem health – felt the return of wolves to Yellowstone was "a symbol of ecological reconciliation, a return to wholeness" (Wilson 1997, 463). In the end, scientists and environmentalists prevailed and fourteen wolves from Alberta were brought to Yellowstone. In the following years, another twenty-seven arrived from British Columbia. As I write this (May 2020), the twenty-five-year anniversary of reintroduction has just passed. Now there are ninety-four wolves in eight packs (though these numbers fluctuate every year)

(Yellowstone National Park 2020), and the park has become a hub of biological research on the wolf. This reintroduction is held up – at least by some – as a triumph of ecological insight over obscurantism.

To Wilson's contention that the reintroduction was about more than the animal itself, I would add that the wolf's return to Yellowstone is also a national story. Put differently, it is framed as one nation – Canada – still alive with nature saving another – the United States – which had all but destroyed it. The wolves that found their way to the "ocean of elk" (Robbins 2020) in Yellowstone National Park were Canadian wolves. As I have recounted elsewhere (2011), on a research trip to Yellowstone some fifteen years ago, American ecotourists asserted that Yellowstone's new wolf population demonstrated Canada's foresight in saving the wild, unlike the United States. This was echoed in media accounts of the reintroduction, where some outlets displayed smugness that Canadian animals were needed to fix the conservation mistakes Americans committed (Pynn 1994). For example, some headlines read "Canadian Wolves Help Save US Wilderness" (Boswell 2003, A7), while others exclaimed "Canadian Wolves a Howling Success" (*Vancouver Sun* 1997, A14). Scientists involved in the reintroduction seemed to feel the same way about these "transplanted Canadian wolves" (Brooke 1996); for instance, Douglas Smith, the National Parks Service wildlife biologist who oversaw the reintroduction and continues to research wolves in Yellowstone today remarked: "I don't know how to describe it. Every day, I have to pinch myself to make sure this is for real. And every day, I thank Canada for sending us these animals. These wolves are truly a symbol of friendship and co-operation between our countries" (Struzik 1998, A1).

But, as we have explored so far, it wasn't inevitable that there would be any wolves left in Canada to transplant to the United States in 1995. Like its southern neighbour, Canadian provinces tried hard to put themselves in the same ecological pickle, exterminating top predators from a range of ecosystems. However, the work of a number of Canadian wildlife biologists sought to change these practices and the ideas that informed them. Chapter 4 turns from fiction to science, thinking about how biologists and conservationists engineered a reimagining of wolves that really took off in the 1960s and 1970s and, to a large extent, has remained with us ever since. This chapter explores how wolf researchers allowed themselves to be curious about wolves in ways that set the stage for understanding the wolf as central to rather than an enemy of ecosystems. They also opened up new possibilities in thinking about nature and nation together, predicated on ideas of "ecological integrity" instead of good and bad animals, ideas that only reached fruition in the 1980s (Mortimer-Sandilands 2009).

THE "AGE OF ECOLOGY"

The story of the reintroduction of wolves to Yellowstone National Park would have been unthinkable before the rise of ecology as an (inter) discipline to understand the dynamics of the natural world. As we saw in chapter 3 and explore again in chapter 7, there were always other ways of encountering wolves. However, these were often actively derided or supressed, made unintelligible in the face of the dominant settler view that wolves – bad animals that stalked, killed, and ate the good – should be marked for extermination. The ascendance of ecology and wildlife biology provided the intellectual scaffolding for a new way of talking about wolves, not as villains or vermin, or as even as beautiful and majestic yet doomed creatures, but as members of ecosystems and as populations to be known and counted. Nevertheless, while opening up new possibilities for predators like wolves to thrive, ecology also circumscribed them in particular ways.

As explored in chapter 2, wolf management in Canada until the 1940s involved the necropolitical practice of killing one species – the wolf – to foster the lives of others: wild and domesticated ungulates. Management, such as it was, was predicated on annihilation through less structured means, like bounties, and more bureaucratized mechanisms, like predator control officers and poisoning programs. These approaches did not suddenly vanish in the 1940s; many provinces had such policies in place well into the 1950s and 1960s, with Ontario maintaining its bounty into the 1970s. But the way these policies and practices were talked about, the certainty with which they were presumed as the most effective and obvious way forward was called into question. And this had much to do with the ascendance of ecology.

As Curt Meine (2010) recounts, Charles Elton and Arthur Tansley were key to early ecological thought. Elton's 1927 book *Animal Ecology* offered the language of ecological interaction that is familiar to us today: "food chains, food webs, trophic levels, the niche, and other basic concepts" (Meine 2010, 10; see also Dunlap 1988). Tansley gifted science with the idea of an ecosystem in 1935, a delicate balance of forces and relationships born through millions of years of evolution (Meine 2010). And, of course, Aldo Leopold was important here too. Leopold's essay "The Land Ethic" asserted the intellectual superstructure that ecologists needed to render their worldview intelligible: "It brought together a scientific approach to nature, a high level of ecological sophistication, and a biocentric, communitarian ethic that challenged the dominant economic attitude toward land use" (Worster 1994, 284). Extending considerability to the land and all its inhabitants, Leopold's ethic makes ecological principles of biotic communities, diversity, energy flows, and holism questions not only of science but also morality: "A land ethic, then, reflects the existence of an ecological conscience, and this in turn reflects a conviction of individual responsibility for the health of the land. Health is the capacity of the land for self-renewal. Conservation is our effort to understand and preserve this capacity" (Leopold 1949, 221). So, for Leopold and those who were swayed by his philosophy – like Douglas Pimlott and later John Theberge – ecology had a central place in explaining the relationships and systems that make up our world and offered the right way of living in it.

Leopold was also central to a reimagining of the role of large predators in ecosystems, especially wolves. However, he did not start out this way. Leopold was a product of his time, one that mandated that deer, as a productive game species, should live and that wolves, as a useless predator that ate deer, should die (Dunlap 1988). In his now-famous essay "Thinking like a Mountain," Leopold (1949, 130) tells the story of shooting the wolf, which changed his life: "I was young then, and full of trigger-itch; I thought that because fewer wolves meant more deer, that no wolves would mean hunters' paradise. But after seeing the green fire die, I sensed that neither the wolf nor the mountain agreed with such a view." He writes that the mountain knows this view is folly, for when there are no wolves, deer over-browse the bushes and trees that grow on its slopes. Once the keystone predator is removed, the ecosystem becomes imbalanced. But before "Thinking like a Mountain" was published, Leopold elaborated more on the relationship between predator and prey in his book *Game Management* (1933), where he noted that these dynamics were rooted in the density and characteristics of prey and predator populations as well as food sources, rather than the inherent nobility or wickedness of prey and predators, respectively. As Dunlap (1988, 88) notes, "predators were now not evil, even a necessary evil: they were evidence of the completeness of that part of the natural world."

By the time *A Sand County Almanac* was published in 1949, some its ideas had found fertile ground. In particular, field biologists were instrumental in fleshing out predator-prey dynamics. During the 1940s and 1950s, we begin to see the recuperation of the wolf in earnest (Harrington and Paquet 1982). Among the first – and serving as the inspiration for many who came after – was Adolph Murie's (1944) research on wolves and their impact on Dall sheep in Mount McKinley (now Denali) National Park in Alaska. From 1939–41, Murie studied wolves and their ecological relationships with not only Dall sheep but also caribou, moose, fox, and other animals by engaging in close field observation, inspection of sheep remains, scat analysis, and skull studies, breaking methodological ground that would be adapted in later studies. Murie wrote the first definitive account of timber wolves in North America, describing their characteristics, pack behaviour (including hunting, howling, breeding, and tolerance for other wolves), and food habits in extraordinary ethological detail (see chapter 2). In the end, Murie determined that wolves did control Dall sheep populations, but not to their detriment. He argued that wolves prey on the old, weak, sick, or very young: "predation would seem to benefit the species over a long period of time and indicates a normal prey-predator adjustment in Mount McKinley National Park" (ibid., 230). He made similar observations about caribou, the wolves' main food source. For Murie, this meant that wolves should be allowed to persist in national parks as "areas dedicated to preserving samples of primitive America" (ibid., 232), unlike the western United States where "it was, of course, necessary that the wolf should go" (ibid., xiii). The recuperation of the wolf was not to interfere with the progress or commerce of the nation.

Ian McTaggart-Cowan, professor in zoology at the University of British Columbia, conducted similar studies in parks of the Rocky Mountains[1] between 1943 and 1946. Following some of Murie's methods, McTaggart-Cowan (1947) included different phases in his study, such as scat analysis, examination of kills, tracking, the use of wardens' counts, and first-hand observations. Like Murie, he traced the specificities of the lives of wolves in these parks, describing their physical characteristics, their movements, their distribution in winter and summer, breeding habits, dens, efforts at territorial defence, hunting behaviour, food habits, and the effects of control programs on their populations. He confirmed Murie's findings that wolves mostly ate game (rather than rodents, as Mowat would have it). He also confirmed that wolves were not, as was imagined, decimating elk populations: "The comparative figures from wolf-inhabited and wolf-free areas reveal that at the present population levels of wolves and ungulates the net effect of wolves on game herd productivity in Banff and Jasper Parks is inconsequential. It is apparent, then, that evidence points to the wolf as being of lesser importance to the survival of game in the parks than are the welfare factors, of which the most important is food supply adequate in amount and in composition. The present overcapacity game herds, inhabiting many parts of the Rocky Mountain parks, developed largely since 1930, at a time when predator control varied from none at all to light, with traps used infrequently, and poison strictly prohibited at all times" (McTaggart-Cowan 1947, 172). McTaggart-Cowan's study showed that the wolves were not even making a dent in the ungulate population. His efforts opened a possibility space to think about predator-prey relationships in the Canadian context. By deploying scientific expertise, he rendered legible the idea that rather than villains, wolves were one actor in the broader ecological webs of the Rocky Mountains. His efforts led others to name him the "father of wildlife management in Canada" (Campbell, Jakimchuk, and Demarchi 2013, 808).

THE LAND THAT CAN GROW A WOLF

If McTaggart-Cowan opened the window for wolves, Douglas Pimlott battered down the door. And there were many similarities between the two. For starters, both did their work in the ecological patchwork of the Canadian parks system. It is perhaps not terribly surprising that both McTaggart-Cowan and Pimlott chose such places to conduct their research; not only were their projects dictated by federal and provincial government agencies but also the parks were more likely to be home to wolves. Parks are also sites where the nation is written and rewritten onto the body of the land. As environmental historian Claire Campbell (2017) has remarked of the first parks in Canada and the United States, "the national park became a useful means of claiming the western interior and in the process acquiring iconic images of territory to nurture a sense of national identity." The making of this national identity involved both physical and epistemic violence (see, for example, Mortimer-Sandilands 2009; Sandlos 2008); indeed, national and provincial parks served as an ideological handmaiden of settler colonialism, both expelling Indigenous Peoples from their traditional territories and transforming them into sites not only of national nature but also of commerce, through logging and tourism. In settler colonial countries like Canada, there are no uncomplicated spaces, but the national and provincial parks are particularly fraught with the entanglement of ideas of nature, nation, and claims to the land. Similarly, Algonquin Provincial Park, which began its life as a national park, was shorn from its cultural surround, instead memorialized as national nature by timber interests, government intention, and public interest in wildlife (Duffy 2002, 71–9). And so, when Pimlott conducted some of the most consequential studies of wolves in Canada on the unceded land of the Algonquins, he inherited this tradition of seeing it as a natural rather than cultural place.

Before Pimlott's research program began in 1958, wolf killing was part of Algonquin Park's approach to wildlife management, accomplished from its founding in the 1890s to the 1920s through poisoning (Douglas H.

Pimlott fonds, n.d.). Following objections that poisoning killed more than just wolves, Algonquin's approach shifted to snaring, which was carried out by park rangers, who caught approximately sixty animals per year in this way (Ontario Department of Lands and Forests 1963). But as Pimlott, Shannon, and Kolenosky note, attitudes toward wolves began to shift in the 1950s, in part because the 1954 Federal-Provincial Conference on Predator Control allowed for a different thinking about wolves in Canada (Pimlott, Shannon, and Kolenosky 1977). There were limits to this reimagination though; as these same authors point out, this move was not based in ecological interest about the lifeways of wolves. Rather, research was mandated to set about controlling (rather than annihilating) wolves (ibid.).

In this context, Pimlott headed the team that studied wolves in Algonquin from 1958–65 (though he left the program in 1963). The goal of the research, funded by the Ontario Department of Lands and Forests, was twofold: to measure the effect of wolf predation on other wildlife and to provide evidence for an appropriate "judicious and efficient program of predator management" (Pimlott, Shannon, and Kolenosky 1977, 5). The researchers realized this would be a challenging project. To be able to answer whether wolf predation impacted ungulates, they had to first answer a series of questions: "How many wolves are there? What do they eat? How much do they eat? How many deer, moose, and beaver are there? How rapidly do they reproduce themselves? What factors influence their numbers in addition to predation by wolves?" (ibid., 56). Pimlott's research team set out to determine, first, the wolf population size through a variety of census methods in both winter and summer, including aerial searching, tracking, marking, and determining location through howling. They also sought to understand the food habits of wolves by locating kills and analyzing scat. They determined that in Algonquin Park, 80.5 per cent of the wolf's diet was deer, distantly followed by moose (8.5 per cent) and beaver (7.1 per cent) with negligible amounts of hare and small rodents (ibid., 36). In terms of age distribution of deer kills, they found seasonal variation: in the summer, wolves ate more fawns, in the winter they were more likely to eat deer that were older than 5.5 years. The researchers also did not find evidence of the surplus or "wasteful" killing that wolves had long been accused of (ibid., 40). Editions of the *Weekly News Release* of the Ontario Department of Lands and Forests (1964) summed up Pimlott, Shannon, and Kolenosky's research along three main points. First, the case for wolf management was dependent on context: in some cases, they would need management; in others, protection. Second, the bounty was ineffective, despite the provincial government spending $42,000 on it over a twelve-year period. Finally, the primary factor for deer decline was habitat loss and harsh winter conditions, rather than the wolf. John Theberge (1979) pointed out the significance of their findings some years later: "The research, from a practical side, showed that the bounty could be removed without wolf populations increasing substantially because of the self-regulation exhibited (no wolves were taken from Algonquin Park during the five years of the study)."

In 1969, when their report was first published, its authors did not let wolves off the hook in terms of their impact on deer in quite the way that was suggested in the Lands and Forests *Weekly News Release* summaries. They were careful to say that wolves were a "major mortality factor," even in the absence of evidence that showed them as the "primary" one (Pimlott, Shannon, and Kolenosky 1977, 56). Yet how this was interpreted mattered. Certainly, wolves impacted deer populations: they were wolves' primary source of food in Algonquin Park. But the real – and profoundly political – question that needed answering was the one alleged by scores of hunters, trappers, and conservationists like Jack and Manly Miner: did they cause steep declines in deer populations, which authorized wolf elimination through the bounty or other means? The answer to that question, as read through scientific inquiry, was a qualified no.

But Doug Pimlott also wished to be less qualified. According to John Theberge (1979), Pimlott joined the University of Toronto's Department of Zoology and Faculty of Forestry in 1963, leaving his wolf research at Algonquin Park behind, because he felt constrained in what he could say as a government employee. Unshackled, Pimlott began pressing his conservation case with more vigour in a range of essays and public talks meant to provoke and change minds. As Tina Loo (2006, 162) remarks, for Pimlott, "conservation was a matter of managing the two-leggeds as well as the four-leggeds"; this would be achieved not only through ecology but also through a public relations (and affective) campaign to explain the ecological importance of the wolf to everyday people.

By way of example, in a 1968 speech to the annual meeting of the St Catharines and Lincoln County Game and Fish Protective Association, Pimlott castigated mainstream conservation as exemplified by the Miners as selfish and self-interested, "ignoble," and rooted only in human desire for "useful" species. For this he blamed misinformation and an unwillingness to get beyond surface understanding of a relationship like predator-prey dynamics. If hunters could be convinced that allowing wolves to live, and in some cases protecting them, did not necessarily mean fewer deer for them, then the sociological rather than scientific problem of wolf hatred might be solved. Pimlott set about explaining the complexities of ecology to those who would listen. For instance, in the same speech in St Catharines, Pimlott emphasized the role of scientific knowledge in making informed wildlife management decisions:

> In any area, and particularly in Ontario and Quebec where we are perched right at the northern edge of deer range, predation is only one of the strands of an intricately interwoven web. Field biologists learn how to determine conditions in a deer yard from evidence that most people cannot see. They know how to read the story of deer survival from a collection of jaws provided by hunters. They can determine the variation in the birth rate of deer in different areas from a study fo [sic] the scars in the ovarian tissue of adult does. In addition, biologists read case histories of game populations around the world in the scientific journals and reports of their profession. They have learned from these that the key to success in wildlife management is invariably found in the condition of the habitat in which animals live. If you have a good habitat you can readily manipulate the secondary factors. If you have poor habitat you are working for a lost cause. Killing predators, juggling hunting seasons, winter feeding, reducing bag limits may serve as pressure valves and sops to conscience but they do not put game in many freezers. (Douglas H. Pimlott fonds)

Pimlott reasoned that having the general public listening to the emerging consensus in ecology would mean fewer dead wolves.

But the Algonquin Park study also killed wolves, albeit in the name of science rather than hatred. At the end of the wolf research, in 1964 and 1965, a "capture program" was initiated to gather data that could not be gleaned by observation or scat analysis alone. The wolves they had so closely followed, observed, and, to some degree, shared life with were rounded up and killed to understand more about their ages and reproductive histories (Pimlott, Shannon, and Kolenosky 1977). This cull in the name of science is biopolitics writ large: some were made to die so that others might live. Some might suggest that the objection to the killing of these animals is sentimental; their sacrifice gave life to many more since the research produced by Pimlott, Shannon, and Kolenosky profoundly reshaped the terrain of wolf control and management in Canada. And yet, there is an unpalatable irony here: in 1964 and 1965, 106 animals – one-third of the population (Link and Crowley 1994) – were trapped and killed to reveal that the bounty should be repealed; with the exception of 1928, this represents a greater number than the annual kill in the years since rangers began killing wolves in the boundaries of the park. Individual animals mattered insofar as they told a bigger story about the value of the species to the ecosystem. As biologists Paul Paquet and Chris Darimont (2010) note, this is not unusual in wildlife conservation. In thinking about the relationship between conservation and animal welfare, they note that an emphasis on different scales – the population or the individual – produces different matters of concern. At the level of the population, the killing of 106 wolves was unlikely to impact species strength, as the Algonquin Park wolf study showed. But at the level of the individual, the weight of this scientific choice is heavy indeed.

The choice is complicated by the fact that Doug Pimlott did see wolves as subjects, not simply as populations. In an interesting chapter in *The World of the Wolf* (Rutter and Pimlott 1968), Pimlott talks about coming to understand wolves as individuals through his experiences with semi-tamed wolves. Early on in the research in Algonquin Park, Pimlott recognized the futility of observing wild wolves full time: they were too elusive and the park was too big. Captive wolves became the solution to this problem. It is strange to imagine that either Pimlott or Rutter considered captive wolves a proxy for those found in the wild. They note that they had to get these wolves as pups to hand raise them, otherwise they would not accept people as part of their pack. And yet, they enthusiastically adopted five wolf pups, each, as described in the book, with its own personality: Dagwood and Blondie were "extroverts"; Kit was shy, unless with children; Lupe was friendly but wouldn't be bossed; and Puppet was the mischievous one (Rutter and Pimlott 1968). The chapter sets about charting the rollicking adventure that Pimlott has with the wolves, including taking them on a camping trip! Dagwood is also used in the wolf howl program and later appears on television. His impact was palpable: "Six years later, visitors to Algonquin Park still ask after Dagwood, who, we think, has probably contributed more toward creating a favorable image of the wolf than any other single wolf in history" (Rutter and Pimlott 1968, 149).

However, this was an experiment that Pimlott would come to regret, even as he notes how his life was made fuller by their individual presences. Although at home with people, the wolves seemed to seek the company of their wild kin, and unless caged, they would run away. If let free, however, these wolves would also visit campgrounds, because, of course, they did not fear and were curious about people. In the liminal space between wild and tame, the intentions of these wolves could not be trusted. Rutter and

Pimlott (1968, 154) remark after Kit visits one such campsite: "That ended her freedom; we could not risk having campers complain about marauding wolves." Some of the stories of what happens to these wolves are as heart-rending as they are perhaps predictable. The best case was Blondie, who went to live with Siberian Huskies owned by someone with the Department of Lands and Forests. Puppet died, ironically, when a reporter came to take photos of the wolves to promote the project and the pup ate an extension cord. Kit was victim to wolf hatred when, running free, she was purposely run over by a motorist. Lupe was shot by a ranger. Pimlott's grief at their loss is clear in *The World of the Wolf*; he loved these creatures. It leads him to believe that wolves should rarely be kept in captivity, and if they are, they should have some autonomy to "permit them to have lives of their own, to be wolves and not dogs" (Rutter and Pimlott 1968, 170). It not hard to understand Pimlott's desire for closeness with and curiosity about the interior lifeworlds of the subjects of his study; we see this same desire in people who own wolf dogs (see chapter 5). Nevertheless, even their individual lives matter insofar as they changed the way we think about wolves. Theberge (1979) writes in his eulogy of Pimlott that he "arranged their lives so that they made a lasting contribution to their species." Even in death, they were required to labour.

Pimlott's work undoubtedly changed the fortunes of wolves in Canada, for which he has been named the country's "father of wolf research" (Link and Crowley 1994, 25). He noted (1961b) in a conservation workshop in Algonquin, later published in *Fish and Wildlife Review*, that the period between the 1940s and 1960s was a period of "dynamic evolution" in ideas about wildlife and game management; he was a key part of this evolution. He proposed the Wolf Specialists Group of the International Union for Conservation of Nature [and Natural Resources]–Survival Services Commission and became its first chairperson. As part of this work, along with others, he developed a "wolf manifesto," which set out a global con-servation ethic for wolf management. It emphasized, quite radically, the right for wolves to live on their own terms: "Wolves, like all other wildlife, have a right to exist in a wild state. The right is in no way related to their known value to mankind. Instead, it derives from the right of all living creatures to co-exist with man as part of natural ecosystems" (Carbyn 1979). Beyond wolf-specific endeavours, Pimlott was a founding member of what is now Nature Canada and the founder of the Canadian Arctic Resources Committee. He invited a curiosity about the natural world that transcended wolves – though perhaps, they were his way in and remained closest to his heart – and he passed this curiosity on to his students.

John B. Theberge was one such student. He did undergraduate research on wolves with Pimlott in the 1960s, and Pimlott became his "intellectual benefactor" (Link and Crowley 1994, 89). Theberge went on to a PhD and a forty-year career as a wildlife biologist at the University of Waterloo, through which he helped to profoundly reshape the landscape for wolves in Ontario. Along with his interlocutor and wife, Mary Theberge, and countless graduate students, he engaged in one of the longest (though not continuous) and most contentious wolf studies in Canada. From 1987–98, the Theberges led a study of thirty-one wolf packs in Algonquin Park and townships just southeast, radio-collaring them to glean answers to questions around whether Algonquin Park was big enough, if wolves limit deer and moose, what impact logging had on wolves, the importance of hybridization, and the degree of competition and co-operation in and among wolf packs.

While Theberge has written and co-authored an enormous number of academic papers on wolves in Algonquin Park, his own voice and politics come through in the book he penned with his wife[2] about their work entitled *Wolf Country*. Like Pimlott's (and Rutter's) *The World of the Wolf*, this is a more personal account; it includes not only details of the scientific study but also his musings on Ontario Ministry of Natural Resources officials (politically motivated), local people (difficult to persuade with evidence), and loggers (bemused and derisive). There is a warmth to the writing in this book that is compelling; Theberge clearly loved his work and felt an affective connection to the wolf. He also showed impatience with those who stood by the adage that "a good wolf is a dead wolf." And his politics, characterized by an emphasis on the importance of scientific inquiry to reveal the truth of nature and the centrality of large, protected areas in wildlife conservation, are embedded throughout. Like the political thrust of conservation biology, Theberge was motivated by urgency: "If you're concerned about these mammal systems, then pretty soon you ask, 'Where are they going to exist in the world in the future?' They aren't going to exist by default. We have to do something. And I guess I follow the same way. As a student of wolves, now I spend equal time in conservation lobbying" (cited in Link and Crowley 1994, 89). Theberge's research aimed not only to generate and extend knowledge about wolves but also to ensure there was a place for them in the world.

As Pimlott did in his work, Theberge traces the contours of his research, providing details of his close observations of the many individual wolves and packs that crossed his path during the decade of work at Algonquin Park. The duration of his study allowed him to come to know the wolves in a new way, offering a multispecies ethnography (Kirksey and Helmreich 2010) before such was named. For instance, he writes of one female wolf that he tracked on and off for seven or eight years, from birth to dispersal to founding of her own pack (1998, 65–7). With others, his acquaintance was shorter. But in all cases, Theberge emphasizes the intimacies of fieldwork, of coming to know another creature in a deep way. Like Pimlott and other wolf researchers, he employed the "habituation model," which involved staying in one place and watching for hours at a time (Link and Crowley 1994). The stories Theberge tells in the book are rich with detail and emotion. Through this approach, Monte Hummel (cited in Theberge 1998, ix) suggests, "the Theberges came as close as any two humans could to knowing the Algonquin landscape as a wolf does – the den areas, rendez-vous sites, deer yards, beaver lodges, moose browse, salt licks, travel routes, game trails, ridges, low spots, rivers, lakes, and the territory of an adjacent pack. They know where the kills are on frozen lakes, how many pups survived the summer in each family group, and when a strange wolf is moving in, not just moving through. But most important, John and Mary know what they don't know, as their research poses an endless stream of puzzles and surprises that leave us all scratching our heads trying to figure out 'what's going on.'" They also offer a celebration of and a plea for more wildlife field research as a way into the lives of animals.

THE AFFECTIVE LOGICS OF CURIOSITY

Both Pimlott and Theberge were intensely curious about wolves. But as Jamie Lorimer (2015, 37) points out, this is not so unusual for field scientists; he contends that fieldwork is full of "passionate interactions" that are "illustrative of the multitude of embodied and affective encounters between skilled humans, other species, and landscapes that underpin conservation." In thinking about how conservation scientists come to know the creatures whose lives they enmesh themselves in, Lorimer suggests that there is a process of and commitment to "learning to be affected" that underpins the encounter. For these scientists, curiosity is the core of this process, which Lorimer (2015, 133) suggests is quite a different affective register than, for instance, awe, because it "focuses on humans and non-human difference in their intimate entanglements in bodies and practices." Curiosity invites a kind of willingness to suspend certainty, an openness to being surprised about what one might encounter in close contact with another. In both Pimlott and Theberge, curiosity also tied them to their research subjects in something that looked a lot like love.

Donna Haraway has also emphasized the importance of not only curiosity but also care in scientific encounters with nonhumans. In her critique of Jacques Derrida's revelation that his cat gazed at his naked body – that it could, in fact, look back with intelligence and comprehension – she writes: "But with his cat, Derrida failed a simple obligation of companion species; he did not become curious about what the cat might actually be doing, feeling, thinking, or perhaps making available to him in looking back at him that morning … Incurious, he missed a possible invitation, a possible introduction to other-worlding" (Haraway 2007, 20). Accepting this invitation, encountering animals in their full complexity, is, for Haraway, an ethical obligation. In her provocative and much-criticized[3] discussion of the possibility of shared suffering in the space of the animal laboratory, Haraway contends that curiosity allows for new ways of relating that attend to the needs of the animals that sacrifice – often their lives – to advance human knowledge. In terms of ethology, Haraway (ibid., 21) notes that the kind of capacious curiosity about the lives of animals demonstrated by primatologist Barbara Smuts or biologist Marc Bekoff has led them to new ways of doing "themselves and their sciences." The "thick mud" of curiosity that emerges among human and nonhuman in the entanglements that Haraway describes lead to spaces of shared (though certainly asymmetrical) responsibility (ibid., 38).

Neither Theberge nor Pimlott would have engaged in the work that they did – over long periods and against strong opposition – unless they felt the itch of curiosity about the lifeworlds of wolves. This curiosity allowed them both to be open to the possibility of the unexpected in wolf habits and behaviour, and to see the animals as more than populations but individuals with agency. For instance, both Pimlott and Theberge were curious about why wolves howl, which led Pimlott to figure out that they would answer human howls and Theberge to devote some of his career trying to determine what those vocalizations meant (for example, Theberge and Falls 1967; Theberge and Theberge 2016). Similarly, Theberge's exploration of the tolerance shown by packs to dispersing "lone" wolves found in their territory was possible because he took time to observe the behaviour of specific animals over a long period and because he approached with inquisitiveness and no preconceived expectation of the outcome: these territorial animals would tolerate intrusion because the interlopers were actually kin – brothers, sisters, aunts, uncles, and cousins. This led Theberge (1998, 60) to assert that wolf societies are more complex and distinct than appeals to instinct might afford and to query whether "dispersion [is] a manifestation of a more flexible social system, sometimes characterized by indifference, sometimes even cooperation."

More than being curious about wolves, Pimlott and Theberge allowed themselves to see the ways in which wolves are curious about each other – and about us. For instance, Pimlott's description of captive wolves like Kit visiting campgrounds was about their curiosity toward humans. Similarly, near the beginning of *Wolf Country*, Theberge (1998, 15) describes an encounter with a radio-collared wolf that was precipitated not by accident or instinct but by purposeful curiosity: "Suddenly, there she [Nahma 1] was, standing face on, watching us. She trotted a few steps, seemingly not alarmed, then disappeared into the brush. Judging by her signal, she stayed within fifty metres or so for the next ten minutes. We sat on a mossy bank waiting to see what she would do. She may have been doing the same thing. Then she left. Curious, cautious, unafraid." He describes many more examples in the book of wolves approaching because they wondered why people were there and what they might be doing.

In different examples, both researchers note that when people howl at them, wolves become curious about the creature making the sound. Pimlott's guess that wolves might respond to the simulated howls of humans raised new possibilities for communication, even if the terrain of call and response is unfamiliar and potentially unbridgeable for the parties involved. Theberge (1998, 31) comments on this in a way that opens up an understanding of a wolf's capacity not only to be affected but also to affect because they are thinking, feeling creatures: "What wolves think when they hear humans howl is unclear. Often they may respond as a reflex and not think, but other times they clearly do. They come to investigate, sometimes howling back first but often arriving silently. We know this from the increasing signal strength of those wearing radio-collars. That happens between one-third and one-half of the times. Then we are a temporary disturbance, probably of little consequence. Wolves discover us, then leave to continue whatever they were doing." It matters, I think, that this wolf language is, for the most part, inaccessible to humans. It signals not only that they will respond to human hailing but also that mostly this conversation is not meant for us. Wolves are curious about and affect each other in ways that are fundamentally unknowable to humans, even to the wildlife biologists who spend years at a time studying them. Their lives are their own, even as they are entangled with the people and politics of Algonquin Park. As Theberge (1998, 3) remarks, "while research will never allow us to fully, or even adequately, understand the wolf, we may understand both ourselves and it better." This willingness to be affected by the wolves they studied led them to good science, but it also led them to advocate on behalf of the animals they came to know so deeply. It was this advocacy that instigated new ways of appreciating wolves as fundamentally Canadian.

THE CULTURAL POLITICS OF NATURE AND NATION

Theberge's advocacy caused a lot of waves. His chapter titled "Bureaucrats, Biopolitics and the Wolf-Killing Ban" opens with this: "Not only data accumulate in any good study, so does animosity" (1998, 178). He wasn't wrong. Both research programs ran afoul of the government agencies that sponsored them, as well as local communities and hunting organizations like the Ontario Federation of Anglers and Hunters and the Whitney Fish and Game Club. In the days of Pimlott's research, this took the form of a conspiracy theory put forward by the Canadian Wolf Control Association, which accused the Ontario Department of Lands and Forests of "propagating wolves" to study them (Ontario Department of Lands and Forests, Wildlife Branch 1970). As Theberge embarked on his research program, Pimlott warned that he would see more of the same, noting "they will throw endless barriers in your way" (cited in Theberge 1998, 181). For the Theberge team, the most significant obstacle was the Ministry of Natural Resources (MNR). According to Theberge, things went sour in 1990 after one of the graduate students involved in the research, Graham Forbes, gave a talk in which he argued that a buffer zone needed to be established around the park because wolves were being killed outside its boundaries. According to Theberge (1998, 183), this caused the MNR to close ranks and try to stop the research, which he asserts was "the government's usual reaction to those whose research points to needed, but politically difficult policy." He contends that the bureaucratic questioning of challenging scientific research follows particular grooves, including questioning of the research objective and methods, efforts to discredit the researchers, and threats to defund or reduce access because of noncompliance with new and poorly communicated rules. Threatened with an end to the project, the Theberge team went public with their research finding around the need for a buffer zone and the MNR backed down because, as an internal memo cited by Theberge notes, "most of his [Theberge's] claims are accurate and we are vulnerable" (cited in Theberge 1998, 191). In 2001, a moratorium on wolf killing was established in the thirty-nine townships that surrounded the park.

As radical as Theberge was about wolf conservation, his politics were less robust for the people whose traditional territory was taken to make Algonquin Park; there were limits to his curiosity. Both Pimlott and Theberge saw the park as a distinctly wild space that should be maintained without human interference, even though it was unceded Algonquin land. During the full period of the Theberge study, the land upon which they laboured was contested as part of the assertion of Indigenous Title by the

Algonquin Anishinaabeg of Ontario. The Algonquin attempts for justice on their lands began with settler colonialism. The Algonquins had been trying to get the British government to engage in a treaty with them since 1772 and made twenty-eight petitions to this effect between 1772 and 1881 (Gehl 2014). As Bonita Lawrence (2012, 21) explores, the long presence of the Algonquins in the Kitchissippi (Ottawa River) watershed had been rendered largely invisible by the state, as settlers sought to control the strategic river, which, she contends, was central to "the formation of Canada itself." With the building of the Opeongo Colonization Road, the upper Madawaska was opened to logging in the 1860s, threatening the Algonquin way of life. As a result, eight Madawaska chiefs petitioned for title to the Madawaska headwaters; land was promised but never received. By the founding of the park in 1893, settler incursion and commercial logging deepened this displacement, making traditional lands uninhabitable. Indeed, until Algonquin Park was legislated into being, those lands had acted as something of a sanctuary (Luckasavitch 2019). As Algonquin land was remade into Canadian nature, Indigenous presence had to be removed; "under pressure from the superintendent of Algonquin Park, it was decided that allowing Algonquins to settle so near the park, where they would surely hunt, would be 'dangerous'" (Lawrence 2012, 234). But Lawrence (2012) recounts via interviews with community members, knowledge holders, and elders that Algonquins continued to make use of the land after the founding of the park – hunting, trapping, harvesting medicines, visiting sacred sites like Rock Lake, and taking part in ceremony on their traditional territory as they had done since earliest memory. The difference was that after Algonquin Provincial Park was decreed, such practices were rendered into trespass and poaching on a site of Canadian nature.

Theberge came to his wolf research in the park at a time when the Algonquins were asserting sovereignty and nationhood on their traditional territories, as they had always done. He likely did not see the two things as connected. Indeed, he read the Algonquin assertion and practice of their rights to the land as intrusion. This view is clear in this passage: "With a change in provincial governments in 1992 came a political decision to give the Golden Lake native people [Algonquins of Pikwakanagan] hunting rights to moose and deer on the eastern third of the park. They are allowed to use trucks, all-terrain vehicles, and snowmobiles anywhere they wish. The decision was made without any consideration of the environmental and biological impacts. Conservation organizations objected, and so did I in the Toronto *Globe and Mail*. To the extent that land is used and wildlife exploited in the park the same way it is outside, there is no reason to have a park at all. However, despite our objections, a new predator entered Algonquin's large mammal system" (Theberge 1998, 70–1). Later on, Theberge (ibid., 164) again articulates the problems of Algonquins hunting in the park, suggesting their ecological impact was greater due to "much-enhanced hunting efficiency, after an absence of one hundred years since the park's creation." Here Theberge buttresses the long-standing and deeply embedded colonial assertion of the separation of nature and culture (Braun 2002; Cronon 1996). But he also, crucially, rehearses the earlier settler notions of Indigenous peoples' overexploitation of the land. In fact, it is almost the same as a decision by the Commissioner of Crown Lands one hundred years earlier, who noted that an Algonquin appeal for a land grant was "denied because, it was argued, their predatory habits would make it 'impossible to keep these Indians, thus situated, from hunting and trapping within the Park'" (cited in Gehl 2014, 39). What Theberge refused to be curious about were the ways that Indigenous engagement with the land might increase instead of decrease biodiversity, ecosystem health, and, perhaps more importantly, relationships based on ethics and the presumption of subjectivity. Time and again, the Algonquins warned loggers and settlers of their exploitation of the land, that their practices were "disrupting the habitat of the Algonquin and all their relations: trees, medicine, bear, beaver, deer, gopher and moose" (ibid.). An emphasis on kinship and responsibility, while specific to each territory, shares a common thread across Indigenous nations that has been asserted in countless struggles across Turtle Island. This is the focus in chapter 7. But if Theberge had been more curious about Indigenous legal orders as well systems of relationality and reciprocity, he might have offered a much more radical politics for people and animals in the lands of the Algonquin Anishinaabeg and elsewhere in Canada – perhaps one acknowledging that justice for wolves is also tied to justice for people who share the land with them. Put differently, it might require an anti-colonial project.

"THE BIOPOLITICS OF WOLF AND WILDERNESS PROTECTION"

At the outset of *Wolf Country*, Theberge (1998, 8) writes admiringly that Doug Pimlott took on the "biopolitical" responsibility of advocating for wolves in Canada and beyond. I am quite sure he did not mean biopolitical in the same register that I do. But he was right to suggest that Pimlott's (and his own) studies of wolves in Canada had a biopolitical purpose. Scientific inquiry was central to the reimagining of wolves in

Canada. That reimaging has had lasting impacts on their life chances. What McTaggart-Cowan, Pimlott, and Theberge offered was a different mode of engagement with wolves, one that hinged on the affective logics of curiosity. What they advanced was a liberation from annihilation, but not from management. Instead, their curiosity led them to an interesting combination of ways of seeing wolves: as populations and individuals, objects of study and subjects of a life. And even as they tried (and succeeded) to protect space for wild wolves to thrive, they did so via intensified intrusion into their lives, through examination of their kills, radio-collaring, and, in Pimlott's case, killing them to understand something bigger about the population. They also sought to regulate people in their biopolitical efforts, changing perceptions of wolves to allow them some space to live out their lives on their own terms. They marshalled the considerable weight of scientific expertise to advocate for these animals when it was neither easy nor politically palatable to do so. In this way, studies of wolf biology and ecology – along with cultural touchstones like *Never Cry Wolf* – opened up a new view on the wolf: an important member of healthy Canadian ecosystems. Their work helped wolves to survive, such that their reintroduction to Yellowstone as an act of Canadian benevolence was rendered not only possible but also legible.

The researchers highlighted in this chapter offered a kind of affirmative biopolitical frame, inviting the public to also be curious about wolf lifeworlds. This invitation was largely accepted, especially by those unlikely to encounter a wolf unintentionally. (Chapter 5 takes this up more fully in its discussion of the popular Algonquin Wolf Howl.) But in so doing, the critique provided of the human relationship to nature continued to operate within a settler colonial frame, being distinctly incurious about ways of coming to know wolves that do not involve the separation of nature and culture. Protecting wilderness might not be the only way to ensure wolf survival, something these wolf scientists cared deeply about. Indigenous teachings about and relations with the wolf might lead to new forms of conviviality that were not imagined by the radical ecologists of the time. Their wisdom and teachings are taken up in chapter 7.

5

Devotion

Wolf Love in Modern Times

Loki the Wolfdog is, by any definition, an internet sensation. Named "one of the most recognized pets on the planet" (Monitz, n.d.), the Husky/Malamute/Arctic wolf mix is a mediagenic superstar, boasting an astonishing two million followers on Instagram as of April 2021. Kelly Lund, Loki's human guardian, purchased his low-content wolfdog in 2012 after surmising that "a wolf hybrid could deliver the kind of challenge-to-reward metric he was looking for in his next companion" (Bookhart 2016). Lund asserts that he grew up "in a family that took dog ownership very seriously" (Loki the Wolfdog, n.d.) and so was familiar with the needs, desires, and specificities of large breeds. But his new dog's wolfish nature demanded more than would a German Shepherd or Golden Retriever: "Loki was different though. Instead of him entering into my world, I felt like I had to listen closely and enter into his world, if this was going to work out. At that time, I decided that I would do everything possible to not leave him behind at the house. We started backcountry snowboarding together when he was four months old, and before his third birthday, he'd seen most of the western US." (ibid.). Lund restructured his life to live with his new companion. He writes that "Loki's instinct is to roam and inevitably that's what he challenges me to do" (Loki the Wolfdog 2017). So Lund quit his job and became Loki's "full-time social media manager," work that involves taking countless pictures of Loki, posting them to online platforms like Twitter and Instagram, and garnering likes, retweets, and followers. It helps that Loki is remarkably beautiful and that Lund is an accomplished photographer with a keen eye for light and staging; the more than 1,600 pictures of Loki on Instagram show him in a variety of settings and activities, such as frolicking in the snow, howling, curling up on the couch, being cuddled by his human companion, and, famously, sleeping in a hammock (@loki, n.d.).[1]

But Loki does more than pose; he is enrolled in the political economy of Instagram influencers and their product endorsements. According to digital anthropologist Crystal Abidin (2015, para. 1), social media influencers are people – or in this case animals – who, "accumulate a relatively large following on blogs and social media through textual and visual narration of their personal lives and lifestyles, engage with their following in digital and physical spaces, and monitise their following by integrating 'advertorials' into their blog or social media posts." In this respect, Loki's Instagram account is no different than that of human influencers, who curate images of their daily activities combined with sponsored content to market and sell a particular kind of lifestyle. In Loki's case, the animal's wolfishness is on offer; what Kelly Lund sells through Loki is bold and adventurous living in the wild. So, interspersed with images of Loki trekking around the American West are brand endorsements and promotional shots for companies like Toyota, Mercedes, REI, I and Love and You organic and raw dog food, Icelantic Skis, and Wolfgang Man and Beast collars and harnesses, each articulating an image of expedition or exploration. Loki also has his own brand of cannabidiol (CBD) pet products to help with canine joint stiffness, anxiety, and seizures (Loki Naturals, n.d.) so that you can keep exploring with your dog best friend for years to come.

How do we make sense of Loki the Wolfdog in the context of the broader arguments laid out in this book? He's a wolf (of a kind) with a massive following of passionate supporters and with at least potential to set trends and shape consumer behaviour. He is a product – quite literally, since he is bought, marketed, and conscripted into selling – of the desire for a wilderness that settlers once sought to eradicate. Loki is also an affective labourer, responsible for generating a range of affects, not only in his companion but also in his millions of Instagram followers. While feminist scholars have long noted the kind of care work that goes into social reproduction, geographer Maan Barua (2018) applies this specifically to animal life: "Corporeal, somatic, and intangible in its products, the affective work of animals becomes particularly visible in the entertainment industry and its regimes of spectacular accumulation." Loki is spectacular, and his adventures may induce feelings of excitement or contentment, ease, and relaxation. But there is also a tangible quality to Loki's work; hidden as playful photos in the wild, Loki's affective labour also hinges on commerce. And so, desire – that old trick of advertising – is invoked here too; if you want a dog as majestic, captivating, and bold as Loki, who matches your own qualities in this regard, there are a variety of items to acquire to help you fulfill this end.

Thought of in concert with the work of the authors and scientists described in chapters 3 and 4, Loki might be evidence that their invitation to a recuperation of the wolf in Canada indeed bore fruit. Tina Loo (2006) argues this new-found embrace of the wolf – perhaps culminating in or perverted by Loki the Wolfdog, depending on your perspective – was more cultural than scientific. She notes saving the wolf was sutured to saving the wild; the rise of environmentalism in the 1960s offered new conditions of possibility not only for wolves but also for the ecosystems they inhabited. Loo (2006, 181) contends that the impact of writers like Farley Mowat and filmmakers like Bill Mason was to reflect back and amplify a larger cultural argument, one they infused with scientific research, the beginnings of which were already evident: "the poisonous war on wolves was a violent manifestation of the twentieth-century triumph of the technocratic and the modern, a reminder of the uncertain benefits of a progress built on extinguishing the wild." Wolves and their extermination became the perfect symbol of destructive relationships to the natural world. Like Loki then, wolves became an almost ghostly presence at the heart of narratives in Canadian environmentalism, ambassadors for some bigger project not of their own design.

This chapter delves into the consequences of this recuperation, or at least how it has been taken up in some quarters. Here I trace two vignettes in the modern devotion to wolves in Canada, thinking about how this can take multiple and divergent forms. First, I look at the rise of the public wolf howl in Algonquin Provincial Park in Ontario, which emerged just at the time that Loo notes ideas about the wild and the creatures who prowl it began to change. As a tool of nature interpretation and scientific communication, I contend that the wolf howl also worked (and continues to work) on the affective registers of wonder and devotion while reinforcing particular ideas about the Canadian nation. Second, I explore the market in dogs that have been hybridized with wolves – like Loki the Wolfdog – which has taken off in recent years. With an emphasis on the quality and quantity of DNA, these dogs have become a somewhat problematic status symbol for people who wish to curl up with a part of Canadian wilderness. I also explore wolfdog sanctuaries as having the potential to offer new ways of relating to animals that were once pets. These examples offer complex variations on attempts to connect to a once-reviled species.

EXPRESSING DEVOTION

What does it mean to be devoted? To something? To someone? How might it foster forms of both intimacy and distance? The *Oxford English Dictionary* tells us that to be devoted is to be "zealously attached or addicted to a person or cause; enthusiastically loyal or faithful. (Of persons, their actions, etc.)" (*OED* 2020). Suresh Emre (2019) contends that it is necessarily experiential, by which he means understood outside of the words we often fail to find to describe it. It might be thought of as an intense and embodied longing, a yearning for intimacy characterized be feelings of admiration, awe, and worship.

It also emerges through specific practices; longing and worship are materialized through forms of ritual. Of course, devotion is most closely associated with religion or, at the very least, spirituality, so this attention to ceremonial practice probably comes as no surprise. But in the cases explored below, devotion and ritual are found in the secular expression of wolf(dog) love.

This chapter teases out these kinds of attachments as they relate to modern wolf love. Visitors to the Algonquin wolf howl and wolfdog owners share a desire for connectivity; people seek avenues to come to know and understand this animal in new ways. But they differ in that the Algonquin wolf howl functions through conditional people-wolf encounters while the purchase of a wolfdog seeks to impart certainty, even one that is unsustainable. In what follows, devotion is felt and performed in polyvalent ways. It can be obsessive or fleeting, contingent or based on enduring bonds of care. It might dissolve at the sign of transgression or be amplified by the recognition that the animal has a mind of its own. It might be fostered through a sense of closeness or invoked because of the very aloofness and elusiveness of the animal one seeks. Devotion is always complicated and unpredictable.

LISTENING FOR WOLVES

Extinguishing a wilderness alive with howling and other sounds of "uncivilization" was one of the primary tasks of settler colonialism. As US environmental historian Peter Coates (2005, 646) contends, the "silencing of the wolf epitomized the taming of the frontier." I have argued elsewhere that the same impetus was present in Canada as the transformation of the landscape replaced one set of sounds with other, more controllable ones (Rutherford 2016); indeed, chapter 1 in part traces how the howling of wolves was only ever understood as a source of terror. And so the notion that people would gather to listen to – and celebrate – the howling of wolves would have been, and was, broadly unthought of until Algonquin Provincial Park started running their Public Wolf Howl in 1963. In fact, wolves were routinely killed by Algonquin Park rangers until 1958, when such "management" was banned to so that research could be done on an undisturbed wolf population (Rutter and Stickland 2002). So, what changed?

As charted in chapter 4, zoologist Douglas Pimlott was a key scientific figure in the recuperation of wolves in Canada. He was also central to a reimagining of how they could be heard. As part of his research on wolves in Algonquin Park in the late 1950s and early 1960s, Pimlott found that if you howled at a wolf, it might just howl back, and the notion gained popularity. For Pimlott and others, this became a very helpful way to track and estimate the number of wolves in the park (Strickland 2004). Park staff wondered about the possibilities it might present for public nature education (Rutter and Strickland 2002). Unsure of the potential response, Russell J. Rutter wrote a notice in the August 1963 issue of *The Raven*, Algonquin Park's newsletter, inviting campers to the event. The short article described the nature of the "outing," but Rutter (Rutter and Strickland 2002, 3) also gestured to the changing views of wolves: "An interest in the wolf and a desire to know more about it has been evident for some time among our summer visitors, and Park Naturalists feel that an important element of the Algonquin environment is being neglected if people do not become better acquainted with what is perhaps the Park's most interesting animal. In Algonquin Park, where there is no hunting, wolves play an important part in regulating the deer population. They also contribute much to the spirit of "wilderness" which is one of the attractions of the Park. To hear a wild pack howling in the night is a never-to-be-forgotten experience." The response was extraordinary – and completely unexpected. Anticipating the popularity to come of Farley Mowat's *Never Cry Wolf* or Bill Mason's *Death of a Legend* and *Cry of the Wild*, the first Public Wolf Howl drew over six hundred listeners; park staff had predicted only a dozen (A. Ingram 2015). Since this first howl, Algonquin Park has become famous for its Canadian "wilderness opera." Listening to wolves – the sounds settlers once attempted to eliminate from the landscape – has now become a marker of Canadian national identity, evidence that Canada remains alive with a nature the rest of the world should encounter.

In terms of the logistics and practice of the Algonquin wolf howl, not much has changed since 1969, when wolf howls became a regular rather than ad hoc part of the park's interpretative program (Strickland 2004). Every Thursday in August a wolf howl is attempted; some are successful, others are not. Wolves are more likely to be heard in August because the pups born in the spring, having outgrown their dens, have been moved to their temporary rendezvous sites, where they remain while the adult members of the pack hunt (Rutter and Strickland 2002; Strickland 2004). A day or two before the scheduled wolf howl, naturalists see if they can track one of the thirty-five or so packs, four of which may be close to Highway 60, the main artery that bisects the park. Whether or not they find a pack, park naturalists give a public lecture on the Thursday evening about the biology and behaviour of the Eastern wolf to between 1,500 and 2,000 people. Following the talk, if naturalists have been successful in their midweek search, attendees drive to a specified site along Highway 60 in what Dan Strickland (2004, 5), former chief park naturalist, described as "a spectacle," noting that "a typical turnout of 2,000 people means 500 cars and these, even when moving at only 50km/h, still stretch for at least 15 kilometres." Everyone gets out of their cars to listen as the naturalists begin their rendition of the howl of a wolf. Amid the chirping of crickets, everyone stands silent, waiting to see if the wolves might respond. If they do, their range of vocalizations potentially include the yips and yelps of pups born in the spring, the long and lilting downward wail of a single adult, and the chorus of many adults. Each voice is different – some pitched higher, some lower; sometimes harmonious, often discordant in their combination.

These are sounds that people not only hear but also feel – often in an embodied way – but can never know for sure what they mean. What we may hear as haunting, mournful, and lonely may be simply an attempt by one wolf to locate the rest of the pack, a "territorial declaration," or a warning to other wolves (Strickland 2004, 2). Indeed, even those who have studied wolf song for decades cannot always be certain: as Harrington and Asa (2003) remark, while howling clearly does something, that function could vary from strengthening social ties, communicating joy at reunion, finding a mate, or attempting to avoid confrontation. Others suggest that wolves may howl "simply to express themselves" (Ford 2009, 19).

Whether or not we can grasp their purpose, many find hearing the howls of wild wolves deeply moving. When I interviewed Rick Stronks, Algonquin's chief park naturalist in 2013, he told me that the Public Wolf Howl changes people forever – it grants visceral and embodied connection to an elusive animal that has now become a symbol of wilderness. Mike Tidwell, writing in the *Washington Post* in 2000, agreed. Rendered in poetic detail, Tidwell (2000) describes his experience of a private wolf howl with Dan Strickland. He notes that he was struck by the simultaneous feelings of apprehension and exhilaration, of wanting to run and remain in place. He writes of this complicated assemblage of reactions: "Chills ran up my legs. I had the overpowering urge to yell, 'Wolves! Wolves! I'm listening to wolves in the wild!' But I couldn't speak at all at that point and instead grabbed and squeezed Strickland's arm as if to steady myself from the shock of this great gift of nature and good fortune." The play of uneasiness and delight described by Tidwell – a kind of loss of equilibrium – is common among wolf howl attendees. Strickland (2004, 5) elaborates on the sentiment beautifully:

> And when a pack of wolves breaks out with a tremendous clamour a few hundred metres away under a star-studded sky, even a seasoned wolf howler is likely to feel as though the hair on the back of their neck wants to stand on end. There is little doubt that the howling of wolves arouses deep emotions in human beings. Perhaps it is the awakening of a buried wish for the wild freedom of remote ancestors; the mystery of an animal that responds to us but which we almost never see; the thrill of direct communication with the legendary outlaw that has resisted for centuries our efforts to destroy it; or the magic of a night in wolf country, including even that tinge of fear carried over from childhood wolf stories. Whatever the exact reason the impact is profound.

It offers an affective trigger for the complicated assemblage of sensations and emotions that wolves produce.

Perhaps because of this embodiment, the Algonquin wolf howl is capacious, holding open the possibility for new wolf-people relations to emerge that do not necessarily recall the practices of domination captured in previous chapters. Geographer Henry Buller (2015, 378) notes that although humans and animals are different, there are some vital ways in which we are the same: "we may not share language with non-humans but we do share embodied life and movement and, in doing so, different – yet both biologically and socially related – ways of inhabiting the world." In listening for wolves, people must be attentive and curious about lupine lifeworlds, mobilities, and temporalities that are very different from our own. Listeners must allow for the fact that they will be affected in sometimes contradictory and complicated ways by the experience. And they must also be open to the fact that sometimes the wolves will not respond to our efforts at communication. For instance, before August 2019, the last successful wolf howl was held in August 2013 – even though during the intervening years park staff found wolves in the days before the public event or for private trips. Rick Stronks (2013) told me that even if the park staff do all the steps necessary so that wolves will be heard, the animals may simply choose not to respond. This is not the first time this has happened; between 1973 and 1984, wolves were also hard to find (Rutter and Strickland 2002). They may simply have moved deeper into the park (Chung 2015). And they may eventually return to areas closer to Highway 60. But even if they do, they still may not answer the people who hail them. For me, it is the contingency – a kind of anticipatory hopefulness at the possibility of communication and connection – that makes this event important in reconfiguring people-wolf relationships. Unlike virtually all other forms of animal tourism, the Algonquin wolf howl does not, and indeed cannot, promise interaction. It operates on the understanding that wolves might answer, based on the coming together of a variety of unpredictable variables. And that if they do, it will be in their language not ours, one that is as opaque as it is captivating. In this way, the wolf howl offers the possibility of enmeshment and devotion defined not only on human terms but also amplified through people accepting – maybe even enjoying – the uncertainty of the encounter.

Note also the kind of devotional mysticism with which the event is described. Attending the Algonquin Public Wolf Howl is something of a pilgrimage for those who love wolves; a rite of passage read through ideas about the Canadian nation and its relationship to nature. This secular pilgrimage – the ritual of which is elaborated through repeated practices of the public lecture, the drive to the listening site, waiting silently, and then the human call and hope for response – demonstrates not only a devotion to wolfiness but also to the wild. The sensations it generates – embodied and visceral – speak to revelations about the fiction of human exceptionalism and the beauty of intact ecosystems in a time of environmental loss.

As many involved in the event over the years have remarked, the Algonquin wolf howl is a barometer of how much public opinion has changed in the last sixty years (Runtz 1997; Rutter and Strickland 2002; Strickland 2004; Stronks 2013). And wolf howling as a key interpretive program is now found in a range of parks in Canada (Strickland 2004). More than just a gauge, however, the Algonquin wolf howl has been important in crafting new human-wolf relationships: "In a very real sense, it can be said that wolves now regularly meet and, through their own howls, convince thousands of park visitors that they deserve a place on our planet" (Strickland 2004, 7). Interestingly, of course, the wolves' mobility, agency, and choices about denning may confound the event's ability to sustain these wolf-people conversations. For instance, one disappointed Algonquin tourist railed against the event on Tripadvisor, noting that the park is not telling people that wolf howls are not being held (contra the information publicly available on this website: www.algonquinpark.on.ca/visit/programs/wolf-howls.php) and that the wolves "aren't what they used to be" since they are now breeding with coyotes (Tripadvisor 2015; see also chapter 6 for more on this panic about wolf-coyote hybrids). But if we are serious about new ways of relating to this once-persecuted predator, then this ambiguity – this wolfy refusal – is something we will need to accept and indeed celebrate.

FOR THE LOVE OF A WOLF(DOG)

If the Algonquin wolf howl demonstrates devotion by way of accepting contingency in human-wolf relations, the recent uptick in interest in pet wolfdogs holds no such ambivalence. For many, owning a wolfdog proceeds almost entirely on human terms, even as these hybrids vigorously assert their agency and individuality. But first, we must think about what a wolf-dog is, which is a more complicated question than one might assume.

The straightforward answer to this question is that these creatures are a hybrid of wolf and dog. Dogs split from wolves on their evolutionary path some 15,000 to 40,000 years ago, with friendly wolves "self-domesticating" to access a reliable supply of food (Addams and Miller 2012; Handwerk 2018). Wolves and dogs remained interfertile: they could continue to breed with one another. However, this rarely happens without human intervention; as territorial animals, wolves are likely to kill rather than mate with any canid that enters their range (International Wolf Center, n.d.a). And yet, wolfdogs are relatively common, with estimates of between 300,000 and 400,000 in the United States alone (Addams and Miller 2012, 100). According to Annie Lowrey (2020), the breeding of dogs to wolves for pets really emerged in the last fifty years or so. Like coywolves, then, wolfdogs are a profoundly human creation.

That said, the wolfdog you might buy today is unlikely to have been mated with a wild or captive wolf. Many wolfdogs are multi-generational: wolfdog mated to wolfdog (Wilde 2004). This is especially relevant as many who want to own a wolfdog suggest a preference for a first- or second-generation dog (F1 or F2) because they believe it is closer to a "pure" wolf (more on this below). These hybrids are then further subdivided among low-, mid-, and high-content categories, with some high-content wolfdogs advertised as 98 per cent wolf (and fetching a premium price because of it).

There is also a less straightforward answer to the question of what a wolfdog is. Two separate considerations illustrate this messiness. First, there is the question of whether the wolfdog is a wolfdog at all. In many cases, they are simply dogs that look quite wolfy. Misrepresentation is common in the industry (Harris 2020), and you might simply be buying a Malamute or Husky. Even if the dog is part wolf, Addams and Miller (2012, 3) call the idea of wolf percentage "arbitrary." They contend that, "since dogs and wolves are so closely related, there is hardly such a thing as 'dog' genes or 'wolf' genes" (ibid., 67). And they note that behaviour cannot be reduced to genetics; a 50 per cent wolfdog will not act like a wolf only half of the time or in half of its behaviours. Genetics are far more complicated than that.

Second, defining the wolfdog is made more complex by the way we think about them in law. Are they domestic pets, exotic pets, wild animals, or something else entirely? A recent case in Finland hinged on this question. In 2015, fifteen men were brought to trial for wolf poaching. However, their defence was predicated not on denial – they freely admitted to killing the canids – but on their definition; the accused suggested that the animals they killed were not wolves, but wolfdogs (Peltola and Heikkilä 2018). Wolves were covered under legislation protecting their status; wolfdog hybrids had no such protection, and indeed, their killing might be warranted to save wolves from genetic swamping (see also chapter 6 on wolf-coyote hybrids). As Peltola and Heikkilä point out, the mechanisms for discerning wolf from wolfdog are flawed; morphology and behaviour are not good differentiators. Genetic testing is also complicated since "the animality, and wildness, of the wolf is presented primarily in mathematical terms," where the question becomes "how much a wolf can have dog DNA and still be considered a wolf" (ibid., 207, 208).

By contrast, in the case of a hybrid bite in Kamloops, British Columbia, the animal's wolfiness mattered in terms of damages. The judge suggested that wolfdogs "as a class 'are not harmless by nature but are animals *ferae naturae*' (of a wild nature)" (Oaks 2011). For this judge, wolfdogs could be counted upon to be more wolf than dog. In still another legal interpretation of the nature of a wolfdog, a judge in Alberta ruled that the owner of a hybrid named Phantom was not in violation of the *Alberta Wildlife Act* for owning an exotic pet. In this case, Phantom was ruled a dog and hence a legal entity. So, the question of what a wolfdog is can hide a remarkable amount of complexity. Like Coppinger, Spector, and Miller's (2009) provocation entitled "What, if Anything, Is a Wolf?," delineating the boundaries – behavioural, morphological, or genetic – of a wolfdog is even murkier. And while the answer may be opaque and vary depending on context, it is one that has teeth. The stakes are high in how a wolfdog is defined, in some cases resulting in the death of the animal deemed an exotic menace.

A FURRY PIECE OF THE WILD

The muddled status of wolfdogs does not seem to worry potential owners very much, at least in the beginning; indeed, it seems part of the appeal. A lot of different theories have been put forward as to why wolfdogs have gained in popularity in recent years. For instance, a spate of articles suggested that *Game of Thrones* was the culprit, as people sought to replicate the Stark family's dire wolves in their own homes, either through wolfdogs (Scott 2019; Lowrey 2020) or breeds like Huskies and Malamutes (Daly 2019). Nicole Wilde (2004, loc. 92), former executive director of the Villalobos Rescue Center for wolves and wolfdogs, has scornfully suggested that owning a wolfdog can serve a variety of aims that have little to do with the animal itself: "Like older men who marry younger 'trophy wives,' getting a wolfdog to show off is selfish and does not speak of a meaningful relationship. Likewise, that macho desire to 'own' a piece of the wild is not a valid reason, and screams insecurity on the owner's part. 'Because they're cool' is a completely immature attitude. Then there are those who feel the wolf is the spiritual totem animal, so they long to share their life with them. While I have a solemn respect for that spiritual belief, I must say this: There is a big difference between a wolf on a spiritual plane and a wolf in your living room. For one thing, your astral guide is not as likely to eat holes in your couch!" These dogs are beautiful and untamed-looking, and their putative wildness comes through in their owner's descriptions of the nature of these animals, in contrast to that of "regular" dogs. Wolfdog enthusiasts emphasize the animal's uniqueness: super smart with a lack of desire to please humans, which makes them particularly appealing. One breeder in the United States puts this desire in more succinct terms: "Everyone who buys one says the same thing: 'I've always wanted a wolf'" (*Toronto Star* 1991). Wild, intelligent, and aloof – wolfdogs appear to be just the kind of untameable spirit that many find appealing and wish they were more like. Owning a wolfdog gives expression to all these different desires. These desires were amplified by the affective work of Mowat and Seton as well as the scientific recuperation of Pimlott and Theberge. Wolves' wildness came to be prized.

Of course, pet ownership of any kind, not just wolfdog ownership, is a complex practice. As Yi-Fu Tuan (1984) has famously suggested, it hinges on axes of affection and domination. As such, it is likely no surprise that pets can sometimes act as surrogates for the self or, at the very least, (increasingly) expensive markers of status. Harriet Ritvo (1987, 86), in her history of the rise of pet-keeping among middle-class Victorians, notes that while the "Victorian cult of pets" was about love, it was also very much about class. In spending upwards of £1,000 on a dog, the middle class could demonstrate its class power in nonhuman form. What has changed in the intervening years is not so much that pets are status symbols but how that gets conveyed and performed. The markers of status have changed, as has the scale of class display via pet. Heidi Nast's (2006, 895) work on the now-global markets for pet commodities illustrates the point: "It is now possible to find your dog or cat a herbal massage or pastries in Bangkok, Tokyo, Chicago, Paris, or London, with the number of private and public venues catering to dog sporting events and physical health increasing exponentially." Devotion to our animal companions is elaborated in hyper-commodified ways. It says less about dog than owner.

Willingness to spend money on a pet is often seen as a marker of devotion (Maharaj, Kazanjina, and Borgen 2018). It is likely no surprise then, given the cachet of wolfdogs, that the price breeders can demand is quite high. For example, in 2015, Sun Valley Wolf Kennels in Kelowna, British Columbia, advertised on their now-defunct website "high-content" – 98 per cent wolf – puppies expected to be born in spring or summer 2016. Reservations for these wolfdogs could be made for an eventual sale price of $3,000 per "cub" (Sun Valley Wolf Kennels 2015a).[2] You can find other breeders online, especially through the site hoobly.com. For instance, one listing from Calgary, Alberta, advertises pups from an "ultra-high content dad" and "Malamute-Husky-Arctic Wolfdog" mom for $1,800 (Hoobly.com 2020b). Another in Saskatoon, Saskatchewan, proffers "very high content litters for spring 2020." Grey or black pups sell for $2,500; Arctic (presumably white) for $3,500 (Hoobly.com 2020a). And there are thousands of these breeders in the United States. Note the emphasis on the degree of wolf blood in each litter and how this both offers a selling point and, seemingly, increases the price. Even as experts note that this articulation of genetic inheritance is unfounded (International Wolf Center, n.d.a; Wilde 2004), as a marketing strategy for a wild animal, it's bang on. And so, like the wolf howl, the devotion associated with wolfdog ownership is secular, but I would contend its rituals are worked in and through capitalism.

This quest for wildness seems to delineate and fix not only wolfdogs but also, in the process, other dogs through biopolitical dividing practices of inclusion and exclusion. More specifically, there appears to be almost a kind of contempt for the domesticated in the celebration of the wild and unbroken. For example, in my research in 2015, I found the following testimonial from Jordanne on the high-content wolf cubs section of the Sun Valley Wolf Kennels website: "I want to have one [a wolfdog] in my life once again, I forgot the love these animals can give uniquely compared to domestics. They have their way of completing the family function and creating home, Sun Valley Wolf Kennels has one in store for me" (Sun Valley Wolf Kennels 2015b). Similarly, Lowrey (2020) notes that the companions of wolfdogs are "stewards more than owners" who revel in the fact that their animals cannot be controlled. And just as wolfdogs aren't your run-of-the-mill pet, by extension, neither are their owners. They are more discerning and perhaps themselves unique. John Davis, president of the United States American Wolfdog Association in the 1990s, indicates: "I'm not interested in a dog that's blindly obedient. I like the free spirit and independence of the American Wolfdog. When I tell my dogs to 'sit' or 'stay,' I want them to ask, 'But why? I have such a better idea'" (Shankovich 1998, W1). What these wolfdog's human companions suggest is that there is something about owning a wolfdog that is more authentic – more reward-ing – than building a relationship with an "ordinary" domesticated dog.

However, while people might think they want to share space with an ungovernable creature that has a mind of its own, they often get more wolf than they bargained for. Wolfdogs can be shy and skittish around people they do not know. They may be difficult to house train. They need an enormous amount of exercise and a great deal of space. They are called "canine Houdinis," jumping over fences or digging under them to escape their confines, particularly if left alone for long periods (Wilde 2004, loc. 315). Beyond these behavioural considerations, the wolfiness of wolfdogs can be amplified, particularly when they outgrow the pup stage and enter sexual maturity. According to the International Wolf Center, during this period, "status becomes much more important, and the animal may begin testing its packmates to achieve a higher-ranking position in the pack" (International Wolf Center, n.d.a). The problem, of course, is that for wolf-dogs, their owners and their families are their pack. Having a wolfdog challenge for dominance can lead to disastrous outcomes, including attacks on children (Hanson 2019). Because of this, some animal protection and welfare organizations have released statements opposing the breed-ing and keeping of hybrids. For example, Humane Canada, the Canadian federation of humane societies, classifies wolfdogs as "dangerously un-predictable," "predatory," and seemingly irredeemable: "Such behaviour in the wolf hybrid is genetically encoded and cannot be eliminated by socialization and training" (Humane Canada, n.d.). Similarly, the British Columbia Society for the Prevention of Cruelty to Animals warns against "high incidence of both predatory and idiopathic aggression toward other animals and humans" (BC SPCA 2009). Both organizations suggest that wolfdogs are always dangerous predators. It is often the combination of wolf and dog traits that makes them so menacing; they have a wolf's predatory instinct and a dog's affinity for humans. According to these animal welfare organizations, that makes wolfdogs particularly challenging as house pets.

Both interesting and telling is that if the above-described characteristics emerge, the range and extent of human devotion to the animal fades. When wolfdogs display an excess of the wildness their owners suggested they prized, the bonds of love are broken. This is perhaps no surprise; animals are often given away if they trespass the boundaries (physical, economic, social, and familial) that their human companions provide for them. Heidi Nast's (2006, 900) work points to this flexibility in pet love, even among those who profess deep affection for the wolfdog's less-predatory kin; she notes that pets are better suited than children for "the mobility and narcissism of postindustrial lives," especially because they can be discarded when they become inconvenient. And because wolfdogs can be exceptionally inconvenient, they are surrendered, abandoned, or euthanized at astonishing rates – in the range of between 60 to 70 per cent, at least in the United States (Lowrey 2020). For instance, it seems that when hybrids become challenging, some human companions choose to see them as wolves rather than dogs, relinquishing the animal back into a wild from which it never came. This appears to be precisely what happened in Bowen Island, BC, in February 2011. Residents reported that they were being terrorized by a wolfdog, presumed to have been abandoned by someone who brought it over on the ferry from Vancouver, which is twenty kilometres away. In its reign of terror, this wolfdog reportedly killed and ate myriad cats, dogs, sheep, deer, geese, and "one of the island's prized swans" (Sullivan 2011, A13). Bowen Islanders went into "lockdown," fearful for their children and pets (ibid.), and set up a "hybrid hotline" to report sightings (Hopper 2011a, A1). The local vet spent months trying to hunt and tranquilize the animal but was unsuccessful. The municipality then hired a trapper who was tasked with humanely trapping the wolfdog; he too failed. Finally, a trapper was hired and authorized to kill the hybrid; he did so within two days (Hopper 2011b, A7). Interestingly, while residents relied on narratives of wildness to describe their encounters with the wolfdog, the BC Conservation Officer Service felt it was too domesticated for their consideration (Sullivan 2011). It seems that for the residents of Bowen Island, this hybrid was clearly too wolfy, yet the Conservation Officer Service felt it was too doggy. What, indeed, is a wolfdog.

DEVOTION, DONE DIFFERENTLY

While many wolfdogs are euthanized or abandoned, a small number are surrendered to rescues or sanctuaries specifically for these hybrids. It is here that we might find the potential for a different kind of devotion, one predicated on constrained intimacy, care, and perhaps something approximating interspecies solidarity. Elan Abrell (2017) and Juno Salazar Parreñas (2018) have written about sanctuaries and rehabilitation centres, respectively, as sites for the emergence of new human-animal relations that recognize contingency and intersubjectivity. For instance, the embodied care and daily attention to the needs and desires of specific animals renders a new kind of relationality, one that Abrell (2017, 4) calls the "praxis of empathic engagement." This is not to suggest that sanctuaries, animal rescues, or rehabilitation centres operate outside the confines of power. They are spaces of captivity and control, even if the goal is to rescue the animal from deeper forms of violence or even from extinction. However, there is an attention to specificity and an ethical imperative around harm reduction that frames the labour of these places. As Abrell (ibid., 5) remarks, this leads to the possibility where "humans and animals can create new systems of meaning together."

One such place is the Yamnuska Wolfdog Sanctuary in Cochrane, Alberta. Like the Algonquin wolf howl, it has become something of a tourist attraction, written up favourably in Travel Alberta and Travel Bliss Now, and awarded the Tripadvisor "Certificate of Excellence" from 2014 to 2018 (Travel Alberta 2017; Travel Bliss Now 2017; Yamnuska Wolfdog Sanctuary 2020b). The sanctuary offers public tours with increasing levels of interaction with wolfdogs. You can choose an interpretative walk and wander around on your own outside the enclosures; an intro tour, which takes you inside one of the enclosures to a viewing platform; and/or an interactive tour, which allows visitors to have an up-close experience of the wolfdogs (Yamnuska Wolfdog Sanctuary 2020b). However, like the wolf howl, the goal of these experiences is education, even as it relies on exhilaration to function. The pedagogical impetus is to teach visitors about wolfdogs and wolf conservation. The wolfdogs are engaged in this labour too; ten of the twenty-five sanctuary residents are deployed as "ambassador wolfdogs … that take front and center stage at events and sanctuary interactions, to help educate the public" (Yamnuska Wolf Sanctuary 2020a). We might also think of these sanctuary denizens as affective labourers of a different kind, less commodified but similarly inspirational.

There are four packs at the sanctuary at the time of writing, each in a one- to two-acre enclosure. Yamnuska's website gives a snapshot of their stories. Most were abandoned because people did not know how to handle them. Others came from the infamous Milk River seizure, in which the Alberta s p c a removed 201 dogs from a rural property, most living chained outside without shelter or much food (c b c News 2015). Experience has taught many of the seized animals to be timid around people. They will not be ambassadors or part of Yamnuska's wolfdog adoption program. They will remain at the sanctuary with their pack – both human and wolfdog – until the end of their days.

More importantly, perhaps, for the new kinds of relationships that Abrell emphasizes, Yamnuska hosts interns who want to work for three months at a time, or more, caring for and getting to know the animals. This labour involves tending to the everyday needs of the wolfdogs – food, shelter, enrichment, sociality – as well as being attentive to their specific personalities and lived experiences. Some are stubborn, others timid, still others "goofy"; some are all three (Yamnuska Wolf Sanctuary 2020a). Those who work with the hybrids need to come to know them as individuals, not as sums of their genetic makeup, status symbols, or beautiful and lucrative lively commodities. And much of that will happen on the wolfdogs' terms. Like the Lockwood Animal Rescue Center in California that runs a program where veterans care for wolfdogs, "each animal determines how much interaction it wants to have with the humans on the property" (Lowrey 2020). It's not uncomplicated, but it is an attempt to come to know animals on their own terms.

BEING AFFECTED

Our relationships with animals are never straightforward; even the animals we share our homes with have interior lives we will misrecognize or be inattentive to. Of course, that also extends to the human animals with whom we may cohabitate. Creatures of all kinds are hard to read.

Coming to know another is challenging, which is why the stories of devotion presented here are complicated and should be treated as such. For instance, an easier approach to analysis might tend to write off the desire to own a wolfdog as just another form of human control over the natural world, from fixation on high-content genetics to abandonment after the wolfdog's behaviour becomes problematic. And I would agree that there is much to criticize in this practice. Its approach to opening space for one another is flawed since it re-centres human desire and animal commodification in the quest for connection. But it is about connection, about expressing a sense of kinship and devotion, even as it becomes mangled through' biopolitical practices of dog breeding and abandonment, rendering, as Nicole Shukin (2009) would say, life into animal capital. The wolf howl is more open to the possibility of beastly refusal, which makes efforts at connection more haltingly uncertain. It is also less obviously commodified, though a wolf howl industry of tours and hotel stays rings Algonquin Park. It too is about connection – about seeking to be affected – by these animals we try, and fail, to understand.

Linda Birke and Jo Hockenhall (2016) plumb some of these depths in a book chapter on the human tolerance for "wayward" behaviour in horses. They note that people build relationships with their horses that often make affordances for acts of defiance, like biting or pushing, to maintain connection, even as they recognize that the agency of the horse reveals the connection would only ever be partial. Drawing in part of Barbara Smuts's lifelong work on animal sociality, Birke and Hockenhall (2016, 135) contend that it is important to understand behaviour and bond in collective rather than singular terms; if we seek to understand another, we should look to their "most important relationships" for clues (Smuts in Birke and Hockenhull 2016, 125). Rather than "connections being continuous," they are made in and through unstable relations that shift and change. In other words, humans and nonhumans learn and relearn how to be affected by one another.

In the iterations of lupine devotion explored here, we see the cultivation of both intimacy and distance. In terms of intimacy, we see the longing for kinship and connection. In the wolf howl, this is evident with listeners standing hushed – bodies tensed – waiting for the wolf to answer their call. In wolfdog sanctuaries, it is in the practices of love and care afforded to animals that have been cast off as a dangerous inconvenience. There are also flashes of shared vulnerability and intimacy, the tendrils of a larger movement toward interspecies understanding, if not solidarity. However, there is distance too. The wolves of Algonquin are there in such concentrations because the park affords them protection from their biggest predator: humans. Given the option, they might choose to live in a different area, more remote and removed from the humans desperate to hear them. Similarly, the wolfdogs selected by eager owners have little say in their life course, which often involves their human companions trying and failing to understand them and, in the process, frustrating their natural inclinations. This distance is amplified in abandonment in the wild or in death. The lucky ones end up in sanctuaries, which also need to function through a kind of distance, even as they seek to know the individual animals in more complex ways. While each of these practices is preferable to the all-out assault waged on wolves until the 1950s and 1960s, these ways of seeking connection and encounter are nevertheless imperfect.

Moreover, there is a distancing implicit in the rendering of animal into synecdoche, which occurs across the examples explored in this chapter. Tracylee Clarke (1999) has traced how wolves are deployed as rhetorical tropes in the conflict over reintroduction in Idaho. She notes that the figure of the wolf was a flexible one, symbolically utilized in contradictory ways. For the Nez Perce, the wolf was a symbol of cultural resurgence on stolen lands; for Sagebrush Rebels, whose ideology was deployed by Idaho House Representative Helen Chenoweth, the wolf signified the threat that environmentalism presents to American values of liberty and economic progress. Clarke's works demonstrate the flexibility of the wolf in cultural discourse; we've seen this throughout the book and also in this chapter. For howlers and wolfdog owners, these animals evoke the wild. And if honouring the wolf carries with it the kind of devotional practice explored here, we see a concomitant dishonouring of the domestic. Celebrated here is an idealized wild, read through the body of a wolf or wolfdog hybrid – one that also reinforced particular notions of wildness as a national character now to be praised instead of tamed. But this synecdochical rendering, while providing a broader cultural impetus to save wild space and animals, does violence to the actual animals themselves, which struggle to exist free from these cultural representations. In this frame, devotion – even as it is worked through affection, admiration, and the desire for connection – is still a dividing and distancing practice.

In the next chapter, we see how a hybrid of a different kind has negotiated its own set of political, cultural, environmental, and affective boundaries, most outside of its own making.

PART THREE

Knowing the Wolf

6

Ambivalence

Dwelling in Multispecies Assemblages

This chapter offers a departure from the rest of the book in that it considers an animal that, strictly speaking, is not a wolf. The coywolf – the polluted and hybrid kin of wolf, coyote, and dog – is our guide in thinking about what our relationships to the canids might look like if they were structured by holding open space for multispecies dwelling. This chapter explores how ambivalence is central to our reaction to this animal that only recently came to share our landscapes as a direct result of human intervention. It is an invitation to think about what the coywolf might mean for our particular practices of apprehension. In this time that we have called the Anthropocene, what can the coywolf teach us about a past littered with the bodies of wolves and a future seemingly at the edge of cascading species collapse? How might we craft new stories that allow both human and nonhuman to flourish? I suggest the coywolf invites us to learn to love the damaged world we share while insisting on a generative conversation about the ways in which our lives are always interspecies collaborations.

In 2014, PBS ran a documentary entitled *Meet the Coywolf*, which introduced its viewers to a new urban predator. But it was an animal many were already familiar with since it was the lead in a series of stories – from Toronto to Chicago – about dog-snatching wolves. Most startlingly, coywolves hit the national media in Canada in 2009, when a nineteen-year-old hiker in Cape Breton Highlands National Park was attacked by two canids, at the time thought to be coyotes. Other hikers came upon the scene and had to scare the animals away from the hiker's body in what clearly appeared to be a predatory event. The woman later succumbed to her injuries. In response, park wardens set traps for coyotes in the attack area and eventually killed one that appeared to be acting aggressively.

Genetic analysis of the animal's body indicated that it was not a coyote, or at least not straightforwardly so. Instead, the hiker was taken down by a critter named, at turns, the "eastern coyote," "northeastern coyote," or "coywolf," a hybrid of eastern wolf and western coyote, with some dog genes thrown in the mix (Way and Lynn 2016; Way, Rutledge, et al. 2010).

This story might have remained a somewhat shocking footnote in the history of Canadian national parks, a stark reminder that wildness still remains. It could have pointed to the ways in which Canadian conservation practice have changed through time, such that animals like the coywolves are not automatically persecuted by biopolitical means like the bounty. Further, it might also have served as an instructive example of what can happen to nonhumans when they transgress human boundaries. But the problem with any such consigning of this story is that coywolves have not stayed in the wilderness. Instead, like raccoons, foxes, bears, and sometimes cougars, they have become part of the multispecies assemblages that make up some of the biggest Canadian and American cities.

I contend that notions of ambivalence and indeterminacy that are sometimes embedded in human perceptions of coywolves can make it seem unnerving and most certainly out of place. In all respects, the coywolf is an "unsettled mixture" (Tsing 2012), crossing the supposed species lines between wolf, coyote, and dog; the spatial assignments of wild, rural, and urban; and the categorizations of valued species and vermin. Its indeterminate classification – its resistance to taxa – makes the coywolf an indistinct and troublesome creature, and one that works to reveal the instability of not just the boundaries that it exceeds but also the project of boundary making in the first place. As a result, some see the coywolf as a form of biological pollution that deserves extermination rather than conservation. While the coywolf can induce disquiet, I suggest that there is a more affirmative place to go and that, in addition, the coywolf might offer an opening that those who care about the more-than-human world would be wise to seize. As Waterton and Yusoff (2017) point out, indeterminacy can work both ways, eliciting all manner of affective response. Talking about "indeterminacy as a site of political possibility" (2017, 6), Waterton and Yusoff show the potential in attending to the unpredictable, unfixed, and incoherent, which requires an acknowledgment not only of the porous relations between animal species but also between human and nonhuman. This indeterminacy and ambivalence is important as we think about the history of the present human-canid relations in Canada. As previous chapters have explored, part of the desire to exterminate wolves had to do with the fact that they crossed settler boundaries because they either terrified their "betters" or stole their property (chapters 1 and 2). Even as love or scientific curiosity about wolves was allowed to bloom, there were still attempts to fix them: as noble yet dying, as beneficial rather than bad animals, or as a bigger version of "man's best friend" (chapters 3, 4, and 5). Chapter 7 shows us that this view was not inevitable; there were always other ways of thinking and knowing about the human-animal relations, but they were actively suppressed. Different ways of knowing and being may be vital as we try to work our way out of the environmental crises we find ourselves in. The coywolf amplifies and insists on this point, demanding both recognition of and invitation to a new way of relating that the history of wolf-settler relations in Canada shows is desperately needed.

MORE-THAN-HUMAN GEOGRAPHIES OF THE ANTHROPOCENE

The coywolf is, I contend, an animal that embodies the idea of the Anthropocene. Now famously defined by Paul Crutzen and Eugene Stoermer (2000) as the proposed geological epoch defined by human intrusion into the biosphere, the concept has taken root across the traditional solitudes in academia, spreading like wildfire in the sciences, but even more so in humanities and social sciences. This is no surprise; as Jenny Turner notes, "it has a luscious mouth-feel, and seems just the thing to bring new urgency and direction to all the tired old arguments about climate change, resource depletion, the future of the planet" (Turner 2017). In attempting to make the case that Earth is in a new geological epoch, a range of evidence has been marshalled. Much of this has come from Will Steffen and a group of like-minded scholars, who published the graphs indicating a "great acceleration" in economic activity, industrial production, urbanization, resource use, pollution, and population that began to spike in the 1950s (Steffen et al. 2015). The Anthropocene Working Group of the International Commission on Stratigraphy agrees, with twenty-nine of the thirty-four members voting to recognize the atomic age at the beginning of a new geological epoch (Subramanian 2019).

The impact of the Anthropocene on nonhuman species has been particularly acute. Habitat fragmentation, over-exploitation, urbanization, agriculture, species introductions, pollution, and climate change have led wild species to the brink of what scientists have called the Sixth Extinction, the next mass extinction event (Kolbert 2014; Eldredge 1998). While there is some debate about how imminent this massive collapse of biodiversity might be, Barnosky et al. (2011, 51) remind us that if the planet does witness another mass extinction event, "recovery of biodiversity will not occur on any timeframe meaningful to people: evolution of new species typically takes at least hundreds of thousands of years, and recovery from mass extinction episodes probably occurs on timescales encompassing millions of years." The converse is true for domesticated species. While their wild kin face extinction, billions of chickens, cows, sheep, pigs, and goats are brought into being each year to be slaughtered for accelerating global meat consumption, which, in turn, contributes to markers of the Anthropocene such as greenhouse gas emissions, pollution, and land-use change. Parallel to biopolitical tracks of life and death, the Anthropocene shapes, limits, reconfigures, and renders animal bodies in complex and intersecting ways.

As a scholar of animal and environmental studies, I take for granted the salience of the Anthropocene concept, acknowledging as it does that my species (or very specific parts of it) have reshaped the world in ways that are indelible, and sometimes irreparable. Of course, the trouble with depicting humans as a geological force is that it is at once awfully self-centred and totalizing. It obscures both differential cause and effect, rendering the racialized, classed, gendered, and imperial forms of violence that have, in part, created and perpetuated this human-defined moment occluded from view (Chiew 2015; Davis and Todd 2017). Instead, an undifferentiated Anthropos has ravaged the wild. It might also be taken to mean that to remedy the worst excesses of the Anthropocene, we need a different yet still totalizing new story to tell. By contrast, Donna Haraway (2016) suggests that we should talk about the Chthulucene, which rejects both the boastfulness of the Anthropocene as well as the end-of-the-world-ishness of the Capitalocene, proposed by Jason W. Moore as an alternative. Haraway is at pains to emphasize the chthonic: that which is of Earth. In so doing, she suggests that the "Chthulucene is made up of ongoing multispecies stories and practices of becoming-with in times that remain at stake, in precarious times, in which the world is not finished and the sky has not fallen – yet" (ibid., 55). So, Haraway points to what is beneath notions of the Anthropocene, hewn as it is to a fiction of separation, as an exaltation of human mastery even as it decries its impacts. Following Bruno Latour, she provides reinforcements here for the broader sweep of her work; the Chthulucene hinges on the notion that we have never been just human, but are always and inevitably an assemblage, a "tentacular" composition constituting and constituted by the more-than-human world.

From my perspective, however, an even more compelling and generative intervention into discussions of the Anthropocene is offered by Heather Davis and Zoe Todd (2017). They assert that the ethical thrust nascent in the term "Anthropocene" is often sidestepped because it is talked about as a new state of being instead of the result of long and violent histories of imperial power. Rather than situating the start of the Anthropocene at the rise of the atomic age, as other Anthropocene scholars would have it, Davis and Todd make the case that the Anthropocene started in 1610 since settler colonialism fundamentally reshaped the peoples and lands of the Americas through dispossession, genocide, and massive transformations of the landscapes, plants, and animals they encountered. Tracing the through line of settler colonialism in our current Anthropocene moment, Davis and Todd (2017, 770, emphasis added) write: "what settler colonialism, and its extensions into contemporary petrocapitalism, does is a *severing* of relations. It is a severing of relations between humans and the soil, between plants and animals, between minerals and our bones. This is the logic of the Anthropocene." This way of conceptualizing the Anthropocene – as neither new nor universal – centres the politics and uneven stakes of what the Anthropocene means in this conversation.

BECOMINGS

Coywolves are recent entrants into the biological record, only emerging in the last hundred years or so. Yet in this time, they have displayed a remarkable degree of evolutionary plasticity and adaptability, seizing on the areas "dewolfed" by the bounty across Canada and the United States. The bounty system in both countries served as a technology of colonization, one tentacle in an all-out assault that replaced a complex web of Indigenous nationhoods, lifeways, knowledges, and practices with European ones. The aim of extermination is rendered legible in the context of the anxieties that wolves induced, both similar and different to anxieties generated by coywolves. For white settlers, the transformation of appropriated lands to "productive" use – forestry, trapping, ranching, farming, and fishing – was the mainstay of their lives. Wilderness – and the people and animals that inhabited these spatial imaginaries – needed to be eliminated: one landscape replaced by another. Wolves (among others, both nonhuman and human) resisted the sweep of colonial transformation, both actually and by what their bodies represented. As chapters 1 and 2 have shown, settler relationships with wolves were dominated by fear and disgust.

The bounties and predator control units in both Canada and the United States achieved a good part of their aim, such that wolves were eliminated from much of their range in both countries at the turn of the twentieth century. As a result, by the early 1900s in Ontario, Canada, the eastern wolf

(*Canis lycaon*) – something of a hybrid itself, or at least subject to taxonomic debate (Grewal et al. 2004) – was hunted for bounty or killed by government predator control units until near extinction. As keystone predators, wolves limited the range extension of coyotes, which were found in the southwestern United States since the Pleistocene (Pennsylvania Game Commission, n.d.). However, the gap created by the bounty meant that coyotes could move east, expanding their population and extending their range. According to Kays, Curtis, and Kirchman (2010, 89), "coyote colonization was fivefold faster via the northern route through Ontario, which exposed them to wolf populations, compared with the southern route through Ohio, where wolves were extirpated prior to coyote expansion." The speed of this colonization was amplified by the landscape change that the coyotes encountered, one in transition to large-scale industrial agriculture. Because their numbers had been so decimated, the remaining wolves began to look upon coyotes – animals normally driven from their territories – as potential mates (Way 2013; Rutledge et al. 2010). In this way, settler persecution of wolves made the coywolf an evolutionary possibility. We created a window for a new species to emerge, one that thrives in wilderness and disturbed ecosystems equally well (White, personal communication) and that, by some estimates, now numbers in the millions in northeastern United States and Canada (*Economist* 2015). Our national necropolitical project gave life to a new creature. In less than one hundred years, they have become the largest predator in the region and have taken their place at the top of the food chain (Kays, Curtis, and Kirchman 2010). But this would not have been possible without the enactment of settler anxieties about wolves and the colonial and national imperative to reshape the land. As Brad White, a geneticist at the forefront of canid research suggests, "this animal is a creation of human impact on the planet" (cited in Vyhnak 2009). Put another way, the coywolf is an animal of the Anthropocene.

That said, there remains much debate in scientific literature and in conservation circles as to whether the coywolf is an actual "thing." By way of example, one might take a quick look at a recent debate that played out in *The Conversation,* an online platform meant to deliver academic research and opinion on a range of issues in an accessible and interesting way. In November 2015, zoologist Roland Kays (2015) wrote a piece for the website contesting the use of the term "coywolf." He takes issue with the word because it imputes, in his view, equal gene contribution from wolves and coyotes. Kays asserts that the coywolf remains mostly coyote (somewhere between 60 and 84 per cent), and in some cases, there are animals with almost no wolf genes. As such, "there is no single new genetic entity that should be considered a unique species" (Kays 2015): hence, no coywolf. He concludes the article with the somewhat testy exhortation, "Call it a distinct 'subspecies,' call it an 'ecomorph,' or call it by its scientific name, *Canis latrans var*. But don't call it a new species, and please don't call it the coywolf" (ibid.). In May 2016, the other side answered. Jonathan Way, who has written extensively on coywolves, including the book *Suburban Howls: Tracking the Eastern Coyote in Urban Massachusetts* (2007), entered the fray. Way argues, contra Kays, that the coywolf is in fact a distinct species and should be hailed not as a coyote variant, but as *Canis oriens* (Way 2016). Way (ibid.) contends that the animals are "significantly different – genetically and physically – from their parental species since the coywolf is about 60 percent coyote, 30 percent wolf, and 10 percent dog; thus, nearly 40 percent of this animal is not coyote." He ends his intervention with the suggestion that coywolves might act as something of conservation role model, demonstrating the importance of protecting species not only that live in wilderness but also with whom we are more likely to share space.

Whereas Kays's argument hinges on similarity – coywolves are too much like coyotes – Way's functions on difference – they are dissimilar enough to be considered their own species. The language seems to matter quite a bit here, working as it does to enforce taxonomic boundaries that reify species' divides. These arguments also suggest that the divisions between species are more calcified than they may actually be. For my purposes, this debate is interesting less as a means to determine the truth of species-hood and more about its insistence that defining whether or not the animal as a distinct species is central to understanding it. And so, I use the term "coywolf" precisely to stick with its indeterminacy, for its inability to be contained either by the geographical imaginaries that are imposed upon it or the species boundaries that its body actively resists.

DWELLING IN-BETWEEN

What is interesting about coywolves is the blend of morphological and behavioural traits they display from their progenitors. For example, they fall between wolves and coyotes in size, weighing somewhere between thirty and fifty-five pounds. They hunt in packs, like wolves, but demonstrate a degree of fearlessness, or at least curiosity, toward humans – more of a coyote trait. They thrive in urban environs, moving along our highway systems, abandoned rail lines, and segmented green space in search of food (Cortorneo 2013). They are opportunistic omnivores, with the ability to eat deer (because of their larger jaws) or urban compost (CBC News, n.d.). There have also been reports suggesting that the animals are "bolder and smarter than regular coyotes" (Vyhnak 2009). And it appears it is their very hybridity that has ensured their evolutionary success; rather than genetic pollution, interbreeding has led to species strength in the form of adaptability (*Economist* 2015). For example, citing Kays, Velasquez-Manoff (2014) asserts that "the Eastern coyote's hybrid ancestry has allowed it to expand its range five times as fast as nonhybrid coyotes could have."

In some cases, the unsettledness of the coywolf has provoked a fearful response that has been part of the media narrative around the coywolf expansion across southern Canada and the northeastern United States. This disquiet follows, at least to some degree, the well-worn grooves laid down by settler interactions with wolves. Like wolves, coywolves are seen as out of place. They occupy places that wild animals should not. For wolves, their very presence marked them for extermination. In the case of coywolves, it is their proximity to the margins of city life that generate affective responses in the humans that encounter them. This is especially true because of their ubiquity. Since their first sighting in central Ontario in 1919, coywolves have in recent years become something of a shadowy fixture in urban and suburban areas. As a result, the interactions between coywolves and humans have grown. While they might be difficult to categorize, for many, especially those who have lost a beloved family pet to their predations, coywolves fit the definition of "urban terrorist" assigned to other "trash animals" (Nagy and Johnson 2013, 2). Predatory wildlife in the city presents challenges to our normative spatial understandings of what belongs where, generating registers of fear and anxiety around wildness radically out of place. As Jennifer Wolch (1996; 2002) suggests, the urban setting offers an illusory sense of separateness from nature, where the ordering and segmentation of space proceeds almost entirely on human terms. But, of course, animals and other nonhumans have always been integral to cities in the form of not only urban wildlife but also pets, livestock, disease vectors like cholera, cockroaches, bedbugs, and so on. Moreover, rather than eschewing contact with humans, some animals may choose to live in close proximity for a number of reasons, such as access to food or safety from hunters (M.S. Thompson 2007). Despite this evidence, the idea that the cities are somehow anti-natural is prevalent, causing Jerolmack to suggest that urban wildlife "signals a cityscape that is not subdued" (2008, 88). As a result, intrusion upon this fiction is often vigorously policed, particularly if the multispecies encounter leads to human loss (property damage, missing pets) or perceived loss ("aesthetic insults")

(Wolch 1996, 35). For example, the flying fox, a large fruit bat native to Australia, has been purged from its chosen home in Melbourne's Royal Botanic Gardens (M.S. Thompson 2007). So too have van Dooren's (2016) "unwelcome crows" in Hoek van Holland. Along the same lines, the coywolf, with its less predatory co-travellers, like raccoons, rats, weasels, feral cats, and foxes, disrupt our narratives about how and on whose terms animals can occupy the world.

Indeterminacy and ambiguity often amplify reactions to coywolves. Writing about coyotes in Toronto, Blue and Alexander (2015, 155) contend that they "refuse to remain within such tidy geographical orderings and imaginaries. In transgressing these categories, coyotes can be viewed as out of place and risk inciting potentially dangerous reactions for the human community." The coywolves' success in using urban infrastructure – moving along remnant green spaces designed for recreation, using highway off-ramps for dens, howling at the sound of fire truck sirens or, in my community of Peterborough, Ontario, train whistles – suggests a sense that they can navigate urban terrain capably and without human awareness. They are synanthropes that have adapted to urban environments and "are able to adjust their behavior to habitat fragmentation and human activities" (Birnie-Gauvin et al. 2016, 417). Put differently, coywolves are novel animals for novel ecosystems that show the kind of phenotypic plasticity that some find so troubling.

To grasp how the coywolf's indeterminacy was storied, I looked at almost 200 media articles between 1995 and 2017 (193 to be exact). I found that the coywolf generated a range of affective responses, often concentrated (though not entirely) around fear and panic. Some articles were reflective think pieces on the emergence of coywolves and their remarkable capacity to live in some of the biggest cities in Canada and the United States (see, for example, Matheny 2015). Others were more focused on the taxonomic classifications that such critters resist (see, for example, M. Miller 2015). However, a good number displayed angst at a new predatory force that seems capable of moving among our spatial and genetic categories with ease. Take, for example, some of the more overwrought headlines:

"Victoria Beach under Siege by a Vicious New Predator" – *Winnipeg Free Press* (B. Owen 2015)

"The Super Coyote Is Here … They Are Here, maybe Right in Your Own Backyard, and They're Bred to Hunt." – *Windsor Star* (City Desk 2013)

"Coyotes Taking over East Haven Backyards" – WTNH Connecticut (Simoni 2014)

"This Is Our Town's Jaws" – *Motherboard* (Knafo 2015)

"Coywolves Have Taken over the Northeast" – *Business Insider* (Welsh 2014)

"Coywolves, Coyote-Wolf Hybrids, Are Prowling Rock Creek Park and D.C. Suburbs" – *The Washington Post* (Dingfelder 2014)

Of course, these are not the only stories telling of human-coywolf encounters. Some media outlets have been far more admiring in their depiction of these canid hybrids. But I would suggest that these stories – the ones that dwell on the affective registers of panic, fear, and horror – are the ones freighted with the most potential to impact the lives of coywolves. While each of these news reports might be read as a hyperbolic lead to attract audiences in a media-saturated market where click-bait is prevalent, the degree of fear and disdain is palpable as one delves further into these news reports. For example, in the case of Chappaqua, New York, an affluent suburb in Westchester that is home to Bill and Hillary Clinton, the presence of coywolves has torn the community in two between those who believe the coywolves should be trapped and killed because of an impending "coyote jihad" (sporting freshly made coyote gloves at town meetings to emphasize the point) and those who suggest that maybe we need to find better ways to live together (Knafo 2015). In the case of Victoria Beach, Manitoba – and in the absence of any documented cases of coywolves – the description given is of a pack of roving (and ravening) canids, completely unafraid of humans (B. Owen 2015). Members of the community indicated they preferred the long-reviled wolf to the coywolf because it stayed away from humans; wolves it seems, unlike their kin, know their place. Citizens of Victoria Beach asserted that they felt "under siege" in having to keep their pets indoors (B. Owen 2015). Similarly, in the central Ontario town of Gravenhurst, resident Lori Kennedy recounts being attacked by a coywolf as she attempted to rescue her pet cat. She remarks that since the attack "the neighbours have all been living in fear" (Kenny 2014). Bette Jean Crew of the Ontario Federation of Agriculture echoes this sentiment: "From what I know talking to farmers, the animals are getting bigger and bolder" (Winsa 2011). The article goes on to suggest that "in recent years, stories have spread about the hybrid eastern coyote, a once solitary animal that now hunts in packs like a wolf and lures off expensive guard dogs so other pack members can move in for the kill" (ibid.). In Carol Kaesuk Yoon's (2010) account, coyotes are also wily, charged with four attacks on children in one summer and leaving the community on alert from this new suburban predator.

Most articles also deal head-on with the indeterminacy of the coywolf, remarking on wolf-coyote hybridity in the United States and Canada in sometimes less overstated but no less important terms. For instance, as far back as the early 1990s, the *Toronto Star* (1990) suggests that "wolves are threatened by a lust for coyotes" in ways that "threaten their genetic integrity." Ron Nowak, a former United States Fish and Wildlife Service zoologist, amplified this concern in a 1995 article for *Canid News*, where he outlined the taxonomic peril from recognizing hybridization: "The wolves of North America are under a severe new threat from an influential group; not the lumber companies, fur trappers, or stockman, but the zoologists, or at least some among them who are keen to publish claims that wolf populations have hybridized with other species" (Nowak 1995, 1). A more recent article about wolves in a national park in western Quebec echoes this lack of distinction, suggesting that in the six packs found in Gatineau Park, the lines between wolf, dog, and coyote are blurred (Spears 2015). Almost all the articles I looked at referenced the "canid soup," the futility in separating out species lines among canid populations, as exemplified by the fight about whether or not coywolves are a distinct species. The presence of the coywolf in the first place, alerts us to the invention of species boundaries.

The discursive signals in these articles work through fear of a new predator or the biological risks it poses, often hinged on the notion of invasion and intrusion – that coywolves represent some kind of biorisk that needs to be eliminated from the urban landscape. This terrain has been expertly covered both with reference to predatory wildlife (Collard 2012) and with the broad literature on "invasive alien species" (Larson 2008). Invasion carries its own lexicon of political prescriptions, but the vast majority dictate extermination of one species for the conservation of another (Ritvo 2017) – the latter being the one "in place" rather than the one exceeding its spatial or species boundaries. Similar to wolves, those species deemed out of place, by virtue of either geography or taxonomy, unsettle the certitude with which humans navigate the world. And yet, in my estimation, it is not just that the coywolf is wild but that it occupies a space in between that gnaws at the edges of normalcy in urban life. The coywolves' success in using urban infrastructure suggests that they make use of the novel ecosystems we have provided for them. Rather than their wildness, I would suggest it is the coywolves' instability that has induced the kind of moral panic we see elaborated in these news reports. At the root of this is the notion that the coywolf is an abject animal. For Julia Kristeva (1982, 4), the abject has to do with "what disturbs identity, system, order. What does not respect borders, positions, rules." The coywolf represents the loss of distinction, of secure moorings with which to define both the human-dominated landscape of the urban and the supposed impermeable divisions between species themselves. The coywolf not only resists our spatial categories but also refuses our notions of genetic purity. Its biggest violation is that it insists on being in the first place. Coywolves, then, can be thought of as an embodiment of the Anthropocene's most interesting conceptual elements. They call into question what Fiona Probyn-Rapsey (2016a) has called the "purifying logic" we apply to the nonhuman world, pointing instead to the evolutionary possibilities of hybridity, of unsettled mixtures, of indeterminacy. They are, as Donna Haraway would suggest, string figures, emphasizing the knottiness of enmeshed living. I think this, if nothing else, is fruitful in the idea of the Anthropocene. For all its conceits around the importance of humans to the stories of Earth, it does invite a recognition (or acknowledgment as Davis and Todd (2017) might point out) that the world only operates via entanglement.

HISTORICIZING HYBRIDITY

As mentioned above, some of the responses to coywolves follow a longer lineage of both fascination and revulsion around hybridity. Hybridity, like the nation, as Homi Bhabha (1995) so famous remarked, is a site of ambivalence. One can see this ambivalence at work when looking at animals, like the coywolf, that unsettle our taxonomic practices. As Caccavale and Reiss (2011) suggest, monsters captivate. Those creatures that do not fit within our classificatory practices are at once bewitching and abhorrent, titillating yet disquieting (see also Ritvo 1998). This ambivalence is often sutured through a re-establishment of the categories that such creatures unsettle. This is very clear in the insistence that the lines between species are distinct and bounded. However, the emphasis on species boundaries is as much an imaginative as biological act, yet an act that is "deeply rooted in our culture" (Caccavale and Reiss 2011). Since Ernst Mayr's elaboration of the biological species concept, based on the notion that species boundaries are calcified through the (im)possibility of breeding, this understanding has become the normative way of conceptualizing species distinction (Mitchell 2016). But, as Mitchell (2016, 34) points out, this move to abstraction can only be maintained by disregarding "the creative promiscuity and proliferation of life forms."

As Mitchell (2016), Latour (1993), and others have signalled, beneath the boundary policing between species, hybridization thrives. Perhaps because of this, efforts at purification may be redoubled. In revealing the historical contingency of species divides, animals like coywolves are rendered unworthy of conservation (Stronen and Paquet 2013) in language that often echoes eugenic desires to purge the body of impure elements (Pêgas 2013), one that recalls the impulse to expel wolves from the newly made nation. Referring to the instability of these notions, as shown by genetic modification, recombinant DNA, and animal hybridization, Caccavale and Reiss (2011) go on to suggest that "this has provoked a deep anxiety among many people, an anxiety that has been variously described as a rejection of the 'unnatural' or a fear of the 'alien' or the 'dangerous.'" Conservation biology is not immune to these views, where, as Rodrigo Vargas Pêgas (2013, 1) attests, hybridization has an "unnatural image." We see this in Nowak's panic around an acknowledgment of hybridization, as well as Giese's (2005, 865) more recent work on coywolves, which asserts that "the wolf now faces a new and unlikely threat. Molecular genetics research suggests that gray wolves have hybridized with coyotes in the northeastern United States." Underpinning this contention is a biopolitical move that carries the resonance of the wolf bounty, but instead of killing wolves, they are saved from genetic swamping. What is interesting, of course, is that this discourse and practice assumes that wolves are somehow a pure species, whereas coywolves are not. This essentialism falls apart once we recognize that the eastern wolf, with whom coyotes bred in the first place, is part of the canid soup that makes up the northeastern United States and southeastern Canada. The politics of purity has no place in the canine world.

Even so, animals like the coywolf – genetically, spatially, and discursively indeterminate – are remade into threats in need of management. For Mitchell (2016, 30), these are the "unloved" creatures of conservation practice, rendered so, in this case, because they thrive where they should not. This unlovability is present in both conservationist and popular discourses of the animal. For instance, it is also not hard to miss the underlying racial logic at play, most obviously in the language of jihad above but also present through an elaboration of the perils of genetic swamping, or "extinction by introgression," that is pinned on this animal. The coywolf is talked about as an agent of invasion. As Probyn-Rapsey (2016b) suggests, "the categories into which animals are made to fit are both cultural and scientific … We have ferals because we have a stubborn insistence on categorical thinking." Livingston and Puar (2011, 7) stick with the implications of the genetic transgression offered by creatures like the coywolf, arguing that attention must be paid to the "social and affective processes when barriers are breached" and "the hierarchical classificatory system is subverted or reworked." In this way, the kind of horror expressed by the residents of some of the towns featured in the news makes a little more sense. In many of the accounts presented in the media and in some scientific understandings, the coywolf's eradication is necessary: it inverts some of the certainties through which we order our lives and throws into relief the futility of these attempts at demarcating the world.

LOVE YOUR MONSTERS

Perhaps the most interesting aspect of this story from the perspective of multispecies encounter is that human action made the coywolf possible. By attempting to exterminate one species, white settlers, invested in the national project of settling the land in specific ways, allowed another to emerge, one that is highly adapted to human socio-ecological relations. The critical question, then, is: if we made it, what is our responsibility to it? The more predictable reaction charted above does not have to be – and indeed is not – the only one. Just as often as people want to trap and kill the coywolves (and make them into silky mittens!), others want to ensure their continued ability to live in the places that they choose. If the coywolf is an animal of the Anthropocene, then, as Collard, Dempsey, and Sundberg (2015, 322) suggest, it invites "the question of how humans ought to intervene in the environment; how to live in a multispecies world." Bruno Latour tells us to love our monsters. He contends that "Dr Frankenstein's crime was not that he invented a creature through some combination of hubris and high technology, but rather that he abandoned the creature to itself" (Latour 2012). What if we take this seriously, accepting both responsibility for and humility to learn with more-than-human critters, like the coywolf? What might it look like if we take attentiveness and enmeshment as the place to start?

The wolf, the coywolf's co-traveller and kin, has played an active role in the lives of humans for millennia, even as we spent centuries trying to eradicate them. There is evidence of the domestication of wolves since at least the Neolithic period. But interestingly, new research contends that wolves domesticated us, rather than the other way around. The notion that wolves approached us first, perhaps hanging around the edges of a cooking fire in 10,000 BCE, suggests a kind of "survival of the friendliest," which is marked by our relationship with dogs today (O'Callaghan 2013).

In the end, we have co-evolved. Throughout much of the history of our relationship with and to wolves, we have attempted to deny this co-evolution, this multispecies assemblage. Some wolves became dogs, and others remained resolutely part of the wilderness that needed taming. But coywolves show us yet another layer of this co-evolution. Fugitives from a feral landscape, their presence jars us into thinking about the stakes of decisions about livability, and how we might rework them – both discursively and materially – if our goal is co-flourishing.

It's good to think with the coywolf precisely because it disconcerts. Put differently, it asks how we learn to love our monsters, beings that upset the neatness of our conceptual boundaries, that function as examples of Kirksey's (2015) emergent ecologies. How can we foster intimacy by way of new forms of attentiveness while at the same time making room for autonomy? What do cohabitation and livability look like for the coywolf? It is here that I think turning to the notion of ferality leads in interesting directions, not to reify a discourse of genetic purity but to deny the political value that an attachment to a fictive purity offers. I contend that the coywolf is feral, but not in the putative sense of a domesticated animal returning to the wild. I would invite a broader interpretation. Ferality points to the ways in which some animals are made possible through human interaction, with that encounter shaping all those doing the relating. In the case of the coywolf, its relationships to humans, to particular kinds of landscapes, and to wolves brought it into being. In my deployment of the notion here, ferality might be a synonym for symbiosis, always entangling multiple actors in a messy and unending negotiation of difference. So, ferality is risky. It shreds certainty and violates limits. Yoon (2017, 136) asserts that the feral "evokes liminal, excessive, inappropriate, and transgressively abject connotations, marking the need to correct, neuter, or even exterminate ecological and political outcasts." It is the unruliness here that I think might be important to hang on to, for in my view, it offers a path forward in the politics (and poetics) of ecological revivification and repair. As Haraway and Tsing (2015) tell us, "resurgence is always a multispecies affair." And it is necessarily relational, often occurring at the "neglected margins or the seams of empire" (Tsing 2012, 155). The coywolf is an animal of the edge, full of the potential that ferality implies.

And yet, there is much to be critiqued in the flat ontologies that often accompany an unambiguous celebration of resilience in nature. This emphasis on enmeshment, on resilience, on the capacity of the more-than-human world to respond to and shape our shared environment can also work to evacuate politics out of questions of human-animal relations. If we acknowledge that humans are not always, as Steve Hinchliffe and Nick Bingham (2008) suggest, the most interesting place to start, then there is the attendant possibility that an emphasis on agency obscures asymmetry, coercion, and domination. As Rosemary Collard, Jessica Dempsey, and Juanita Sundberg (2015) have so insightfully shown, mainstream conservation is becoming both more "neoliberal and postnatural" in its embrace of the Anthropocene, emphasizing ecosystem services over biodiversity protection, where the more-than-human world becomes instrumentalized through new forms of green governmentality. A potential hazard, then, of this posthumanist celebration of entanglement, co-constitution, assemblage, and biopolitical collectivities is that it actually perpetuates the very circumstances that require nonhuman resilience in the first place. There are better ways of relating to the fact that we are necessarily and inevitably entangled with the nonhuman and that it has everything to do with reciprocity, exchange, improvisation, and liveliness rather than doubling down on the kind of technological utopianism espoused by the folks at the Breakthrough Institute through their *Ecomodernist Manifesto* (Asafu-Adjaye et al. 2015). Conservation triage or de-extinction are not, in my view, options. We need to find another way.

Put differently, when I say we need to love our monsters, I am gesturing to the ways that rejecting Western humanism is a political project – one with real stakes not only for nonhumans but also those people who, through the epistemic violence of the nature-culture divide, have found themselves on the wrong end of that boundary. How do we open space for all parts of creation – human, nonhuman, biotic, abiotic, person, polar bear, and lichen? How do we invite a curiosity and attentiveness to the world outside of the human, a world that fundamentally co-constitutes us even as we have sought to deny this material reality? How do we make life liveable for each other? In this context, the coywolf may offer an example of the degree to which some humans have intruded on and shaped the biosphere, but our reaction to it need not continue along this thread. The coywolf is illustrative of the precarity that the Anthropocene implies, but also of the ways that there is life in the midst of death. Said differently, the coywolf could be considered an agent of "genetic rescue" (Stronen and Paquet 2013, 391) in the context of the rate of extinction we have wrought. While the Anthropocene presents us with a dire indictment of violence against the nonhuman world, it also may not be the end of this story. For J.B. MacKinnon, "a story of loss is not always and only a lament; it can also be a measure of possibility" (cited in Collard, Dempsey, and Sundberg 2015, 327). This does not provide an alibi for the destruction of the natural world; rather, it gives a place to go that sidesteps the politics of purity. Instead of balking at the environmental change that the coywolf represents or denying the role of the colonial project in producing it, those whose lives are enmeshed with coywolves might seek a productive and generative attention to difference and livability in the context of that difference. Rather than panic and issue exhortations around genetic pollution or animals out of place, there could be an embrace of the kind of resilience the coywolf exemplifies, while also recognizing that we need to do more for those animals that cannot live in such close proximity to humans. In cities, this might mean, at a minimum, the acknowledgment that the urban is a space constituted by multispecies encounters, which cries out for a "transspecies urban theory" (Hovorka 2008). At a concrete level, and at the very least, planners could extend spaces for the coywolf and other predators to survive – establishing nodes, buffers, and corridors – where wildness is a characteristic defined not by proximity but by the chance for autonomy and self-determination (Collard, Dempsey, and Sundberg 2015). Or, instead of embarking on ecological restoration projects that deny the value of novel ecosystems, there might be an acknowledgment that humans sometimes increase rather than decrease biodiversity or, at the very least, allow for different kinds of biodiversity to emerge and thrive. Some of us may be required to accept the potential for loss – particularly of beloved pets – if we allow them to roam outdoors, negotiating the knotty entanglements of sharing space.[1] Further still, the possibilities for urban wildlife to thrive might be made manifest if we see them not as pests or wildlife out of place, or even as victims displaced through the Anthropocene, but as individual animals that may have chosen to occupy the city on their own terms. More broadly, Stronen and Paquet (2013, 394) offer an option that is at once common sense and challenging: "Where hybrids have filled the ecological niche (or parts thereof) of one or more extirpated parent taxa, such as the eastern coyote in the northeastern United States and parts of southeastern Canada, the focus should be on preserving the ecological role currently held by these hybrids."

One wonders about the possibilities for interspecies exchange that are opened up when we allow for the fact that all animals, human and otherwise, make choices to pursue their own lifeways. In this context, the existence of the coywolf gives us some reason for hope; they might be our accomplices in dwelling well in the Anthropocene. Either way, it seems, the coywolf invites us to unfix our conceptual rigidity, offering what Livingstone and Puar (2011, 11) call a "politics of curiosity and vulnerability," where risky and contingent attachments may be formed and reformed in a continuous negotiation of mutual responsibility. There is need for care here; as David and Todd point out, the study of the Anthropocene has reinforced rather than disrupted the colonial logics from which it arises. They "call here for those studying and storying the Anthropocene to tend to the ruptures and cleavages between land and flesh, story and law, human and more-than-human ... for a tending once again to relations, to kin, to life, longing, and care" (2017, 775). And so perhaps a bigger story in the embrace of the coywolf is that it requires attending to the severing practices of settler colonialism in Canada. Put another way, it requires reimagining the nation on these lands.

Working out how we might make our choices around animal life less asymmetrical and more about flourishing is, in my view, the critical task of our time, for both humans and nonhumans. Curiosity and vulnerability can be put into practice through the politics of encounter where we come to relationality bereft of assumption. Maan Barua (2015, 266) sketches eloquently what this could mean: "Encounters point to taxa being occurrents, inseparable from the heterogeneous bodies, technologies and practices through which they are articulated. Multiple modes of knowledge are fused in classificatory schemes, evident when plicated histories of encounters between colonizer and colonized are unraveled. Encounters scramble genealogical trees: introgression and horizontal gene transfer happen across phyla and scales. They herald involutions, organismic filiations based on contagion and symbiosis." The choice to encounter requires something of us; apathy becomes an unacceptable response. There is hope here, but not the kind that is blind to the perils we face or the enormity of the task at hand. As Davis and Todd (2017) point out, the stakes are high, but some people have been living with these stakes for a long time and have lessons to impart on living better. Learning to love our monsters is an iterative process, one that we will almost certainly get wrong again and again. Paying attention to one another in ways that are intimate but also allow for autonomy will be difficult. The likely result will be an inevitably flawed effort to come to know another animal in a way that grants it has lifeways that we may not understand but that are worth attending to. So then, it is important to deploy hope as a verb, as an ethical obligation, and, for my purposes, as a way of doing research. If, as Haraway (n.d., 1) contends, "it has become literally unthinkable to do good work in any interesting field with the premises of individualism, methodologically individualism, and human exceptionalism," then political hope must be a relational multispecies affair.

7

Empathy

Indigenous Teachings Offer a Way Out (and In)

In 2012, a lone coastal wolf appeared in Victoria, British Columbia. He navigated the city streets and suburban backyards for a couple of months and eventually swam two kilometres to the Tl'ches archipelago (Discovery and Chatham islands), part of the traditional territory of the ləkʷəŋən People, known as the Songhees Nation. There, the wolf, who would come to be known as both stqéyə and Staqeya (the ləkʷəŋən word for wolf), made its solitary existence for eight years.

Staqeya was an unusual wolf, even among coastal wolves, which are a genetically distinct population of grey wolves (McAllister and Read 2010). That he lived alone for eight years without leaving the island to seek a mate is remarkable enough (Collins, Alexander, and Darimont 2019), but he also exhibited other distinctive behaviours. He preyed almost exclusively on marine mammals, like otter and seal, and, amazingly, dug wells in the summer months to find a source of fresh water at a time when none was available on the island (Cecco 2020). He howled frequently, although lone wolves are usually much less chatty for fear of drawing the attention of stronger packs (ibid.). And he occupied far less space than a typical wolf pack's territory. As Collins, Alexander, and Darimont (2019, 3) note, Staqeya's life demonstrates "significant plasticity in the life history of wolves." Lived in such proximity to humans, Staqeya's life provided a window into the myriad ways that wolfiness is inhabited.

For some, like wildlife photographer Cheryl Alexander, who spent years tracking, studying, photographing, and interacting with the wolf, Staqeya was a beautiful reminder of wildness close at hand. But for the Songhees, this wolf was a relative. Chief Robert Sam, who worked to protect the islands that the wolf inhabited as part of the Songhees traditional territory, died the summer before the wolf appeared. Some Songhees thought that Staqeya was the spirit of their chief returned in the body of a wolf, continuing his work of protecting their nation (Counter 2017). Indeed, this might explain his behaviour; while odd for a wolf, it makes sense in the context of an ancestor protecting unceded lands. Many Songhees are wolf clan and thus recognized Staqeya as kin (ibid.). Quoted in a story on the CTV Vancouver Island website, Chief Ron Sam noted: "We took it as a sign that he showed up there for some reason. You really wonder why he was out there alone. There was something out there for him" (Kelly 2020). After two failed attempts in 2012 and 2013 to trap and relocate Staqeya amidst Songhees objections, the Nation asserted its jurisdiction over their unceded lands and asked that the wolf be left alone (Lavoie 2013). Provincial authorities complied, and Staqeya lived – protected – on Songhees territory until 2020.

Staqeya's life, however, was not without incident. In 2016, although dogs were banned from the island, a family visited Chatham Island with their pet (Counter 2017). This apparently was not uncommon; many people walked their dogs off-leash on the island's beaches. On this occasion, they encountered a wolf that was not particularly afraid of, and moreover quite curious about, them and the animal they brought with them. Like other wolves that feature in this book, Staqeya had learned that he did not need to be fearful of humans and no doubt thought of the pet dog as a potential mate, or at least a play-mate. And so Staqeya followed the family. Alarmed, they called for help, and Staqeya's situation suddenly became precarious. Again, the Songhees advocated for the wolf, and he was allowed to remain on their territory.

However, in January 2020, Staqeya decided to leave the archipelago. No one knows why. Some, like biologist Chris Darimont, think he might have finally decided to find a mate. Others, like Cheryl Alexander, think that he did not intend to leave permanently (Cecco 2020). Either way, like the coywolves of chapter 6, Staqeya was rendered illegible as a wild wolf once he returned to Victoria. Instead, he became a threat to public safety, even as conservationists noted that he posed little risk (Hunter 2020). Once he left the protection of Songhees territory, Staqeya was trapped in a backyard in Victoria, and the decision was made to relocate him. Once again, the Songhees Nation came forward, advocating for the wolf's return to their territory, but this time the BC Conservation Officer Service reckoned that his habituation necessitated his removal from proximity to humans. Staqeya was moved near Port Renfrew on the west coast of Vancouver Island, about one hundred kilometres from Victoria. Conservation officers hoped he would thrive and maybe find a mate, even as another Indigenous community, this time the Pacheedaht First Nation of Port Renfrew, said he should be given more protection in a provincial park further to the north (Pynn 2020).

What happened next is unclear. Staqeya was spotted occasionally but mostly it was thought that he had a new and better life away from humans. Then, in March 2020, Staqeya was found near Shawnigan Lake where he was legally shot and killed. The hunter who shot Staqeya skinned him and took his head and feet to be preserved as a taxidermy trophy (Hall 2020).

The response to Staqeya's death was an almost uniform lament. The wolf had captivated not only people in Victoria and British Columbia but also across Canada. It also generated a bigger conversation about why it was possible in BC to kill any wolf, not just Staqeya, for a trophy. But the pain felt by the Songhees was both deeper and more profound. They had lost kin, and quite possibly the spirit of their late chief. The Nation reached out to the hunter, and he returned Staqeya's body to the Songhees, who privately honoured him with ceremony and laid his body to rest (Pynn 2020).

The story of Staqeya is heartbreaking on its own terms. This wolf was an enigmatic and resilient survivor who was given voice and celebrity status, most particularly by the work of Cheryl Alexander. His death also mattered in that Staqeya came to stand in for the plight of wolves and other animals whose lives were no more valuable than a head adorning a wall. He stood as a representative for a bigger population rendered killable by provincial law. But Staqeya's death also illuminates the way that animals come to matter in both settler and Indigenous cultures in fundamentally different, and often incommensurate, ways. The capacious way in which the Songhees first understood Staqeya's presence on their territories, to their advocacy for and protection of his life, to the way in which they honoured his death, speaks to a relational engagement with the nonhuman not premised on what animals lack but what is gained when animals are encountered as relatives. Their understanding of Staqeya as kin – either quite literally as the embodied spirit of their former chief or as a part of Songhees wolf clan – opened up specific obligations to help Staqeya thrive, to recognize him as an individual who could make his own choices and deserved the space to do so. At every turn, the Songhees enabled his choices. They knew he was there for a reason that, while perhaps not accessible to people, should be honoured.

The way in which Staqeya was welcomed and known by the Songhees is not an anomaly. The teachings about and modes of engagement between wolves and Indigenous Peoples were – and remain – radically different from those of settlers and wolves. There is complexity and nuance, and a fundamentally more robust sense of agency than is seen in settler texts, either at the beginning of the bounty or now. In this assertion, it is not my intention to hold up a kind of mythical pan-Indigenous embrace of

all things wolf; there are, of course, multiple and varied ways of relating
to wolves (and all plant and animal nations) in Indigenous communities,
and I am not an expert in any of them. But there are common threads
that rely on notions of respect and reciprocity, kinship and relationality
(LaDuke 1999; Nelson 2008; Kimmerer 2013; Simpson 2017). As Kyle
Whyte (2020, 267) explains: "Indigenous traditions focus on details of
how our bonds with others really work. Kin relations are like ideal family
bonds, and are composed on types of relationships and qualities of relationships." Beyond these modes of engagement being profoundly different
from settler accounts of the wolf, they were considered so radical that
they were understood to be a threat, one that, like the wolf itself, needed
to be eliminated.

THE COLONIALITY OF POSTHUMANISM

In recent years, scholars keen to disrupt human exceptionalism have turned
to posthumanism and its variations to account for the fact that nonhumans
are political actors who are not only shaped by but also actively shape the
natural world. But in its insistence that new ways of thinking and being
are required to see the world as it actually is – entangled, lively, agential –
posthumanism ignores the fact that an emphasis on relational ontologies
has underpinned (and continues to underpin) Indigenous teachings,
philosophy, and legal orders. Kim TallBear (2011), Vanessa Watts (2013),
and Zoe Todd (2016) have all pointed to the ways in which academic theorizing about the nonhuman in its various forms – posthumanism, object-oriented
ontology, new materialism, and so on – draws on, but crucially does not
credit, important elements of Indigenous thought. Smith, Tuck, and Yang
(2019, 14) name this succinctly: "There have been several 'turns,' including
the ontological turn, the material turn, the spatial turn, each of which is
actually a turn to where Indigenous people have always been"; or as Rosiek,
Snyder, and Pratt (2019, 2) suggest more irreverently: the posthuman turn
is evidence that "Columbus discovers non-human agency." In my own
discipline, Juanita Sundberg (2014) has cautioned geographers to recall
that what they are saying is not precisely new, and often reasserts the colonial dividing practices it seeks to destabilize. By claiming, as much of the
literature in more-than-human geographies does, that the divide between
nature and culture has been universal, posthumanist thought can erase
ways of knowing that are not structured in this manner while also reifying
the very Euro-American dualism being critiqued. This move, Zoe Todd
(2016, 16) contends, is not innocent but has real impacts: "So it is important

to think, deeply, about how the Ontological Turn – with its breathless 'realisations' that animals, the climate, water, 'atmospheres' and non-human presences like ancestors and spirits are sentient and possess agency, that 'nature' and 'culture,' 'human' and 'animal' may not be so separate after all – is itself perpetuating the exploitation of Indigenous peoples."[1]

It is not only the scholars who identify with the posthuman turn who have often disregarded Indigenous thinkers as they call for a more fulsome accounting of all the actors and forces that make up our world. The failure to engage with Indigenous thought may have also led to a rather thin conception of nonhuman agency. Rosiek, Snyder, and Pratt (2019) contend that Euro-American scholars are so caught up in trying to prove that animals, plants, bacteria, and more have the ability to act in the world – a start rather than end point in Indigenous ontologies – that they often do not get around to the ethical questions that this agency compels. Getting stuck in proving that agency exists instead of why it matters is compounded by the fact that for many Euro-American scholars, agency is conceptualized as a "general abstraction" rather than a characteristic revealed through a deep understanding of place (Rosiek, Snyder, and Pratt 2019, 7). Vanessa Watts (2013, 21) explains this idea in her notion of place-thought, defined as the understanding that "the land is alive and thinking and that humans and non-humans derive agency through the extensions of these thoughts." Rather than agency, then, perhaps a better word for what Watts and others describe is "personhood" as worked through place-thought, which allows for a deeper understanding of what the roles and responsibilities are in understanding the liveliness of the world. Watts (2013, 23) goes on to assert: "Thus, habitats and ecosystems are better understood as societies from an Indigenous point of view; meaning that they have ethical structures, inter-species treaties and agreements, and further their ability to interpret, understand and implement. Non-human beings are active members of society. Not only are they active, they also directly influence how humans organize themselves into society. The very existence of the clan systems evidences these many historical agreements between humans and non-humans." In this definition, there is a much more capacious understanding of the social and political lives of the nonhuman. This is a harder thing to see and know with a cursory understanding of the land and what systems of relationality it fosters.

There is much for settler scholars like me to learn from Indigenous understandings of personhood. Engaging in these ontologies might bring about a fuller understanding of what might be ethical, place-dependent responses to the intersecting environmental crises we face. And, I think, there is a call for more humility than has been displayed, to be open and non-defensive to the suggestion that this work, which many of its adherents think of as radical, has done real harm to Indigenous Peoples. But there are also risks in a rush to deploy Indigenous thought outside of its cultural surround. As Eve Tuck (Smith, Tuck, and Yang 2019, 15) notes, settlers have "read Indigenous work extractively, for discovery." This echoes objections to the ways that Traditional Ecological Knowledge (TEK) has been taken and repurposed in academia to help secure environmental futures that afford no place for the people whose knowledge determines them. With reference to TEK, Winona LaDuke (cited in McGregor 2004, 395) notes: "We who live by this knowledge have the intellectual property rights to it, and we have the right to tell our stories ourselves. There is a lot to learn from our knowledge, but you need us to learn it." Watts (2013) remarks that non-Indigenous scholars are increasingly interested in the lessons that can be learned from Indigenous epistemology, but how it is accessed and deployed often works to buttress non-Indigenous power over the telling and the way it can be received. Todd (2016, 9) notes the bind here: "So there is a very real risk to Indigenous thinking being used by non-Indigenous scholars who apply it to Actor Network Theory, cosmopolitics, ontological and posthumanist threads without contending with the embodied expressions of stories, laws, and songs as bound with Indigenous-Place Thought or Indigenous self-determination ... However, there is a risk as well, to Indigenous thinking not being acknowledged at all." Navigating this line between appropriation for settler gain and recognition of the depth of Indigenous ontologies requires non-Indigenous scholars not only to utilize Indigenous teachings to understand settler futures but also to amplify the voices of Indigenous scholars and activists who have been elaborating and refining ideas about human-animal relations much longer than the so-called posthuman turn. I do not expect Indigenous teachings to save settlers from ourselves, but I do think that settler scholars like myself need to "become accountable" (Sundberg 2014, 35) in new ways, in part by being explicit about whose ideas we draw from and how. Beyond the importance of citational practice, non-Indigenous scholars who engage with Indigenous thought must also demonstrate solidarity with actual Indigenous Peoples. Rosiek, Snyder, and Pratt (2019, 4) put this impetus well: "We will know if that respect has moved beyond a desire to possess knowledge Indigenous communities have, to a respect for the lives that are the source of this knowledge, if it is accompanied by an increase in solidarity with the self-determined political projects of Indigenous communities." The example offered below of

Indigenous teachings about the wolf demonstrate the ways in which wolf and Ojibwe futures are tied together. The quest for justice for one necessitates justice for the other.

INDIGENOUS TEACHINGS ABOUT WOLVES

Indigenous understandings of human-wolf relationships have much to tell about what respecting the personhood of animals actually looks like. Although the story of wolves as both villain and vermin is the one settlers in Canada are most familiar with, there were and are other stories that existed before, concurrently with, and after the pursuit of wolf extermination. These teachings are here with us today. For example, Inuit peoples, reliant on caribou for their survival, see the relationship between wolves and caribou as an important one:

> According to the textbooks, a wolf is a hunter, an animal of prey. But the Inuit, the people of the North, take a different view of it. They have their own idea of why the wolf was created. In the beginning – so the legend says – there was a man and a woman, nothing else on the Earth walked or swam or flew. And so the woman dug a big hole in the ground and she started fishing in it. And she pulled out all of the animals. The last animal she pulled out was the caribou. The woman set the caribou free and ordered it to multiply. And soon the land was full of them. And the people lived well and they were happy. But the hunters only killed those caribou that were big and strong. And soon all that was left were the weak and the sick. And the people began to starve. And so the woman had to make magic again, and this time she called Amorak, the spirit of the wolf, to winnow out the weak and the sick, so that the herd would once again be strong. The people realized that the caribou and the wolf were one, for although the caribou feeds the wolf, it is the wolf that keeps the caribou strong. (Canada's Polar Life 2002)

In the case of the Inuit, the wolf has a special place in their understanding of the world: an agent that made the caribou stronger rather than weaker, and a hunter to be emulated. Separated from the Inuit by thousands of miles, the Nuu-Chah-Nulth on the west coast of Vancouver Island have a different but equally reverential relationship with wolves. Their key winter ceremony was the Tlkwa:na, or Wolf Ritual, in which young novices would be captured by a supernatural wolf warrior, gain its power, and return to their people imbued with the essence (but not the wild spirit) of the wolf (Kruger 2003). In some versions of a creation story that belongs to the Nehiyawak (Plains Cree), the wolf was the Earth maker, diving deep into the waters left by a great flood until he found moss at its bottom, which became the foundation for Turtle Island (K.R. Jones, *Wolf Mountains*, 2003). In the teaching about wolves and people that I learned from Haudenosaunee scholar Dan Longboat as part of his class on Indigenous environmental studies, it is the wolf that walks with humans and teaches them how to live (Longboat 2017). In each of these iterations, wolves are recognized as valued persons, as part of animal nations that are imbued with gifts like "fidelity, perseverance, and guardianship" (Johnston 2008, 57, 53) and unparalleled hunting skill. These are not stories of slavering killers that need to be put down for a nation to be born. In these ways of knowing the wolf, it is seen and recognized as a being who is a powerful hunter and a teacher for those willing to listen. And for many, the wolves are part of a nation, as are all plants and animals, that requires diplomatic relations with humans. Here, wolves are seen aren't terror generating or awe inducing. Rather, they are simply *seen*.

MA'IINGAN/MA-EN'-GUN/MYEENGUN (THE WOLF)

The place where I live is Anishinaabe Aki: Michi Saagig Anishinaabeg territory covered by the Williams Treaties. For the Anishinaabeg, and especially the Ojibwe, the lives of wolves (ma'iingan) and humans are intertwined. As Peter David writes, "wolf enters the Ojibwe Creation Story early and dramatically" (2009, 267). In Anishinaabe Elder Edward Benton-Banai's *The Mishomis Book: The Voice of the Ojibway* (1988), he gives the teaching about Original Man, who the Creator places on Earth and tells him to wander, naming the plants, animals, and landforms he encounters. Benton-Banai writes:

> In his travels, Original Man began to notice that all the animals came in pairs and they reproduced. And yet, he was alone.
> He spoke to his Grandfather the Creator and asked, "Why am I alone? Why are there no other ones like me?"
> Gitchie Manito answered, "I will send someone to walk, talk and play with you."
> He sent Ma-en'-gun (the wolf).
> With Ma-en'-gun by his side, Original Man again spoke to Gitchie Manito, "I have finished what you asked me to do. I have visited and

named all the plants, animals, and places of this Earth. What would you now have me to do?"

Gitchie Manito answered Original Man and Ma-en'-gun, "Each of you are to be a brother to the other. Now, both of you are to walk the Earth and visit all its places."

So, Original Man and Ma-en'-gun walked the Earth and came to know all of her. In this journey they became very close to each other. They became like brothers. In their closeness they realized they were brothers to all of Creation.

When they had completed the task that Gitchie Manito asked them to do, they talked with the Creator once again.

The Creator said, "From this day on, you are to separate your paths. You must go your different ways.

"What shall happen to one of you will also happen to the other. Each of you will be feared, respected and misunderstood by the people that will later join you on this Earth."

And so Ma-en'-gun and Original Man set off on their different journeys. (Benton-Banai 1988, 7–8)

Joe Rose Sr, an elder in the Bad River Band of Lake Superior Chippewa and part of the Great Lakes Indian Fish & Wildlife Commission, gave the same teaching, which was recorded by the Timber Wolf Alliance:

Original Man
    and the wolf
    were brothers
And the Great Spirit
    told them
He said, Original Man
        Anishinaabe
    The wolf
        Ma'iingan
He said, In many ways
    you are alike
He said, When you take a mate
    you mate for life
He says, Your social structure
    will be the clan system
He said, Both of you will be
    good hunters

And he said, Later on
    there will be others who will come
      who will misunderstand
      both of you.[2] (Cerulli 2017, 252)

The wolf and the Anishinaabeg are linked in the original instructions shared by Benton-Banai and Rose Sr; their fates are shared. Peter David, writing about Anishinaabeg in Wisconsin (though one imagines both the wolves and the Anishinaabeg have little interest in reifying those colonial borders), suggests that the capacity of the Anishinaabeg to see the wolf not only as an equal but also a creature that shares characteristics with them opened up possibilities for relationships based on respect rather than fear or disgust. This view would have been unthinkable in settler society, where domestic animals became forms of agricultural capital and, as we have seen, wolves were only thought of as wanton destroyers of their way of life. David (2009, 268) notes that "the Ojibwe, in contrast, recognized that wolves embodied many of the qualities that they themselves needed to survive on a demanding landscape. While a person of European descent is likely to be insulted by being called a wolf, an Ojibwe may take this as an extreme compliment for who has greater knowledge of the natural world, who hunts with greater stamina and skill, who works in greater cooperation, and who goes to greater extreme to provide for their young than ma'iingan?" In Wisconsin (as well as Minnesota and Michigan), these different ways of seeing wolves – as persons and brothers rather than populations and numbers – are relevant to the conflict between Anishinaabeg and the US Fish and Wildlife Service. The status of "recovered" as defined by the Endangered Species Act is what drives the management strategies of the Fish and Wildlife Service. But for the Anishinaabeg, David notes, this cannot account for their understanding of the wolf because its fate is intertwined with their own. David (2009, 274) asks perhaps a more fundamental question based on Anishinaabe epistemology, one that has the potential to reshape how wildlife management is practised: "The differences are clear to those who can truly understand the Ojibwe ontology of 'what happens to the wolf, happens to you.' How different might state management plans be if they had been written in the belief that they would be shaping not only the future of wolves but the human community as well."

Ma'iingan's story is not mythic nor only of the past – as many settlers might imagine. It is a truth of Ojibwe life, relevant today and into the future. Benton-Banai (1988, 8) directly signals the story's continued relevance: "The last teaching about the wolf is important for us today.

What the Grandfather said to them has come true. Both the Indian and the wolf have come to be alike and have experienced the same thing. Both of them mate for life. Both have a Clan System and a tribe. Both have been hunted for their wee-nes'-si-see' (hair). And both have been pushed very close to destruction." This shared fate makes recovery a matter not just of conservation or preserving pieces of wilderness but also of survival. But wolf recovery must proceed on Anishinaabeg terms. For example, the White Earth Nation's tribal council in northern Minnesota has actively resisted attempts to delist wolves from their protected status as endangered, asserting their treaty rights and sovereign nationhood as well as the importance of their ecological knowledge in naming their territory a wolf sanctuary (White Earth Land Recovery Project, n.d.). There is an active making of space for the nonhuman with the recognition that we can only flourish when we know how to co-exist together. That co-existence is premised on a deep understanding of the land and the persons – human and nonhuman – that share it. It is also a clear articulation of a different view of nationhood and a strong assertion of co-management rights on tribal land. For settlers, wolves are also tied to the nation, first as a discommodity and then as a marker of environmental foresight. But in neither iteration is the wolf – or any other animal – recognized as subject, agent, person, or member of a nation that is deserving of relational ethics on their own terms. Indigenous ontologies are the only ones I have seen in which wolves are recognized as more than the ways they are deployed for a variety of ends.

The Anishinaabeg teachings around the wolf do not end with that of Original Man. There are others in which wolves come to teach humans how to be in the world and what actions lead to, in Anishinaabemowin, *mino bimaadiziwin* – a healthy or good life. This is important because humans were the last of the creatures to arrive on Earth and, like all newborns, required the most teaching. As Vanessa Watts (2013, 25) emphasizes: "in many Indigenous origin stories the idea that humans were the last species to arrive on earth was central; it also meant that humans arrived in a state of dependence on an already-functioning society with particular values, ethics, etc." Animals, then, teach people how to survive, thrive, and relate to the world: "Without the animals the world would not have been; without the animals the world would not be intelligible" (Johnston 2008, 49). In the case of wolves, then, part of their job, at various times, is to teach humans how to hunt, how to follow social protocols, how to parent, how to listen, how to be humble, and how to be patient and restrained (Usik 2015). Put differently, wolves provide guidance about how to live in the world. In these stories, wolves save human lives time and again. As

Kenny Ausubel (2008, xxii) suggests, the original instructions provided by creation stories like this one "remind us that it's not people who are smart. The real intelligence dwells throughout the natural world and in the vast mystery of the universe that's beyond our human comprehension. Humility is our constant companion."

These teachings stand in radical opposition to those that would most often be told by settlers, and certainly the stories that precede them in this book. The story of Ma'iingan offers the possibility for animals to have an active role in shaping our worlds in significant ways. Instead of human domination, there is co-evolution and equality, where humans are often the least important actors in the story. There is also recognition that we have more similarities than differences with animals; both the presumed radical alterity and atomistic nature of the human subject is unsettled in the teachings offered by Ma'iingan. As Katherine Usik (2015, 17) suggests: "In traditional narratives, it is not wolf that is an anthropomorphized projection of human culture, but is rather one of the original models for humanity." It is only through relationships with the nonhuman that we can actually become human: it is a joint project all the way down. We have never simply been human – we are, and always have been, a confluence of connection and encounter with the more-than-human world. So, as Indigenous scholars have been reminding posthuman scholars like me for quite some time now, this relational ontology is not new but ancient, and it continues to grow and change, extending its relevance now and into the future.

My retelling here of these original instructions does not account for the intricacies and understandings of agency between the Anishinaabeg and the wolf. It was not a story given to me through teachings by an elder nor is it a story that stems from or that can be easily understood from my settler colonial standpoint. My intention is not to interpret the story's teachings on the basis on Anishinaabeg epistemology, political organization, or legal orders – I have neither the wisdom nor the permission. But I do think that the teachings around the wolf offer not only lessons in conceptualizing what human-animal relationships based on ethical engagement might be but also how such lessons might figure into destabilizing settler colonial claims to both nature and nation. I am thinking here in particular, but not solely, about Indigenous recognition of plant and animal nations. Nicholas Reo and Laura Ogden's work on Anishinaabe perspectives on "invasive" species among the Sault Ste Marie Tribe of Chippewa and Bay Mills Indian Community in Michigan has been especially helpful to me in thinking through how nationhood is not always already an oppressive idea. In their work, Reo and Ogden (2018) explored how Anishinaabe elders, knowledge keepers, and community members understood and engaged with the presence of phragmites and hybrid cattail in their territories. These plants, much like the coywolf or wolfdog, are seen as both "aggressive" and out of place – invading wetlands, displacing native plants, and reducing biodiversity (Invasive Species Centre, n.d.; Wisconsin Department of Natural Resources, n.d.). While some of the people they interviewed saw these species as threats, Reo and Ogden (2018, 1446) contend that Anishinaabe teachings offer a different starting point with the new plants found on their territories: they "assemble in 'nations' as compared to the Western scientific notion of species." From this perspective, the presence of aquatic plants on the landscape is an invitation to be curious; as the authors point out, in Anishinaabe thought, people are the ones who are meant to figure out why the plant or animal is here and what the relationship to it should be. One of their research participants makes this explicit by offering: "I wonder if any has bothered to ask the Asian carp … or hybrid cattail … why they are here?" (Reo and Ogden 2018, 1447). The elders and knowledge holders who participated in this project described as out of place not the hybrid cattail or phragmites but the "invasive land ethic" premised on colonial logics of private property and the reimagining of nations into natural resources (Reo and Ogden 2018, 1449).

It is this way of seeing the land – and all its animate and inanimate aspects – as fungible and ownable that is aggressive. It is also a new story. It is not among the ones that have informed the relations on this land long before the onset of settler colonialism – indeed, since time immemorial. It was not inevitable; it could have been otherwise. But this way of seeing – and the way this logic has cohered into the idea of Canada as a nation – has led to deep and indelible harm to the plants, animals, people, waters, and lands in this place, as well as to the relationships among them. Cree poet and scholar Billy-Ray Belcourt (2015) names this when he notes that the human-animal relations that posthuman and other animal studies scholars object to – in particular, but not only, animal agricultural and other practices of speciesism – are fundamentally underwritten by settler colonialism. Tying together anthropocentrism, settler colonialism, capitalism, and white supremacy, Belcourt contends that efforts at reforming settler colonialism only work to shore it up, making it less vulnerable to critique. Instead, Belcourt offers a decolonial ethic rooted in Indigenous ontologies and epistemologies as the best path forward to the liberation of both people and animals. For Belcourt (2015, 10), decolonization is a project that must proceed "through the non-speciesist and interdependent models of animality envisioned in Indigenous cosmologies."

Put another way, it could be that the most ethical ways of reimagining the relationship to wolves – or, indeed, all the creatures of the lands – is by embracing a decolonial politics of nationhood, one designed and led by Indigenous People and epistemologies. Leanne Betasamosake Simpson (2017, 8–9) explains the Anishinaabe view of nationhood as one rooted in relationality and reciprocity: "Our nationhood is based on the idea that the earth gives and sustains all life, that 'natural resources' are not 'natural resources' at all, but gifts from Aki, the land. Our nationhood is based on the foundational concept that we should give up what we can to support the integrity of our homelands for the coming generations. We should give more than we take. It is nationhood based on a series of radiating responsibilities." This is not a conception of the nation currently at work in the halls of the Canadian parliament, nor in the legal manoeuvrings around treaty negotiations with Indigenous People in this country. As Simpson remarks, this notion of nationhood calls into question the very idea of Canada itself. But it seems to me we cannot continue as we have. We need a new treaty, one in which settlers aim to keep up their end of the agreement and one that also recognizes animals and plants as nations that need to be parties to any treaty. Explicit in the teaching about ma'iingan is an invitation to take the agency of both the human and nonhuman worlds as the place to start rather than the place where theorizing stops. Beginning here means, as the Creatures Collective (Hernández et al. 2020, 5) notes, that "just responses to global scale violence begin from ongoing struggles for Indigenous sovereignty and self-determination in specific places." That may seem difficult to imagine. But the alternative – which seems to be very quickly leading us to a mass extinction event likened to the disappearance of the dinosaurs as well as 75 per cent of life on Earth – is equally unimaginable. Settler ways of interacting with animals have led to death, for people and the planet. It's time to heed epistemologies that disrupt the violence of settler colonialism and extractivist logic. Robin Kimmerer (cited in Whyte 2020, 269) tells us that "the living world is understood, not as a collection of exploitable resources, but as a set of relationships and responsibilities. We inhabit a landscape of gifts peopled by nonhuman relatives, the sovereign beings who sustain us, including plants."

Sustained and radical Indigenous resistance to the violence of settler colonialism on land and bodies – and the relationships between them – has always offered settlers a different understanding of what it means to live ethically, as well as possibilities for acting in solidarity. As Nick Estes (2019) tells us, in its long history and many iterations, the Indigenous struggle for life and land was usually met with settler erasure. Attending to the lessons of Indigenous activism, which has continued in the face of the settler state's efforts to eliminate it,[3] offers a way forward for settlers to act in solidarity with the Indigenous Peoples who, all this time, have been showing us how to live in ethical ways with each other and the natural world. Such alliances are the best way to deal with the interlocking crises in justice that have characterized our present condition. This is the notion of nationhood we need right now.

Epilogue

The Hazards of a Symbol

We cannot help viewing wolves in symbolic terms, but symbols change.
The wolf was once widely seen as a symbol of the depravity of wildness; it is
now to many a symbol of the nobility of nature. Largely by the use of symbols,
we nearly eradicated the wolf. Largely by manipulating symbols, we may
yet save it.

Peter Steinhart (1995, 344)

As Peter Steinhart attests, there are stakes to seeing wolves as symbols. The
stories told in this book are about how seeing wolves symbolically has
evoked particular feelings that have led to all sorts of biopolitical strategies
to manage and sometimes contain those feelings. But wolves were and are
always more than the symbology used to describe them. The particularity
of wolves has shaped responses to them: biology eliciting affect, affect
circulating to produce means of fostering life or making death, and strategies cohering into narratives of nationhood at particular times in particular
ways. There is a violence in making something a symbol; the complexity
of wolves and their relationships with humans is rendered into a simplistic
representation, a part rather than a whole. This was the case with the settlers who saw wolves as terrorizing beasts, with the predator control officers
who thought of them as disgusting vermin, and with the writers who adored
the image rather than the animal. It was also the case with the scientists
who sought to reveal the truth of the wolf while seeing them mostly in
terms of aggregations, or in the idea that owning a wolfdog reveals something significant about the owner. And when coywolves are seen as forever
out of place, exceeding the boundaries afforded to them, this logic operates
once again. So, I agree with Steinhart: seeing wolves as symbols of wickedness has historically led in one necropolitical direction. But unlike Steinhart,
I think seeing them only as symbols of virtue is dangerous too. Seeing
them – *actually seeing them* as described in chapter 7 – might lead to different and more life-affirming political, social, and ecological relations.

OF MANHUNTERS AND JUNKYARD DOGS

The way various people have understood the story of Kenton Carnegie's death shows the hazards of continuing to see wolves as symbols rather than agents whose lives are sometimes tightly woven with humans in unpredictable ways. In the autumn of 2005, Kenton Carnegie was a twenty-two-year-old University of Waterloo geological engineering student. He had travelled to Points North Landing, Saskatchewan, a staging point for mining exploration, to complete a work term for his degree. On the afternoon of 8 November, he decided to take a walk around a nearby lake. He never returned. His body was found some hours later with obvious signs of animal predation.

The story received much attention. The tragedy of such a young life lost, and one so full of potential, seemed breathtakingly cruel. This was compounded by the grisly violence of his death. Carnegie was literally eaten alive by wild animals; the pathologist's report indicated that he "lost 25 to 30 per cent of his body mass during the attack" (J. Jackson 2020). It seems Carnegie became aware he was being stalked since footprints show he started to run but was surrounded and pulled down twice (H. Johnson 2020; McKean 2007). It was as if the pages of *Rod and Gun* had come to life. But what was particularly unnerving, at least for the scientific and wolf conservation community, was that Kenton Carnegie's death was described as the first time in one hundred years that a healthy (non-rabid) wild wolf killed a human being in North America (J. Jackson 2020). This truism – one to which I previously adhered – was often repeated: wolves had never killed a human in living memory, and the threat they posed was overstated by those who wanted them exterminated (Boyd, n.d.).

And yet, accounts of wolf fearlessness had been piling up for some time. According to a report written by Mark E. McNay (2002) for the Alaska Department of Fish and Game, credible stories had been increasing since the 1970s, culminating in the biting incident of a six-year-old in Alaska, which prompted his study. Covering the period from 1900 to 2000, McNay crafted a typology of wolf behaviour (aggressive and non-aggressive) across incidents he gleaned from a variety of sources, including interviews with witnesses, wildlife biologists, and law enforcement officers, as well as historical records. In the eighty cases he examined, McNay (2002, 1) found that "thirty-nine cases contain elements of aggression among healthy wolves, 12 cases involve known or suspected rabid wolves, and 29 cases document fearless behavior among nonaggressive wolves. In 6 cases in which healthy wolves acted aggressively, the people were accompanied by dogs. Aggressive, nonrabid wolves bit people in 16 cases; none of those bites was life-threatening, but in 6 cases the bites were severe." In the cases McNay describes, wolves engaged in threat display, prey testing, and predatory behaviours, and showed investigative behaviours – curiosity toward people and their belongings.

In Canada, many of these human-wolf encounters took place at or near provincial or national parks (McNay 2002). Banff, Riding Mountain, and Pacific Rim national parks were all sites of recorded wolf interactions, as was Mount Robson Provincial Park in British Columbia. By far the most incidents have occurred at Algonquin Provincial Park, with five since 1987 and two serious attacks involving predatory interest in children (Strickland 1997; 1999). These are likely an unintended effect of the longer sweep of wolf policy in the park, which moved from control to protection in the late 1950s (Strickland 1999; see also Rutherford 2013). The killing of wolves by park staff created spaces for dispersing wolves to claim (Strickland 1999). When this practice ceased, lone wolves were pushed to the margins of the park by other packs. This meant that campgrounds became new-found sources of food. Given that many people visiting Algonquin actively seek wolves – and come to the park to hear them howl – the prospect of these chance encounters is likely more welcomed than it should be. Some wolves became habituated to and less fearful of humans. That can lead to rare violent encounters, where human exceptionalism does not prevent us from being seen as "meaty prey species" (Walker 2013, 48).

Like Algonquin Park, the site of Kenton Carnegie's killing was one of multispecies mingling that led to increased habituation. Harold Johnston, in his recent book about Carnegie's death and its aftermath, notes that the wolves that Carnegie encountered that day were unafraid of – or at least curious about – humans. It is likely that they had a meeting with a different ending just three days before, when two different members of the camp had an interaction with wolves that unnerved them, with the wolves' behaviour being variously described as "aggressive ... and posturing" (H. Johnson 2020, 22) or "retreating defensively" (Paquet and Walker, cited in Lukas 2018, 70). It also seems that Carnegie was curious; he was reported to have taken pictures of four wolves a few days earlier that he showed around the camp (McKean 2007). Andrew McKean (2007), writing in *Outdoor Life* in an article inauspiciously titled "Manhunters," cites trucker Bill Topping who, after seeing the photographs, told Carnegie that "he was lucky to be alive. I told him these wolves up here are hungry and they don't fear people. They [Carnegie and his friend] thought it was something to be that close to wolves."

The problem seems to have been that these wolves weren't wolves at all; they had become something else through their association with people. They were, instead, "opportunistic junkyard dogs" (McKean 2007) drawn to the area of the garbage dump that serviced the mine, which also provided easy food for animals like bears and wolves (H. Johnson 2020). Like coywolves, they had become otherwise, tainted with the stain of civilization. Wildlife biologist Tim Trottier sums up this position well: "These wolves lived in a very unnatural state, so it's not that surprising that they might behave unnaturally ... We don't consider this a widespread problem in Saskatchewan. It's localized abnormal behavior associated with these dump sites" (McKean 2007). The wolves that attacked Carnegie were "brazen," acting like "garbage hounds" that "didn't consider humans a threat so much as a food source. But habituated wolves still have the characteristics and instincts of large predators, and that spells problems for people" (McKean 2007). The problem is not so much that people change the ecological conditions to which wolves are adapted, but that the wolves allow themselves to be reconfigured by an easy meal and proximity to people. Michael Lukas (2018, 74) puts this well in his excellent exploration of the case: "The only way to account for the wolves is through tropes that domesticate their behavior such that they become 'bad dogs' rather than adaptable wolves. Or, to put it another way, they cannot be wolves, but must be something else, perhaps werewolves, or more properly, wolf-men or lycanthropes who become more human. Curiously, the humans are not regarded as having changed at all – they are not 'junkyard men' or some other non-civilized or changed humanity in their actions of wanting to interact with the wolves." Instead, these wolves are "unnatural, liminal canines" (Lukas 2018, 69) – and that's what allowed them to kill and eat Kenton Carnegie.

Harold Johnson sets forth a surgical (and lawyerly) opprobrium of the wildlife biologists who argued that a bear rather than wolves was responsible for this man's death. Johnson contends that these biologists were blinded by what ungulate biologist Valerius Geist (2008), in his equally trenchant writing on the matter, has called "the benign wolf hypothesis," in which wolves never kill more than they need to survive, and certainly do not see people as prey. In the end, I am less interested in who is right and wrong in this case. Instead, I am curious what it tells us about the persistence of symbolic thinking in relationships with wolves. To some, these wolves, by virtue of their species, were already condemnable. For others, they were rendered so by straying from nature into the culture. And there are those who would never believe wolves could be responsible for such violence, regardless of the circumstance, or how accustomed they became to the people transiently living in their territory. Toward the end of his book, Johnson addresses this. He writes that these narratives of villain or hero "aren't the true story of the wolf. He's a wild animal … we have to accept the wolf as he is" (cited in J. Jackson 2020). As I did in chapter 7, Johnson turns to Indigenous teachings to help repair relationships with wolves (though he is Cree and I am a settler). He cites Tr'ondëk Hwëch'in Elder Percy Henry in Adam Weymouth's book *Kings of the Yukon: An Alaska River Journey* on the changing relationships between wolves and caribou in the context of colonial policies of annihilation:

> "They are finding a lot of caribou dying, because the doctor quit bothering with them."
> "Who is the doctor?" I say.
> "The wolf is the doctor of all animals," he says. "He chase caribou. He don't kill 'em right there. He could. But his mother train him, you don't kill 'em till one falls aside. That's a weak one. So that's how they stay healthy. Make 'em sweat. You see that Yellowstone Park. Animal there were half dead. So they took some wolf in there and all the animals were happy. Bring their life back to where it should be."
> But now, Percy says, the young wolves don't know what to do. It began when the state started culling wolves as a way of protecting caribou. They shot the old wolves, the ones that train the pups. Now Percy sees wolves coming into yards to attack dogs, he sees wolves chasing skidoos. They haven't been taught fear; they've had no education from their elders. (Weymouth as cited in H. Johnson 2020, 138)

Tayohseron:tye Nikki Auten, one of my MA students and now my friend, said something strikingly similar to me once, for which I am deeply indebted. It has stayed in my mind ever since. She came to a talk I gave about wolf narratives. In it, I noted that wolves sometimes engage in what's called "surplus killing," in which they tear through an entire pen of sheep, for instance, killing many more than they could ever consume. I suggested that this upends romantic narratives, often credited to Farley Mowat, that read wolves as noble and majestic but never profligate or wasteful. She took away this aside and sat with it for two months. Then she e-mailed me. From her Haudenosaunee perspective, she wondered if wolves engaged in surplus killing because they too had been colonized. She asked: "Does the wolf know the sheep don't belong in North America and this is protecting its homelands? You see what I'm saying? Would a precolonial wolf have ripped through an entire herd of deer for example? Has the wolf been colonized as well and is now affected by the greed that infects the rest of the colonized world? Has colonized man taken so much of its habitat and prey that it is retaliating? Resisting? Is the lone wolf that takes a herd of sheep the renegade of its people?" I didn't have the answers to these provocative questions; I still don't. But what Nikki pointed to is the imbrication of humans and animals in settler colonialism in ways that make no assumptions about who has agency and who has the capacity to affect or be affected. Her questions changed the trajectory of this book.

At the beginning of this book, I asked: what would Canada be without wolves? The answer, in my view: much less, even as settlers tried their hardest to make that a reality. This much is probably obvious; I too have been shaped by the affective tendrils extended by canids. But I have also tried to show that the story of wolves in Canada contains bigger lessons about nature, nation, and the possibility for justice on these lands. Elimination of the wolf was tied to articulations of nationhood animated by specific kinds of affects that continue to do violence to people, animals, lands, and waters. Tracing the affective entanglements of wolves and people has shown how the logics of settler colonialism, inflected through fear, disgust, and sometimes desire, offered no place for beings that fell outside of this way of encountering the land. In contrast, co-existing and flourishing alongside the wolf was always another possibility for the place that became Canada. In this version, wolves were understood as members of their own nation, with their own legal orders, treaties, and diplomatic relations to guide their relationships not just with people but also with other plant and animal nations. What forms of justice might emerge if the wisdom – the brilliance, as Leanne Betasamosake Simpson (2017) has noted – of Indigenous-designed and -led approaches to nationhood were central? What might it mean to be accountable not just to wolves but also to the people who have been fighting for them and the rest of creation on Turtle Island? Accountability is not always about the absence of harm but about recognition of mutual obligation, respect, and solidarity, a posture that has been absent in settler colonial–animal relations as well as in relations among people. And so, justice and love for the wolf might look a lot like decolonization on these lands; indeed, finding ways for all of us to thrive in the so-called Anthropocene demands it.

We live in a time characterized by environmental grief, despair, and inaction. We are in the midst of a "biological annihilation" (Carrington 2017) named the Sixth Extinction, with a fourth of all species on Earth facing disappearance (IPBES 2019). Ronald R. Swaisgood and James K. Shepherd (2010) talk about "conservation despair," a kind of contagious affect whereby biologists and the general public succumb to the doom of our extinction condition. I see this in my students, and I feel this grief myself. It threatens to swallow hope. This is probably no surprise: conservationists now talk about triage, an approach in which some species are left to go extinct in order to focus the limited conservation dollars on species with higher chances of survival in the face of human-induced systemic change (Hagerman et al. 2010). Despair seems like a pretty reasonable response for both the scale and the severity of the crisis.

And yet, I think we owe a different kind of affective engagement in our posture toward and encounter with wildlife – those on the edge of extinction, as well as those that thrive in the novel ecosystems of our anthropogenically altered world. We owe them more than our grief at their regrettable but inevitable demise. At the very least, we could harness this grief to ethically reorient ourselves. Put differently, it could be a call to action. In her writing on ecological grief, Pamela Banting (2018) uses the literary device of peripeteia – a sudden turning point – to think about how the rapid environmental changes collected under the umbrella of the Anthropocene might interrupt the narratives of power that have brought us to this place. In this way of thinking, there might be the possibility for something productive in the collective mourning, both for our fellow humans and for the ways of engaging with the world that we are now witnessing. In Thom van Dooren's work on the extinction of Hawaiian crows, he contends that grief is about relearning our place in a shared world, a transformation that necessitates a changed posture and new modes of engagement. He writes: "Mourning offers us a way into an alternative space, one of acknowledgment and respect for the dead that undoes any pretense towards exceptionalism by drawing us into an awareness of the multispecies continuities and connectivities that make life possible for everyone inside our shared world" (van Dooren 2014, 275–6) Might this mourning teach us how to be kinder to our kin, human and nonhuman? More specific to this book, will it teach those of us who need them, new ways of relating to wolves as they are, rather than as we have imagined them to be? I don't know the answer, but I hope so, because that path is alive with radical possibility for humans and nonhumans alike.

Notes

INTRODUCTION

1 Over the years, *Rod and Gun* went by a variety of names, including *Rod and Gun in Canada*, *Rod and Gun and Motor Sports in Canada*, and simply *Rod and Gun*.

CHAPTER ONE

1 For further discussion on the strengths and weaknesses of Douglas's analysis, see chapter 2.
2 Susanna Moodie had much to say about Michi Saagiig lands she claimed as her own, beyond them being home to wolves. Anishinaabe writer and scholar Leanne Betasamosake Simpson (2017) offers an important intervention that traces the colonial, racist narratives that Moodie trafficked in and how she continues to be upheld as part of the canon in Canadian Studies.

CHAPTER TWO

1 From Straight 1950, 16–17, 35.
2 Nick Estes notes a similar practice on the US plains where, as part of the wholesale slaughter of buffalo, their carcasses were then poisoned to kill vermin like wolves and coyotes.
3 The efficacy of this approach has been the subject of fierce scientific debate. For instance, Gilbert Proulx (2017, 6) contends the wolf cull to protect the Little Smoky caribou herd in Alberta was "based on economics and politics, not on scientific evidence," which would have suggested habitat protection as the appropriate (if more costly and politically difficult) strategy. There is

also a debate over the article by Serrouya et al. (2019), which supported the BC cull. Harding et al. (2020, 3051) dispute this "unbalanced analytical approach that omitted a null scenario, excluded potentially confounding variables and employed irreproducible habitat alteration metrics."

CHAPTER THREE

1 For instance, *Wild Animals I Have Known* (1898) had numerous editions and was translated into fifteen languages (www.thecanadianencyclopedia. ca/en/article/wild-animals-i-have-known).
2 In the documentary entitled *The Wolf that Changed the America* (Gooder 2008), Attenborough recognizes some of the fictional elements of Seton's tale. For example, instead of weighing 150 pounds, Lobo was a more average 75 pounds. Instead of being bountied at $1,000, his pelt fetched $15.
3 Many thanks to one of McGill-Queen's University Press's anonymous reviewers who pushed me on this point.

CHAPTER FOUR

1 The Rocky Mountain parks included Jasper, Waterton Lakes, and Banff national parks in Alberta and Yoho and Kootenay national parks in British Columbia.
2 Mary Theberge's part in writing the book is a little opaque. She was certainly involved in the research itself and is listed as the illustrator of the book; however, her role in scientific knowledge production is obscured. And much of the book is written in the first person, with "I" being John Theberge.
3 A representative critique here is found in Zipporah Weisberg's (2009, 22) assessment that Haraway's position on animal testing offers "disturbing collusion with the very structures of domination she purports to oppose." Indeed, Weisberg asserts that Haraway shores up and provides justification for those practices (like animal testing, but also dog breeding and agility training) that reinscribe a hierarchical division between human and nonhumans.

CHAPTER FIVE

1 There are some doubters as to Loki's authenticity as a low-content wolfdog (see, for example, www.neogaf.com/threads/the-truth-about-loki-the-wolfdog.1349997; and https://ivar-the-real-wolfdog.tumblr.com/

post/151686410869/is-loki-the-wolf-dog-on-instagram-a-real-wolf).
Indeed, as will become clear, the delineation of wolfdog from dog is a tricky
business.

2 It is unclear whether this kennel still operates. While the website domain
has expired, on LinkedIn, Keyhan Modaressi still lists himself as the owner/
operator of Sun Valley Wolf Kennels. The Facebook page for the kennel has
not posted anything since January 2018.

CHAPTER SIX

This chapter is an adapted version of a previously published article:
S. Rutherford, "The Anthropocene's Animal? Coywolves as Feral
Cotravelers," *Environment and Planning E: Nature and Space* 1, nos. 1–2
(2018): 206–23.

1 I speak from experience in this regard. I lost my own cat, the incomparable
and beloved outdoor cat Biggie, in the summer of 2020 from what was
likely coywolf predation.

CHAPTER SEVEN

1 Scholars in Black Studies offer a different, though related, register of
critique. They have also shown that the exhortation to "move beyond the
human" re-instantiates the humanity of whiteness alone. For instance,
Zakiyyah Iman Jackson (2015, 215) writes: "What and *crucially* whose
conceptions of humanity are we moving beyond? Moreover, what is entailed
in the very notion of beyond? Calls to become 'post' or move 'beyond the
human' too often presume that the originary locus of this call, its imprima-
tur, its appeal, requires no further examination or justification but mere
execution of its rapidly routinizing imperative." Similarly, Tiffany Lethabo
King (2017, 162, 166) contends that posthumanism shores up the "power
to confer the identity of human onto some bodies while denying access to
this identity to Black and Native/Indigenous bodies" and questions whether
posthumanism can ever "be accountable to Black and Indigenous peoples."

2 Tovar Cerulli has used ethnopoetic transcription in an attempt to capture
the performative elements of Joe Rose Sr's comments.

3 See, for example, the long history in Canada where Indigenous resistance,
often to extractive capitalism, was met with swift and disproportionate state
violence: Oka in 1990, Ipperwash in 1995, Burnt Church in 1999–2002,
Elsipogtog in 2013, and Wet'suwet'en in 2019–present. These are a very
limited number of recent examples. There are countless more.

References

ARCHIVAL SOURCES

Library and Archives Canada

Canadian Parks Service fonds, RG 84-A-2-a, vol. 2134, microfilm reel T-16472, file U266 NC, part 1, "Universal – Animals – Wolves – Clippings," 1930–52.

Canadian Parks Service fonds, RG 84-A-2-a, vol. 2134, microfilm reel T-16472, file U266, part 3, "Universal – Animals – Wolves," 1930–68.

Canadian Parks Service fonds, RG 84-A-2-a, vol. 181, microfilm reel T-9393, file U300, part 1, "Universal – Predator Control – Training for Park Wardens," 1950–56.

Department of Indian Affairs and Northern Development fonds, RG 85-D-1-A, vol. 1083, file 401-1-1, part 1B, "Bounties on Animals – Wolf Bounty – Northwest Game – Department of the Interior NWT and Yukon (Dominion Park No. 301.5)," 1918–21.

Department of Indian Affairs and Northern Development fonds, RG 10, vol. 8411, microfilm reel C-13829, file 1/20-16-5, parts 1 and 2, "Correspondence on Wild Life Predator Control," 1949–57, 1957–66.

Department of the Interior fonds, Dominion Lands Branch Registry, RG 15-D-II-1, file 1854319, microfilm reel T-14624. "Henry MacKay Re: Bounty for Killing Wolves and Coyotes," 1909.

Department of the Interior fonds, Dominion Lands Branch Registry, RG 15-D-II-1, vol. 1097, microfilm reel T-14659, file 2590052, "Commission for Conservation of Natural Resources," 1912.

Archives of Manitoba

Deputy Minister of Natural Resources office files, G 545, "49.3.1 Game Branch – Wolves & Bears, Bounties, etc.," 1933–52.
Deputy Minister of Natural Resources office files, L-8-7-14, "49.1.3 – Game Branch – Wolves and Bear Bounty," 1962.
Minister of Finance office files, L-7-1-19, "49.0 – Wolf Bounty – Organized Territory," 1922–24.
Minister of Finance office files, L-7-1-19, "50.0 – Wolf Bounty – Unorganized Territory," 1923–24.
Premier's office files, G 303, "Wolf Bounty," 1954–57.

Archives of Ontario

Department of Lands and Forests & Ministry of Natural Resources, RG 1-243, "Weekly Press Releases," 1948–75.
John Macfie photographs of the Patricia District, series C 330-10, 1949–56.
Live Stock Branch administration files, RG 16-90, "Predator Control and Wolf Bounty (Wolf Compensation Act)," 1972–73, 1974.
Ontario Game and Fisheries Commission, RG 18-50, boxes 1 and 2, "Reports of the Ontario Game and Fisheries Commission," 1909–10, 1911.
Premier John P. Robarts general correspondence, RG-3-26, "Lands and Forests, Department of – Wildlife Branch – Wolf Problem," 1961–67, 1968–71.
Wildlife Branch wildlife program files, RG 1-443-2, "Wildlife Branch – wildlife program deer files," 1950–76.

BC Archives

Department of Indian Affairs, RG 10, vol. 6731: "Application of Game Laws to the Indians in Manitoba, Saskatchewan and Alberta," ref. GR-0934.75, reel B01860, 1915–39.
Department of Indian Affairs, RG 10, vol. 6731: "Fur Conservation – Destruction of wolves including the question of bounty and suggestions on trapping predatory animals," ref. GR-0934.75, reel B01860, 1927–44.
Provincial Game Warden records, "Teit, J. – re bounty on wolves; Hyland W. – re trapping," GR-0446, box 16, file 2, 1908–.
Provincial Game Warden records, "List [by category] of Game Act convictions: Game Warden's report for 1912 – typescript with rough drafts and additional information re: effect of bounties on wolves, cougars, etc.," GR-0446.38.2, box 38, file 2, 1912–.

Provincial Game Warden records, "Muir, Douglas – information on hunting panthers and wolves," GR0446.36.9.5, box 36, file 9, 1912–.

Provincial Archives of Alberta

Canadian Wolf Defenders fonds, "Outgoing Correspondence," "Incoming Correspondence 1967–1968," "Incoming Correspondence, 1969," PR0181, 1962–71.
J.D. Waring fonds, "Wolves and Coyotes (21/54) – articles, clippings, reports," PR1964.0007/0111, 1948–57.

Trent University Archives

Ernest Thompson Seton collection, ref. 85-005, boxes 1 and 2, 1886–1984.
John Wadland fonds, ref. 81-014, box 1, 1880–1976.

University of Toronto Archives and Records Management

Douglas H. Pimlott fonds, ref. UTA 1664, 1913–87, acc. nos. B1978-0020, B1990-0023, B1995-0003.

PRINTED SOURCES

@loki. n.d. *Loki the Wolfdog*. Accessed 25 April 2021. www.instagram.com/loki/?hl=en.
Abidin, Crystal. 2015. "Communicative ♥ Intimacies: Influencers and Perceived Interconnectedness." *Ada: A Journal of Gender, New Media and Technology*, no. 8. http://doi.org/10.7264/N3MW2FFG.
Abrell, Elan. 2017. "Introduction: Interrogating Captive Freedom: The Possibilities and Limits of Animal Sanctuaries." *Animal Studies Journal* 6, no. 2: 1–8.
Addams, Jessica, and Andrew Miller. 2012. *Between Wolf and Dog: Understanding the Connection and the Confusion*. Wenatchee, WA: Dogwise Publishing.
Addison, Courtney. 2019. "Compound 1080 (Sodium Monofluoroacetate)." *Fieldsites,* 27 June. https://culanth.org/fieldsights/compound-1080-sodium-monofluoroacetate.
Agamben, Giorgio. 2004. *The Open: Man and Animal*. Stanford: Stanford University Press.

Agricultural Environmental Partnership Initiative. 2005. "Mitigating Cattle Losses Caused by Wild Predators in British Columbia." BC Cattlemen's Association. www.cattlemen.bc.ca/docs/mitigating_cattle_losses_a_field_guide_for_ranchers_smaller_file.pdf.

Ahmed, Sara. 2004. "Affective Economies." Social Text 22, no. 2: 117–39.

– 2014. The Cultural Politics of Emotion. 2nd ed. Edinburgh: Edinburgh University Press.

AHS. 1910. "The Future of Algonquin Park." Rod and Gun in Canada 11, no. 9: 790–4.

Anderson, Ben. 2016. Encountering Affect: Capacities, Apparatuses, Conditions. London and New York: Routledge.

Anderson, Benedict. 2006. Imagined Communities: Reflections on the Origin and Spread of Nationalism. London, UK: Verso.

Anderson, Kay. 2000. "'The Beast Within': Race, Humanity, and Animality." Environment and Planning D 18: 301–20.

Armstrong, L.O. 1907a. "Canadian Timber Wolf Hunts in Midwinter." Rod and Gun and Motor Sports in Canada 8, no. 8: 697–9.

– 1907b. "The Ontario Wolf Hunt." Rod and Gun and Motor Sport in Canada 8, no. 10: 887–91.

– 1907c. "Paper on Wolves." Rod and Gun in Canada 8, no. 10: 863–6.

– 1908. "The CPR Wolf Hunt of 1908." Rod and Gun in Canada 9, no. 10: 957–60.

Artelle, Kyle A. 2019. "Is Wildlife Conservation Policy Based in Science?" American Scientist, January–February. www.americanscientist.org/article/is-wildlife-conservation-policy-based-in-science.

Asafu-Adjaye, John, Linus Blomqvist, Stewart Brand, Barry W. Brook, Ruth De Fries, Erl E. Ellis, Christopher Foreman, et al. 2015. "An Ecomodernist Manifesto." April. www.ecomodernism.org/manifesto-english.

Asdal, Kristen, Tone Druglitrø, and Steve Hinchliffe. 2017. "Introduction: The 'More-than-Human' Condition: Sentient Creatures and Versions of Biopolitics." In Humans, Animals and Biopolitics: The More-than-Human Condition, edited by Kristen Asdal, Tone Druglitrø, and Steve Hinchliffe, 1–29. New York: Routledge.

Askewbud, Hannah, and Bud Napoleon. 2019. "The Caribou Are Our Four-Legged Cousins." Centre for International Governance and Innovation, 27 June. www.cigionline.org/articles/caribou-are-our-four-legged-cousins.

Atwood, Margaret. 1972. Survival: A Thematic Guide to Canadian Literature. Toronto: House of Anansi Press.

Balibar, Etienne. 1990. "The Nation Form: History and Ideology." Review (Fernand Braudel Center): 329–61.

Banting, Pamela. 2018. "Suddenly." *NICHE: Network in Canadian History & Environment/Nouvelle initiative canadienne en histoire de l'environnement*, 17 January. https://niche-canada.org/2018/01/17/suddenly.

Barad, Karen. 2003. "Posthumanist Perfomativity: Towards Understanding How Matter Comes to Matter." *Signs* 28, no. 3: 801–31.

Barager, C.P. 1944. "An Experience with Wolves." *Rod and Gun in Canada* 46, no. 8: 6–7.

Barnosky, Anthony D., Nicholas Matzke, Susumu Tomiya, Guinevere O.U. Wogan, Brian Swartz, Tiago B. Quental, Charles Marshall, et al. 2011. "Has the Earth's Sixth Mass Extinction already Arrived?" *Nature* 471: 51–5.

Barua, Maan. 2015. "Encounter." *Environmental Humanities* 7: 265–70.

– 2018. "Animal Work: Metabolic, Ecological, Affective." *Cultural Anthropology*, 26 July. https://culanth.org/fieldsights/animal-work-metabolic-ecological-affective.

BC SPCA. 2009. *Position Statement on Wolf-dog Hybrids*. https://spca.bc.ca/programs-services/leaders-in-our-field/position-statements/position-statement-wolf-dog-hybrids.

Belcourt, Billy-Ray. 2015. "Animal Bodies, Colonial Subjects: (Re)locating Animality in Decolonial Thought." *Societies* 5, no. 1: 1–11.

Benton-Banai, Edward. 1988. *The Mishomis Book: The Voice of the Ojibway*. Hayward, WI: Indian Country Communications.

Berger, Carl. 1966. "The True North Strong and Free." In *Nationalism in Canada*, edited by Peter Russell, 3–26. Toronto: McGraw-Hill.

Bhabha, Homi. 1990. *Nation and Narration*. London: Routledge.

– 1995. *Location of Culture*. London: Routledge.

Birke, Linda, and Jo Hockenhull. 2016. "Moving (With)in Affect: Horses, People, and Tolerance." In *Affect, Space and Animals*, edited by Jopi Nyman and Nora Schuurman, 123–39. London and New York: Routledge.

Birnie-Gauvin, Kim, Kathryn Peiman, Austin J. Gallagher, Robert de Bruijn, and Steven Cooke. 2016. "Sublethal Consequences of Urban Life for Wild Vertebrates." *Environmental Reviews* 24: 416–25.

Black, W.D., and Ontario Special Committee on Game Situation. 1933. *Report of the Special Committee on the Game Situation*. Toronto: The Legislative Assembly of Ontario.

Blue, Gwendolyn, and Shelley Alexander. 2015. "Coyotes in the City: Gastro-Ethical Encounters in a More-Than-Human World." In *Critical Animal Geographies: Politics, Intersections and Hierarchies in a Multispecies World*, edited by Kathryn Gillespie and Rosemary-Claire Collard, 149–63. London and New York: Routledge.

Bookhart, Ty. 2016. "How Loki the Wolfdog Became an Instagram Star."
    Outside, 20 December. www.outsideonline.com/2143756/how-loki-wolfdog-became-instagram-star.

Borich, Barrie Jean. 2013. "On Nonfiction and Consequence." *TEXT* 18: 1–16.

Boswell, Randy. 2003. "Canadian Wolves Help Save US Wilderness."
    The Vancouver Sun, 30 October, A7.

Boyd, Diane K. n.d. "Wolf Habituation as a Conservation Conundrum."
    A Companion to Principles of Conservation Biology. 3rd ed. Accessed
    7 May 2020. http://sites.sinauer.com/groom/article24.html.

Braverman, Irus. 2015. *Wild Life: The Institution of Nature*. Redwood City, CA:
    Stanford University Press.

– 2016. "The Regulatory Life of Threatened Species Lists." *Digital Commons @
    University at Buffalo School of Law*. https://digitalcommons.law.buffalo.edu/
    cgi/viewcontent.cgi?article=1082&context=book_sections.

– 2017. "Anticipating Endangerment: The Biopolitics of Threatened Species
    Lists." *BioSocieties* 12, no. 1: 132–57.

Brazier-Tompkins, Kali Shakti. 2010. "Superspecies: Bears and Wolves
    in Charles G.D. Roberts's Short Animal Stories." MA Thesis, University
    of Saskatchewan. https://ecommons.usask.ca/bitstream/handle/10388/etd-
    07222010-131944/SuperspeciesThesis.pdf?sequence=1).

British Columbia Caribou Recovery Program. 2019. "Predator Reduction for
    Caribou Recovery – Consultation." www2.gov.bc.ca/assets/gov/environment/
    plants-animals-and-ecosystems/wildlife-wildlife-habitat/caribou/predator_
    reduction_letter_central_selkirk.pdf.

Brook, Ryan K., Marc Cattet, Chris T. Darimont, Paul C. Paquet, and Gilbert
    Proulx. 2015. "Maintaining Ethical Standards During Conservation Crises."
    Canadian Wildlife Biology and Management 4, no. 1: 72–9.

Brooke, James. 1996. "Dangerous Path; Transplanted Canadian Wolves Are
    Roaming beyond Yellowstone's Borders Where Ranchers Are Waiting with
    Guns and Lawyers." *Edmonton Journal*, 18 February, E7.

Buller, Henry. 2015. "Animal Geographies II: Methods." *Progress in Human
    Geography* 39, no. 3: 374–85.

Burroughs, John. 1998. "Real and Sham Nature History." In *The Wild Animal
    Story*, edited by Ralph Lutts, 129–43. Philadelphia: Temple University Press.

Burton, Antoinette, and Renisa Mawani. 2020. "Introduction: Animals,
    Disruptive Imperial Histories and the Bestiary Form." In *Anamalia:
    An Anti-Imperial Bestiary for our Times*, edited by Antoinette Burton
    and Renisa Mawani, 1–16. Durham, NC: Duke University Press.

Caccavale, Elio, and Michael Reiss. 2011. *Miracles, Monsters and Disturbances*.
    https://v2.nl/archive/articles/miracles-monsters-and-disturbances/view.

Calgary Daily Herald. 1922. "Trapper Torn to Pieces by Timber Wolves after Grim Battle for his Life." 17 April.

Cameron, Emilie. 2015. *Far Off Metal River: Inuit Lands, Settler Stories and the Making of the Contemporary Arctic.* Vancouver: UBC Press.

Campbell, Claire. 2017. "The Wisdom of our National Parks." *The Walrus,* 16 January. https://thewalrus.ca/the-wisdom-of-our-national-parks.

Campbell, R. Wayne, Ronald D. Jakimchuk, and Dennis A. Demarchi. 2013. "In Memorium: Ian McTaggart-Cowan, 1910–2010." *The Auk* 130, no. 4: 807–9.

Canada's Polar Life. 2002. *The Wolf and the Caribou.* www.arctic.uoguelph.ca/cpl/Traditional/traditional_frame.htm.

Canadian Wildlife Federation. 1993. *Wolf.* www.hww.ca/en/wildlife/mammals/wolf.html.

Carbyn, Ludwig N. 1979. "A Wolf Manifesto for the World." The Douglas H. Pimlott fonds, University of Toronto Archives. acc. no. B95003, box 003, file 09.

Carrington, Damian. 2017. "Earth's Sixth Mass Extinction Event Under Way, Scientists Warn." *The Guardian,* 10 July. www.theguardian.com/environment/2017/jul/10/earths-sixth-mass-extinction-event-already-underway-scientists-warn.

Cartwright, George, and Marianne P. Stopp. 2016. *George Cartwright's The Labrador Companion.* Montreal and Kingston: McGill-Queen's University Press.

CBC News. 2015. "201 Dogs Rescued from Acreage near Milk River, Alta." 28 January. www.cbc.ca/news/canada/calgary/201-dogs-rescued-from-acreage-near-milk-river-alta-1.2935550.

– n.d. "Wolf/Coyote/Coywolf: A Comparison." *The Nature of Things.* Accessed 15 June 2017. www.cbc.ca/natureofthings/features/wolf-coyote.

Cecco, Leyland. 2020. "Canada Mourns Takaya – The Lone Sea Wolf Whose Spirit Captured the World." *The Guardian,* 27 March.

Cerulli, Tovar. 2017. "'Ma'iingan Is Our Brother': Ojibwe and Non-Ojibwe Ways of Speaking about Wolves." In *Handbook of Communication in Cross-Cultural Perspective,* edited by Donal Carbaugh, 247–60. New York: Routledge.

Chapeskie, A.H.J. 1973. "Ontario Deer Preservation Committee." Bulletin no. 5, November.

Chiew, Florence. 2015. "The Paradox of Self-Reference: Sociological Reflections on Agency and Intervention in the Anthropocene." In *Animals in the Anthropocene: Critical Perspectives on Non-human Futures,* edited by The Human Animal Research, 1–18. Sydney, Australia: Sydney University Press.

Chrulew, Matthew. 2017. "Animals as Biopolitical Subjects." In *Foucault and Animals*, edited by Matthew Chrulew and Dinesh Joseph Wadiwel, 222–38. Leiden, The Netherlands: Brill.

Chung, Emily. 2015. "Algonquin Park Public Wolf Howls Cancelled 2 Years in a Row." CBC News, 14 September. www.cbc.ca/news/technology/algonquin-wolf-howl-1.3227035.

City Desk. 2013. "The Super-Coyote Is Here." *Windsor Star*, 7 February. https://windsorstar.com/entertainment/the-super-coyote-is-here.

Clarke, Tracylee. 1999. "Constructing Conflict: The Functioning of Synecdoche in the Endangered Wolf Controversy." *Wicaso Sa Review* 14, no. 1: 113–27.

Cluff, Dean, and Dennis L. Murray. 1995. "Review of Wolf Control Methods in North America." In *Ecology and Conservation of Wolves in a Changing World*, edited by Ludwig N. Carbyn, Steven H. Fritts, and Dale R. Seip, 491–504. Edmonton: Canadian Circumpolar Institute, occasional paper no. 35.

Coates, Peter. 2005. "The Strange Stillness of the Past: Toward an Environmental History of Sound and Noise." *Environmental History* 10, no. 4: 636–65.

Coleman, Jon T. 2004. *Vicious: Wolves and Men in America*. New Haven, CT: Yale University Press.

Collard, Rosemary-Claire. 2012. "Cougar-Human Entanglements and the Biopolitical Un/Making of Safe Space." *Environment and Planning D: Society and Space* 30, no. 1: 23–42.

Collard, Rosemary-Claire, and Jessica Dempsey. 2013. "Life for Sale: The Politics of Lively Commodities." *Environment and Planning A: Economy and Space* 45, no. 11: 2682–99.

Collard, Rosemary-Claire, Jessica Dempsey, and Juanita Sundberg. 2015. "A Manifesto for Abundant Futures." *Annals of the Association of American Geographers* 105, no. 2: 322–30.

Collard, Rosemary-Claire, Jessica Dempsey, and Mollie Holmberg. 2020. "Extirpation Despite Regulation? Environmental Assessment and Caribou." *Conservation Science and Practice* 2, no. 4: 1–10.

Collins, Dylan, Cheryl Alexander, and Chris T. Darimont. 2019. "Staqeya: The Lone Wolf at the Edge of Its Ecological Niche." *Ecology* 100 (1): 1–4.

Colpitts, George. 2002. *Game in the Garden: A Human History of Wildlife in Western Canada to 1940*. Vancouver: UBC Press.

Coppinger, Raymond, Lee Spector, and Lynn Miller. 2009. *What, If Anything, Is a Wolf?* http://faculty.hampshire.edu/lspector/pubs/what-wolf-preprint.pdf.

Cortorneo, Christian. 2013. "Meet the Coywolf: Susan Fleming Looks at the Hybrid in Our Midst." *Huffington Post,* 2 August. www.huffingtonpost. ca/2013/02/08/coywolf-susan-fleming-film_n_2567531.html.

Counter, Rosemary. 2017. "The 'Rock Star' Wolf of Juan de Fuca." *Macleans,* 12 March.

Cowan, C.G. 1904. "With the Indian." *Rod and Gun in Canada* 6, no. 6: 273–7.

Cowie, Isaac. 1913. *The Company of Adventurers.* Toronto: Williams Briggs.

Cox, Sarah. 2020a. "BC Partners with First Nations to Create New Park in Habitat for Endangered Caribou Herds, Threatened Species." *The Narwhal,* 21 February. https://thenarwhal. ca/b-c-partners-with-first-nations-to-create-new-park-in-habitat-for-endangered-caribou-herds-threatened-species.

– 2020b. "The Complicated Tale of Why B.C. Paid $2 Million to Shoot Wolves in Endangered Caribou Habitat this Winter." *The Narwhal,* 25 April. https://thenarwhal.ca/ the-complicated-tale-of-why-b-c-paid-2-million-to-shoot-wolves-in-endangered-caribou-habitat-this-winter.

– 2020c. "'A Dangerous Road': Coastal GasLink Pays to Kill Wolves in Endangered Caribou Habitat in BC Interior." *The Narwhal,* 13 April. https:// thenarwhal. ca/a-dangerous-road-coastal-gaslink-pays-to-kill-wolves-in-endangered-caribou-habitat-in-b-c-interior.

Cronon, William. 1996. "The Trouble with Wilderness; or, Getting Back to the Wrong Nature." In *Uncommon Ground: Rethinking the Human Place in Nature,* edited by William Cronon, 69–90. New York: W.W. Norton & Company.

Cross, E.C. 1930. "Wolf! Wolf!" *Rod and Gun in Canada* 31, no. 9: 746.

Crutzen, Paul J., and Eugene F. Stoermer. 2000. "The 'Anthropocene.'" *Global Change Newletter* 41 (May): 17–18.

Dalley, Hamish. 2018. "The Deaths of Settler Colonialism: Extinction as a Metaphor of Decolonization in Contemporary Settler Literature." *Settler Colonial Studies* 8, no. 1: 30–46.

Daly, Natasha. 2019. "In Game of Thrones Fans' Pursuit of Real-Life Dire Wolves, Huskies May Pay the Price." *National Geographic.* www.national geographic.com/animals/2019/05/game-of-thrones-dire-wolf-fans-buying-huskies.

Daschuk, James W. 2019. *Clearing the Plains: Disease, Politics of Starvation, and the Loss of Indigenous Life.* Regina: University of Regina Press.

David, Peter. 2009. "Ma'iingan and the Ojibwe." In *Recovery of Gray Wolves in the Great Lakes Region of the United States*, edited by Adrian P. Wydeven, Timothy R. van Deelen, and Edward Heske, 267–77. New York: Springer.

Davis, Heather, and Zoe Todd. 2017. "On the Importance of a Date, or Decolonizing the Anthropocene." *ACME: An International Journal for Critical Geographies* 16, no. 4: 761–80.

Dean, Misao. 2013. "Political Science: Realism in Roberts's Animal Stories." In *Greening the Maple: Canadian Ecocriticism in Context*, edited by Ella Soper, 369–86. Calgary: University of Calgary Press.

Deloria, Philip Joseph. 1998. *Playing Indian*. New Haven, CT: Yale University Press.

Department of Indian Affairs. 1944a. "Correspondence from RA Gibson, Deputy Commissioner." *Game Laws – General Government Publications regarding Federal and Provincial Game and Fisheries Act and Regulation*. 16 February.

– 1944b. "Correspondence from R. Armit from the Department of Mines and Resources." *Game Laws – General Government Publications regarding Federal and Provincial Game and Fisheries Act and Regulation*, 6 February.

– n.d. Reel B01860-150-4. "Fur Conservation – Destruction of Wolves Including the Question of Bounty and Suggestions on Trapping Predatory Animals." GR-0934.79.

Destination Canada. 2018. *Canadian Signature Experiences*. Accessed 26 June 2020. https://caen-keepexploring.canada.travel/canadian-signature-experiences.

– n.d. "Five New Canadian Signature Experiences Showcase Canada's Diverse Adventures from Coast to Coast." Accessed 13 February 2020. www.destinationcanada.com/en/news/five-new-canadian-signature-experiences-showcase-canadas-diverse-adventures-coast-coast.

Dickson, James. 1902. "Ontario's Game and Game Laws." *Rod and Gun in Canada* 4, no. 1: 5–9.

Dingfelder, Sadie. 2014. "Coywolves, Coyote-Wolf Hybrids, Are Prowling Rock Creek Park and D.C. Suburbs." *The Washington Post*. 1 July. www.washingtonpost.com/express/wp/2014/07/01/coywolves-coyote-wolf-hybrids-are-prowling-rock-creek-park-and-d-c-suburbs.

Douglas, A.R. 1910. "The Wolf." *Rod and Gun in Canada* 11, no. 12: 1186.

Douglas, Mary. 1966. *Purity and Danger: An Analysis of the Concepts of Pollution and Taboo*. London, UK: Arc Paperbacks.

Douglas H. Pimlott fonds. n.d. "A History of Wolves in Algonquin." University of Toronto Archives. Acc. no. B1995-003, box 009.

Dre Anderson Photography. 2019. *We Are Bringing Them Back.* www.youtube.com/watch?v=FkltCTrCkzc.

Dunlap, Thomas R. 1983. "The Coyote Itself: Ecologists and the Value of Predators, 1900–1972." *Environmental Review* 7, no. 1: 54–70.

– 1988. *Saving America's Wildlife: Ecology and the American Mind 1850–1990.* Princeton: Princeton University Press.

– 1992. "The Realistic Animal Story: Ernest Thompson Seton, Charles Roberts, and Darwinism." *Forest & Conservation History* 36, no. 2: 56–62.

Dyar, Dorothy P. 1910. "Experiences of a Woman Homesteader: An Adventure with a Timber Wolf." *Rod and Gun in Canada* 12, no. 2: 228, 230.

Eadie, W.A. 1926. "A Few Facts and Figures about Wolf Destruction." *Rod and Gun in Canada* 27, no. 12: 782.

The Economist. 2015. "Greater than the Sum of its Parts." 31 October. www.economist.com/news/science-and-technology/21677188-it-rare-new-animal-species-emerge-front-scientists-eyes.

Emre, Suresh. 2019. "What Is Devotion?" 28 November. https://medium.com/@sureshemre/what-is-devotion-7d3e1e29efeb.

Erickson, Bruce. 2011. "A Phantasy in White in a World that Is Dead: Grey Owl and the Whiteness of Surrogacy." In *Rethinking the Great White North: Race, Nature and the Historical Geographies of Whiteness in Canada*, edited by Laura Cameron, Audrey Kobayashi, and Andrew Baldwin, 19–38. Vancouver: UBC Press.

Esposito, Roberto. 2008. *Bíos: Biopolitics and Philosophy.* Minneapolis: University of Minnesota Press.

Estes, Nick. 2019. *Our History Is the Future.* London and New York: Verso.

Fiamengo, Janice. 2007. "The Animals in this Country: Animals in the Canadian Literary Imagination." In *Other Selves: Animals and the Canadian Literary Imagination*, edited by Janice Fiamengo, 1–25. Ottawa: University of Ottawa Press.

Finney, Carolyn. 2014. *Black Faces, White Spaces: Reimagining the Relationship of African Americans to the Great Outdoors.* Chapel Hill: The University of North Carolina Press.

Follett Hosgood, Amanda. 2020. "The Secret to Caribou Recovery? Indigenous Leadership." *The Tyee*, 25 September. https://thetyee.ca/News/2020/09/25/Caribou-Recovery-Indigenous-Leadership.

Foran, Max. 2018. *The Subjugation of Canadian Wildlife: Failures of Principle and Policy.* Montreal and Kingston: McGill-Queen's University Press.

Ford, Ray. 2009. "Wolfsong." *ON Nature* (Summer): 16–21.

Forests, Lands, Natural Resource Operations and Rural Development. 2017.
 "Factsheet: Mountain Caribou and Wolves." BC Gov News, 24 January.
 https://news.gov.bc.ca/factsheets/mountain-caribou-and-wolves.
Foucault, Michel. 1979. Discipline & Punish: The Birth of the Prison. New
 York: Vintage Books.
– 1990. The History of Sexuality. Volume 1: An Introduction. New York:
 Vintage Books.
– 1996. "Passion According to Werner Schroeter." In Foucault Live: Interviews
 1961–1984, edited by S. Lotringer, 313–21. New York: Semiotext(e).
– 2001. Fearless Speech. New York: Semiotext(e).
– 2007. Security, Territory and Population: Lectures at the College de France,
 1977–1978. New York: Palgrave Macmillan.
– 2008. The Birth of Biopolitics: Lectures at the College de France 1978–1979.
 New York: Palgrave.
Fritts, Steven H., Edward E. Bangs, Joseph A. Fontain, Wayne G. Brewsterm,
 and James F. Gore. 1992. "Restoring Wolves to the Northern Rocky
 Mountains of the United States." In Ecology and Conservation of Wolves in
 a Changing World, edited by L.N. Carbyn, S.H. Fritts, and D.R. Seip, 107–25.
 Edmonton: Canadian Circumpolar Institute, University of Alberta.
Fuller, Todd K., L. David Mech, and Jean Fitts Cochrane. 2003. "Wolf
 Population Dynamics." In Wolves: Behavior, Ecology, and Conservation,
 edited by L. David Mech and Luigi Boitani, 161–91. Chicago: University
 of Chicago Press.
Gage, Andrew. 2012. "West Coast Questions Legality of Wolf-Kill Contest."
 West Coast Environmental Law, 12 December. www.wcel.org/blog/
 west-coast-questions-legality-wolf-kill-contest.
Gehl, Lynn. 2014. The Truth that Wampum Tells: My Debwewin on the
 Algonquin Land Claims Process. Toronto: Fernwood Publishing.
Geist, Valerius. 2008. "Death by Wolves and Misleading Advocacy. The Kenton
 Carnegie Tragedy." Skinny Moose, 22 April. www.skinnymoose.com/
 bbb/2008/12/30/
 death-by-wolves-and-misleading-advocacy-the-kenton-carnegie-tragedy.
Gibb, Samuel. 1903. "Slaughter of Deer." Rod and Gun in Canada 4, no. 8: 298.
Giese, Collette L. Adkins. 2005. "The Big Bad Wolf Hybrid: How Molecular
 Genetics Research May Undermine Protection for Wolves under the
 Endangered Species Act." Minnesota Journal of Law, Science & Technology 6,
 no. 2: 865–72.
Gillam, G.E. 1929. "Suggestions for Curbing Canada's Wolves." Rod and Gun
 in Canada 30, no. 9: 693, 714–16.

Gillespie, Kathryn, and Yamini Narayanan. 2020. "Animal Nationalisms: Multispecies Cultural Politics, Race, and the (Un)Making of the Settler Nation-State." *Journal of Intercultural Studies*: 41, no. 1: 1–7.

Globe and Mail. 1926. "Menace of Wolves Said to Be Serious." 22 October, 5.

– 1938. "Wolves Are Blamed as Kinloss Sheep Killed." 25 August, 4.

– 1947. "Wolves Chase Two Trappers, Maintain Seige during Night." 17 January, 8.

Globe. 1902. "The Ranch and the Farm." 6 May, 8.

– 1904. "Attacked by Wolves." 6 February, 5.

– 1906. "Tragedy of the North." 27 October, 13.

– 1908. "Boy Killed by Wolves." 31 March, 1.

– 1911. "Trapper Probably Eaten by Wolves." 28 January, 15.

– 1912. "Mail Carrier Eaten by Wolves." 5 March, 4.

– 1914. "Indian Trapper Eaten by Wolves in North." 9 January, 1.

– 1922. "Wolf Pack Devours Trapper and Indians Sent out in Search." 28 December, 1.

– 1923. "Wolf Attacks Girls in Sasaktoon Streets." 22 February, 1.

– 1924. "Sheep Farmers Quit Because of Wolves." 26 November, 6.

– 1926a. "Predatory Wild Animals May Again Worry Farmer." 25 February, 14.

– 1926b. "Saved from Wolves by Sacrificing Dogs." 9 January, 14.

– 1927a. "Lumberman Saved by Warden from Pack of Howling Wolves." 6 January, 2.

– 1927b. "Miners Entrapped in Shaft by Marauding Wolf Pack." 7 March, 1.

– 1927c. "Wolves Worrying Renfrew Sheepman." 12 January, 16.

– 1928. "Manitoulin Wolves Take Toll on Sheep." 11 February, 7.

– 1929. "Menace of Wolves Stops Sheep Farms." 14 May, 22.

– 1936. "Wolves Killing Sheep in Parry Sound Area." 22 May, 1.

– 1934. "Wolves Ravaging Flocks in Belleville District." 20 October, 1, 3.

Goddard, John. 1996. "A Real Whopper." *Saturday Night*, 46–54.

Godin, Edwin. 1931. "Letter in Around the Stove Box." *Rod and Gun in Canada* 32, no. 8: 575.

Gooder, Steve, dir. 2008. *Lobo: The Wolf that Changed America*. Produced by Brian Leith.

Grewal, Sonia K., Paul J. Wilson, Tabitha K. Kung, Karmi Shami, Mary K. Theberge, John B. Theberge, and Bradley N. White. 2004. "A Genetic Assessment of the Eastern Wolf (*Canis lycaon*) in Algonquin Provincial Park." *Journal of Mammology* 85, no. 4: 625–32.

Gunson, John R. 1992. "Historical and Present Management of Wolves in Alberta." *Wildlife Society Bulletin (1973–2006)* 20, no. 3: 330–9.

Habitat Conservation Trust Foundation. 2020. "Habitat Restoration across the
     Klinse-Za Caribou Herd Range." *Project Profiles,* 11 August. https://hctf.ca/
     habitat-restoration-across-the-klinse-za-caribou-herd-range.
Hagerman, Shannon, Hadi Dowlatabadi, Terre Satterfield, and Tim McDaniels.
     2010. "Expert Views on Biodiversity Conservation in an Era of Climate
     Change." *Global Environmental Change* 20, no. 1: 192–207.
Hall, Sandy. 2020. "BC Conservation Service Finds Discovery Island Wolf Was
     Hunted Legally." *C-FAX 1070.* 29 May. www.iheartradio.ca/cfax-1070/news/
     bc-conservation-service-finds-discovery-island-wolf-was-hunted-
     legally-1.12536263.
Hambleton, Jack. 1929. "Flocks Are Ravaged by Packs of Wolves on
     Manitoulin Island." *The Globe,* 25 December, 1.
Handwerk, Brian. 2018. "How Accurate Is Alpha's Theory of Dog
     Domestication?" *Smithsonian Magazine,* 15 August. www.smithsonianmag.
     com/science-nature/how-wolves-really-became-dogs-180970014/.
Hanson, Kendall. 2019. "Husky-Wolf Dog Attacks 3-year-old Nanaimo Boy."
     Chek News, 11 May. www.cheknews.ca/husky-wolf-dog-attacks-3-year-old-
     nanaimo-boy-559730.
Haraway, Donna. 2007. *When Species Meet.* Minneapolis: University of
     Minnesota Press.
– 2016. *Staying with the Trouble: Making Kin in the Chthulucene.* Durham,
     NC: Duke University Press.
– n.d. "Anthropocene, Capitalocene, Chthulucene: Staying with the Trouble."
     Accessed 10 January 2020. https://mawa.ca/pdf/Talk_by_Haraway_
     Anthropocene-Capitalocene-Chthulucene-Staying-with-the-Trouble-Donna-
     Haraway.pdf.
Haraway, Donna, and Anna Tsing. 2015. "Tunnelling in the Chthulucene:
     Resurgence on a Damaged Planet. Paper presented at the American Society
     for Literature and Environment Biennial Conference." Moscow, ID,
     23–27 June.
Harding, Lee E., Mathieu Bourbonnais, Andrew T. Cook, Toby Spribille,
     Viktoria Wagner, and Chris Darimont. 2020. "No Statistical Support
     for Wolf Control and Material Penning as Conservation Measures for
     Endangered Mountain Caribou." *Biodiversity and Conservation* 29:
     3051–60.
Harrington, Fred H., and Cheryl S. Asa. 2003. "Wolf Communiction: Behavior,
     Ecology, and Conservation." In *Wolves: Behavior, Ecology and Conservatiom,*
     edited by L. David Mech and Luigi Boitani, 96–9. Chicago: University of
     Chicago Press.

Harrington, Fred H., and Paul C. Paquet. 1982. "Preface." In *Wolves of the World: Perspectives of Behavior, Ecology and Conservation*, edited by Fred H. Harrington and Paul C. Paquet, v–vii. Park Ridge, NJ: Noyes Publications.

Harris, Alix. 2020. Yamnuska Wolfdog Sanctuary. Personal communication, 25 January.

Haynes, Melissa. 2013. "Regulating Abjection: Disgust, Tolerance and the Politics of *The Cove*." *English Studies in Canada* 39, no. 1: 27–50.

Hebblewhite, Mark. 2017. "Billion Dollar Boreal Woodland Caribou and the Biodiversity Impacts of the Global Oil and Gas Industry." *Biological Conservation* 206: 102–11.

Hernández, K.J., June M. Rubis, N. Theriault, Z. Todd, A. Mitchell, Bawaka Country, L. Burarrwanga, et al. 2020. "The Creatures Collective: Manifestings." *Environment and Planning E: Nature and Space* (online first): 1–25.

Hillwood, Amanda. n.d. "A Tale of Two Countries." *Wolf Song Alaska*. Accessed 19 September 2019. www.wolfsongalaska.org/two_countries.html.

Hinchliffe, Steven, and Nick Bingham. 2008. "Securing Life: The Emerging Practices of Biosecurity." *Environment and Planning A* 40: 1534–51.

Hobson, Julia Haggerty, Elizabeth Lynne Rink, Robert McAnally, and Elizabeth Bird. 2018. "Restoration and the Affective Ecologies of Healing: Buffalo and the Fort Peck Tribes." *Conservation and Society* 16, no. 1: 21–9.

Hoobly.com. 2020a. "Very High Content WD Pups for Spring 2020 Expect Black/Grey/and Arctic." www.hoobly.com/p/CtNUE.

– 2020b. *Wolfdog Pups Spring*. www.hoobly.com/p/1PdlL.

Hope, John Arthur. 1907. "Why Our Deer Are Vanishing." *Rod and Gun in Canada* 8, no. 11: 989–93.

Hopper, Tristan. 2011a. "Hunting the Wolf-Dog of Bowen Island." *National Post*, 26 May, A1.

– 2011b. "Wolf-Dog Shot and Killed by Trapper after Beast's Return to Sheep Farm." *The Vancouver Sun*, 28 May, A7.

Hovorka, Alice. 2008. "Transspecies Urban Theory: Chickens in an African City." *cultural geographies* 15: 95–117.

Howtohunt.com. 2019. *I Killed 200 Wolves*. 13 March. www.youtube.com/watch?v=jmWNvpQ1lXY.

Hubbard, Tasha. 2009. "'The Buffaloes Are Gone' or 'Return: Buffalo? – The Relationship of Buffalo to Indigenous Creative Expression." *The Canadian Journal of Native Studies* XXIX, nos. 1–2: 65–85.

Humane Canada. n.d. *Wolf-Dog Hybrids*. Accessed 27 February 2020. www.humanecanada.ca/wolf_dog_hybrids.

Hunter, Justine. 2020. "An Uncertain Ending for Victoria's Lone Wolf."
The Globe and Mail, 28 February. www.theglobeandmail.com/amp/canada/
british-columbia/article-an-uncertain-ending-for-victorias-lone-wolf.

Hutton, Hubert. 1916. "Suggestions for Trapping Fur Bearers." *Rod and Gun*
18, no. 7: 802–6.

Imbler, Sabrina. 2020. "A Canadian Province Killed 463 Wolves for No Good
Reason." *The Atlantic*, 14 July. www.theatlantic.com/science/archive/2020/07/
how-simple-statistical-error-killed-463-wolves/614134.

Ingram, Angelica. 2015. "The Wolves of Algonquin: A History of a
Misunderstood Animal." 24 November. www.haliburtonecho.ca/
the-wolves-of-algonquin-a-history-of-a-misunderstood-animal.

Ingram, Darcy. 2013. *Wildlife, Conservation, and Conflict in Quebec, 1840–
1914*. Vancouver: University of British Columbia Press.

International Wolf Center. 2020. *Canada at a Glance*. https://wolf.org/wow/canada.

– n.d.a "Wolf-Dog Hybrids." Accessed 21 February 2020. https://wolf.org/wolf-
info/basic-wolf-info/wolves-and-humans/wolf-dog-hybrids.

– n.d.b "Wolf FAQ's." Accessed 15 August 2020. https://wolf.org/wolf-info/
basic-wolf-info/wolf-faqs.

Invasive Species Centre. n.d. "Invasive Phragmities." Accessed 26 April 2021.
https://invasivespeciescentre.ca/invasive-species/meet-the-species/invasive-
aquatic-plants/phragmites.

IPBES. 2019. *Summary for Policymakers of the Global Assessment Report
on Biodiversity and Ecosystem Services*. Edited by S. Díaz, J. Settele,
E.S. Brondízio, H.T. Ngo, M. Guèze, J. Agard, A. Arneth, P. Balvanera,
K.A. Brauman, S.H.M. Butchart, K.M.A. Chan, L.A. Garibaldi, K. Ichii, J. Liu,
S.M. Subramanian, G.F. Midgley, P. Miloslavich, Z. Molnár, D. Obura,
A. Pfaff, S. Polasky, A. Purvis, J. Razzaque, B. Reyers, R. Roy Chowdhury,
Y.J. Shin, I.J. Visseren-Hamakers, K.J. Willis, and C.N. Zayas. Intergovernmental
Science-Policy Platform on Biodiversity and Ecosystem Services, Bonn,
Germany: IPBES secretariat. https://ipbes.net/sites/default/files/2020-02/
ipbes_global_assessment_report_summary_for_policymakers_en.pdf.

The Jack Miner Migratory Bird Foundation. n.d. Accessed 22 August 2019.
https://jackminer.ca.

Jackson, James. 2020. "The Story of UW Student Killed by Wolves Revisited."
The Record, 28 February. www.therecord.com/
news-story/9869183-the-story-of-uw-student-killed-by-wolves-revisited.

Jackson, Zakiyyah Iman. 2015. "Outer Worlds: The Persistence of Race in
Movement 'Beyond the Human.'" *Gay and Lesbian Quarterly (GLQ)* 21,
nos. 2–3: 215–18.

Jasen, Patricia. 1995. *Wild Things: Nature, Culture and Tourism in Ontario, 1790–1914*. Toronto: University of Toronto Press.

Jerolmack, Colin. 2008. "How Pigeons Became Rats: The Cultural-Spatial Logic of Problem Animals." *Social Problems* 55 (1): 92–4.

Jervis, H. 1906. "Wolves on the Trail." *Rod and Gun and Motor Sport in Canada* 8, no. 7: 549–50.

Johnson, Abel. 1902. "Why Partridge Are so Scarce." *Rod and Gun in Canada* 4, no. 7: 261.

Johnson, Brian. 2007. "Ecology, Allegory, and Indigeneity in the Wolf Stories of Roberts, Seton, and Mowat." In *Other Selves: Animals and the Canadian Literary Imagination*, edited by Janice Fiamengo, 333–52. Ottawa: University of Ottawa Press.

Johnson, Harold R. 2020. *Cry Wolf: Inquest into the True Nature of a Predator*. Regina: University of Regina Press.

Jones, Karen. 2002. "Fighting Outlaws, Returning Wolves." *History Today* 52, no. 3: 38–40.

– 2003. "*Never Cry Wolf*: Science, Sentiment, and the Literary Rehabilitation of *canis lupis*." *The Canadian Historical Review* 84, no. 1: 1–16.

Jones, Karen R. 2003. *Wolf Mountains: A History of Wolves along the Great Divide*. Calgary: University of Calgary Press.

Jones, Manina. 2008. "Wildlife Writing? Animal Stories and Indigenous Claims in Ernest Thompson Seton's *Wild Animals I Have Known*." *Journal of Canadian Studies* 42, no. 3: 133–49.

Kaseuk Yoon, Carol. 2010. "Mysteries that Howl and Hunt." 27 September. www.nytimes.com/2010/09/28/science/28coyotes.html.

Kaufmann, Eric. 1998. "'Naturalizing the Nation': The Rise of the Naturalistic Nation in the United States and Canada." *Comparative Studies in History and Society* 40, no. 4: 666–95.

Kays, R. 2015. "Yes, Eastern Coyotes Are Hybrids, but the 'Coywolf' Is Not a Thing." *The Conversation,* 13 November. https://theconversation.com/yes-eastern-coyotes-are-hybrids-but-the-coywolf-is-not-a-thing-50368.

Kays, Roland, Abigail Curtis, and Jeremy J. Kirchman. 2010. "Rapid Adaptive Evolution of Northeastern Coyotes via Hybridization with Wolves." *Biology Letters* 6: 89–93.

Keller, Betty. 1984. *Black Wolf: The Life of Ernest Thompson Seton*. Vancouver and Toronto: Douglas & McIntyre.

Kelly, Alanna. 2020. "Remembering Staqeya, the Lone Wolf of Discovery Island." CTV *Vancouver Island*. 29 March. https://vancouverisland.ctvnews.ca/remembering-staqeya-the-lone-wolf-of-discovery-island-1.4870541.

Kenny, Kelly. 2014. "Woman Survives Coyote Attack in Front of Her Home." 3 September. www.muskokaregion.com/news-story/4821031-woman-survives-coyote-attack-in-front-of-her-home.

Kim, Claire Jean. 2015. *Dangerous Crossings: Race, Species and Nature in a Multicultural Age.* Cambridge: Cambridge University Press.

Kimmerer, Robin Wall. 2013. *Braiding Sweetgrass: Indigenous Wisdom, Scientific Knowledge and the Teachings of Plants.* Minneapolis: Milkweed Editions.

King, Thomas. 2003. *The Truth about Stories: A Native Narrative.* Minneapolis: University of Minnesota Press.

King, Tiffany Lethabo. 2017. "Humans Involved." *Critical Ethnic Studies* 3, no. 1: 162–85.

Kirk, Robert G.W. 2016. "The Birth of the Laboratory Animal: Biopolitics, Animal Experimentation, and Animal Wellbeing." In *Foucault and Animals*, edited by Matthew Chrulew and Dinesh Wadiwel, 193–221. Leiden, The Netherlands: Brill.

Kirksey, Eben. 2015. *Emergent Ecologies.* Durham, NC: Duke University Press.

Kirksey, Eben, and Stefan Helmreich. 2010. "The Emergence of Multispecies Ethnography." *Cultural Anthropology* 25: 545–76.

Knafo, Saki. 2015. "Predator Politics." *Motherboard*, 22 June. http://motherboard.vice.com/read/predator-politics-coywolves.

Kristeva, Julia. 1982. *Powers of Horror: An Essay on Abjection.* New York: Columbia University Press.

Kruger, Arnold. 2003. "To Find a Treasure: The Nuu-chah-nulth Wolf Mask." *American Indian Culture and Research Journal* 27, no. 3: 71–86.

Kyle, C.J., A.R. Johnson, B.R. Patterson, P.J. Wilson, K. Shami, S.K. Grewal, and B.N. White. 2006. "Genetic Nature of Eastern Wolves: Past, Present and Future." *Conservation Genetics* 7. https://doi.org/10.1007/s10592-006-9130-0.

LaDuke, Winona. 1999. *All Our Relations: Natie Struggles for Land and Life.* Cambridge, MA: South End Press.

Larson, Brendon M.H. 2008. "Friend, Foe, Wonder, Peril." *Alternatives Journal* (January). www.alternativesjournal.ca/energy-and-resources/friend-foe-wonder-peril.

Latour, Bruno. 1993. *We Have Never Been Modern.* Cambridge, MA: Harvard University Press.

– 2012. "Love Your Monsters." *The Breakthrough Institute* (Winter). https://thebreakthrough.org/index.php/journal/past-issues/issue-2/love-your-monsters.

Lavoie, Judith. 2013. "Trap Set for Discovery Island Wolf, but Songhees Want It Left Alone." *Times Colonist*, 6 February. www.timescolonist.com/news/local/ trap-set-for-discovery-island-wolf-but-songhees-want-it-left-alone-1.68637.

Lawrence, Bonita. 2012. *Fractured Homeland: Federal Recognition and Algonquin Identity in Ontario*. Vancouver: UBC Press.

Lay, Al. n.d. *Investigation and Evaluation of Predator Kills and Attacks*. Alberta Conservation Officer Service.

Lemieux, E.E. 1911. "Some Trips to Petawawa." *Rod and Gun in Canada* 13, no. 6: 647.

Lemke, Thomas. 2015. "New Materialisms: Foucault and the 'Government of Things.'" *Theory, Culture & Society* 32, no. 4: 3–25.

Leopold, Aldo. 1933. *Game Management*. New York: Scribner's.

– 1949. *A Sand County Almanac and Sketches Here and There*. New York: Oxford University Press.

Lewis, Harrison F. 1930–1955. "Memorandum on Wolf Control by Harrison F. Lewis." Parks Canada File U266 Universal Wolves. Library and Archives Canada.

Link, Mike, and Kate Crowley. 1994. *Following the Pack: The World of Wolf Research*. Stillwater, MN: Voyageur Press.

Linklater, M. n.d. "Experimental Wolf Poisoning Program in Kenora District." Wildlife Branch – Wildlife Program Moose/Caribou Files, file 88-7A-2.

Linton, James M., and Calvin W. Moore. 1984. *The Story of Wild Goose Jack: The Life and Work of Jack Miner*. Toronto: CBC Enterprises.

Livingston, Julie, and Jasbir K. Puar. 2011. "Interspecies." *Social Text* 29, nos. 1–106: 3–14.

Loki Naturals. n.d. *Loki Naturals – We Are SDC*. Accessed 25 April 2021. https://wearesdc.com/lokinaturals.

Loki the Wolfdog. 2017. "Wolfgang and Loki the Wolfdog." 18 October. www.youtube.com/watch?v=1Q1eAUKHFww.

– n.d. *Loki the Wolfog – About Us*. Accessed 3 Febuary 2020. https://lokithewolfdog.com/pages/about.

Longboat, Dan Roronhiake:wen. 2017. Personal communication, 30 September.

Loo, Tina. 2006. *States of Nature: Conserving Canada's Wildlife in the Twentieth Century*. Vancouver: UBC Press.

Lorimer, Jamie. 2015. *Wildlife in the Anthropocene: Conservation after Nature*. Minneapolis: University of Minnesota Press.

Lowman, Emma Battell, and Adam J. Barker. 2015. *Settler: Identity and Colonialism in 21st Century Canada*. Halifax and Winnipeg: Fernwood Publishing.

Lowrey, Anna. 2020. "What Do Wolfdogs Want?" 2 February. www.theatlantic.
com/ideas/archive/2020/02/what-do-wolfdogs-want/605896.

Luckasavitch, Christine. 2019. "A Brief History of the Madaoueskarini
Algonquin People." *NorthBayNipissing.com*, 6 June. www.northbaynipissing.
com/community-story/9422211-a-brief-history-of-the-madaoueskarini-
algonquin-people.

Lukas, Michael. 2018. "The Rhetoric of Wolves." PhD dissertation, University
of Victoria.

Lutts, Ralph H., ed. 1998. *The Wild Animal Story*. Philadelphia: Temple
University Press.

MacDonald, Graham A. 1995. "Manitoba History: 'Kootenai' Brown in the
Red River Valley." *Manitoba Historical Society* (Autumn). www.mhs.mb.ca/
docs/mb_history/30/kootenaibrown.shtml.

MacDonald, Robert H. 1998. "The Revolt against Reason: The Animal Stories
of Seton and Roberts." In *The Wild Animal Story*, edited by Ralph H. Lutts,
225–36. Philadephia: Temple University Press.

MacEachern, Alan. 1995. "Rationality and Rationalization in Canadian
National Parks Predator Policy." In *Consuming Canada: Readings in
Environmental History*, edited by Chad Gaffield and Pam Gaffield, 197–212.
Toronto: Copp Clark Ltd.

Mackey, Eva. 2000. "Death by Landscape: Race, Nature, and Gender in
Canadian Nationalist Mythology." *Canadian Women's Studies* 20, no. 2:
125–30.

Mackintosh, Alex. 2017. "Foucault's Menagerie: Cock Fighting, Bear Baiting,
and the Genealogy of Human-Animal Power." In *Foucault and Animals*,
edited by Matthew Chrulew and Dinesh Joseph Wadiwel, 161–89. Leiden,
The Netherlands: Brill.

MacLean, W.A. 1926. "The Wolf Menace." *Rod and Gun in Canada* 27, no. 8:
507.

MacLeod, Andrew. 2015. "Wolf Cull Needed to Save Caribou, Province Says."
The Tyee, 16 January. https://thetyee.ca/News/2015/01/16/BC-Wolf-Cull.

Maharaj, Nandini, Arminee Kazanjina, and William Borgen. 2018. "Investing
in Human-Animal Bonds: What Is the Psychological Return on Such
Investment?" *Loisir et Société/Society and Leisure* 41, no. 3: 393–407.

Malaher, G.W. 1952. "Wolf Control." Archives of Manitoba. 5 February.

Martin, Sandra. 2014. "Acclaimed Canadian Author Farley Mowat Dead at 92."
Globe and Mail, 7 May.

Matheny, K. 2015. "Michigan's Mysterious, Misundertood Coywolves."
Detroit Free Press. 28 February. www.freep.com/story/news/local/
michigan/2015/02/28/coywolfcoyote- wolf-hybrid/24186739.

Mbembé, Achille. 2003. "Necropolitics." Translated by Libby Meintjes. *Public Culture* 15, no. 1: 11–40.

McAllister, Ian, and Nicholas Read. 2010. *The Sea Wolves: Living Wild in the Great Bear Rainforest.* Victoria: Orca Book Publishers.

McDougall Tait, W. 1921. "Wolfing in Western Canada." *Rod and Gun in Canada* 22, no. 9: 1018–22.

McGoogan, Ken. 2011. "Our Own Ancient Mariner." *Literary Review of Canada* (May). http://reviewcanada.ca/magazine/2011/05/our-own-ancient-mariner.

McGregor, Deborah. 2004. "Coming Full Circle: Indigenous Knowledge, Environment, and Our Future." *The American Indian Quarterly* 28, no. 3: 385–410.

McHugh, Susan. 2011. *Animal Stories: Narrating across Species Lines.* Minneapolis: University of Minnesota Press.

McKean, Andrew. 2007. "Manhunters." *Outdoor Life,* 18 September. www.outdoorlife.com/articles/hunting/2007/09/manhunters.

McNay, Mark E. 2002. *A Case History of Wolf-Human Encounters in Alaska and Canada.* Wildlife Technical Bulletin, Juneau, AK: Alaska Department of Fish and Game, Wildlife Conservation.

McTaggart-Cowan, Ian. 1947. "The Timber Wolf in the Rocky Mountain National Parks of Canada." *Canadian Journal of Research* 25: 139–74.

McVeigh, E.J. 1910. "The Lone Trapper and His Story." *Rod and Gun in Canada* 12, no. 6: 789–93.

– 1911. "Sickly Sentimentality." *Rod and Gun in Canada* 13, no. 3: 303–6.

Mech, L. David. 2011. "The Scientific Classification of Wolves: Canis Lupus Soupus." *International Wolf* 21, no.1: 4–7.

Meine, Curt. 2010. "Conservation Biology: Past and Present." In *Conservation Biology for All*, edited by Navjot S. Sodhi and Paul R. Ehrlich, 7–26. Oxford: Oxford University Press.

Miller, M.L. 2015. "Wolf? Coyote? Coywolf? Understanding Wolf Hybrids Just Got a Bit Easier." *Cool Green Science,* 3 August. https://blog.nature.org/science/2015/08/03/wolf-coyote-coywolf-understanding-wolf-hybrids-just-got-a-bit-easier.

Miller, William Ian. 1998. *The Anatomy of Disgust.* Cambridge, MA: Harvard University Press.

Miner, Jack. 1909. "The Big Game in Northern Ontario." *Rod and Gun and Motor Sport in Canada* 10, no. 11: 1051–2.

– 1912. "The Wolves and the Game Laws." *Rod and Gun in Canada* 13, no. 11: 1360–2.

– 1929. "Deer or Wolves." *Rod and Gun in Canada* 30, no. 8: 612–14, 630.

Miner, Manly F. 1972. "Manly Miner Says 'We Must Control the Timber Wolf.'"
    In *Deer and Wolves in Ontario*, by Jack Miner, Jasper W. Miner, and Manly F.
    Miner, 6–8. Kingsville, ON: Jack Miner Migratory Bird Foundation.

Ministry of Forests, Lands, Natural Resource Operations and Rural
    Development. 2017. "Factsheet: Mountain Caribou and Wolves." *BC Gov
    News*, 24 January. https://news.gov.bc.ca/factsheets/
    mountain-caribou-and-wolves.

– 2020. "Governments, First Nations Enhance Caribou Protection." *BC Gov
    News*, 21 February. https://news.gov.bc.ca/releases/2020FLNR0018-000305.

Misner, J.W. 1907. "Why Our Deer Are Vanishing: A Reply to J.A. Hope." *Rod
    and Gun and Motor Sports in Canada* 8, no. 11: 989–93.

Mission: Wolf. n.d. *History of Wild Wolves*. Accessed 22 October 2020.
    https://missionwolf.org/wild-wolves.

Mitchell, Audra. 2016. "Beyond Biodiversity and Species: Problematizing
    Extinction." *Theory, Culture & Society* 33, no. 5: 23–42.

Monitz, Lauren. n.d. *Living Loki: An Exclusive Interview with the Internet's
    Insta-famous Adventure Pup*. Accessed 3 February 2020. www.iexplore.com/
    experiences/adventures/loki-the-wolf-dog.

Moodie, Susanna. (1852) 2003. *Roughing it in the Bush*. Project Gutenberg.

Moody, W.J. 1929. "Ontario Hunters Disappointed." *Rod and Gun in Canada*
    30, no. 12: 992.

Moorhouse, Hopkins J. 1906. "Western Ontario Woods in 1830." *Rod and Gun
    and Motor Sport in Canada* 8, no. 5: 340–2.

Morgan, Philip Dwight. 2019. "Race, Privilege, and the Canadian Wilderness."
    The Walrus, 24 January. https://thewalrus.ca/
    race-privilege-and-the-canadian-wilderness.

Morris, Michael. 2002. "Do Mountain Caribou Matter?" *Columbia Mountain's
    Institute of Applied Ecology*, 15 May. https://cmiae.org/national-park-feature-
    article/do-mountain-caribou-matter.

Morrison, Alex. 1928. "Sheep and Wolves." *The Globe*, 12 May, 4.

Mortimer-Sandilands, Catriona. 2009. "The Cultural Politics of Ecological
    Intergrity: Nature and Nation in Canada's National Parks: 1885–2000."
    International Journal of Canadian Studies 39–40: 161–89.

Moss, Laura F.E., ed. 2003. *Is Canada Postcolonial: Unsettling Canadian
    Literature*. Waterloo: Wilfred Laurier University Press.

Motley, W.C. 1928. "The Predatory Animal Pest Considered." *Rod and Gun
    in Canada* 30, no. 7: 542–3.

Mowat, Farley. (1952) 2004. *People of the Deer*. Boston: Da Capo Press.

– (1963) 2009. *Never Cry Wolf*. Toronto: McClelland Stewart.

Murie, Adolph. 1944. *The Wolves of Mount McKinley.* Washington, DC: United States Government Printing Office.

Musiani, Marco, and Paul C. Paquet. 2004. "The Practices of Wolf Persecution, Protection, and Restoration in Canada and the United States." *BioScience* 54, no. 1: 50–60.

Nagy, Kelsi, and Phillip Johnson II. 2013. "Introduction." In *Trash Animals: How We Live with Nature's Filthy, Feral, Invasive and Unwanted Species,* edited by Kelsi Nagy and Phillip Johnson II, 1–27. Minneapolis: University of Minnesota Press.

Nast, Heidi J. 2006. "Critical Pet Studies?" *Antipode* 38, no. 5: 894–906.

Nelson, M.K. 2008. *Original Instructions: Indigenous Teachings for a Sustainable Future.* Rochester, VT: Bear & Company.

Ngai, Sianne. 2005. *Ugly Feelings.* Cambridge, MA: Harvard University Press.

North, Roy. 1913. "A Plea for Moose: An Article on the Abuse of Moose Hunting by the Swampy Cree Indians." *Rod and Gun in Canada* 15, no. 7: 695–6.

Nowak, Ron. 1995. "Hybridization: The Double-Edged Threat." https://redwolves.com/wp/wp-content/uploads/2016/01/12-Nowak-1995.pdf.

Nyman, Jopi, and Nora Schuurman. 2016. "Introduction." In *Affect, Space and Animals,* edited by Jopi Nyman and Nora Schuurman. London and New York: Routledge.

Oaks, Gary. 2011. "For Half-Wolves, There's No Such Thing as a Free Munch." 15 February. www.theglobeandmail.com/news/british-columbia/for-half-wolves-theres-no-such-thing-as-a-free-munch/article581159.

O'Callaghan, Tiffany. 2013. "Survival of the Friendliest." *Slate,* 11 March. www.slate.com/articles/health_and_science/new_scientist/2013/03/the_genius_of_dogs_brian_hare_on_friendliness_intelligence_and_inference.html.

Omand, D.N. 1950. "The Bounty System in Ontario." *The Journal of Wildlife Management* 14, no. 4: 425–34.

Ontario Department of Lands and Forests. 1963. "Weekly News Releases." RG 1-243. Archives of Ontario.

– 1963. "Weekly News Releases, 1963–1966." Ontario Government Record Series – Archives of Ontario. RG-1-243 B740923.

– 1964. "Weekly News Releases, 1963–1966 – Predator Research and Management in Ontario." Ontario Government Record Series – Archives of Ontario. RG-1-243 B740923, 19 April.

Ontario Department of Lands and Forests, Wildlife Branch. 1970. "The Wolf Problem (file)." RG 3-26, box 280747, Premier John P. Robarts general correspondence papers. Toronto: Archives of Ontario.

Ontario Game and Fisheries Commission. 1912. *Final Report of the Ontario Game and Fisheries Commission, 1909–1911.* Government Document, Toronto: LK Cameron.

Orr, James E. 1908. "An Adventure with a Wolf." *Rod and Gun and Motor Sports in Canada* 10, no. 6: 552.

– 1909. "Experiences of Pioneers." *Rod and Gun in Canada* 10, no. 8: 747–9.

– 1910a. "An Old Lady's Story of Pioneer Days." *Rod and Gun in Canada* 11, no. 11: 1048–50.

– 1910b. "Some Old Time Stories from Old Ontario." *Rod and Gun and Motor Sports in Canada* 11, no. 9: 704–8.

– 1911. "Old Time Reminiscences in Old Ontario." *Rod and Gun in Canada* 13, no. 7: 808–10.

– 1913. "Old Pioneers' Stories: Collected and Written for *Rod and Gun*." *Rod and Gun in Canada* 14, no. 10: 1087–9.

Owen, Bruce. 2015. "Victoria Beach under Seige by a Vicious New Predator." *Winnipeg Free Press,* 22 September. www.winnipegfreepress.com/local/under-siege-328744901.html.

Owen, Robert. 1903. "The Coming North." *Rod and Gun in Canada* 5, no. 7: 379–83.

Pacific Wild. 2018. "With Your Help, We Can Stop the Ongoing Persecution of Wolves across the Province." https://vimeo.com/249045982.

Pagé, Josh. 2018. "BC Caribou Herds Stabilizing Where Wolves Are Culled, Forest Ministry Says." CBC, 23 November. www.cbc.ca/news/canada/british-columbia/caribou-wolf-cull-1.4915683.

Paquet, Paul C., and Christopher T. Darimont. 2010. "Wildlife Conservation and Animal Welfare: Two Sides of the Same Coin?" *Animal Welfare* 19: 177–90.

Parks Canada fonds. 1947. "Wolf Bounties – Saskatchewan." Library and Archives Canada. 30 June.

– n.d. "Summary of Discussion on Wolves and Wolf Control at the 10th Conference of the Provincial and Dominion Wildlife Officials, Ottawa, February 23, 1945." Parks Canada – Universal Wolves File U266. Library and Archives Canada.

Parr, Sadie, and Paul Paquet. 2017. "BC Government Scientists Admit Wolf Cull Is Inhumane, Then Propose to Expand It." *National Observer,* 1 February. www.nationalobserver.com/2017/02/01/news/bc-government-scientists-admit-wolf-cull-inhumane-then-propose-expand-it.

Parreñas, Juno Salazar. 2018. *Decolonizing Extinction: The Work of Care in Orangutan Rehabilitation.* Durham, NC: Duke University Press.

PBS Nature. 2008. *The Wolf that Changed America*. Directed by Brian Leith. www.pbs.org/wnet/nature/the-wolf-that-changed-america-introduction/4260.

Pêgas, Rodrigo Vargas. 2013. "A Review on Animal Hybridization's Role in Evolution and Conservation: *Canis rufus* (Audubon and Bachman) 1851 – A Case Study." *International Scholarly Research Notices*, vol. 2013, article ID 760349, 6 pages. https://doi.org/10.1155/2013/760349.

Peltola, Taru, and Jari Heikkilä. 2018. "Outlaws or Protected? DNA, Hybrids, and Biopolitics in a Finnish Wolf-Poaching Case." *Society & Animals* 26: 197–216.

Pennsylvania Game Commission. n.d. *Eastern Coyote Wildlife Note*. Accessed 18 December 2017. www.pgc.pa.gov/Education/WildlifeNotesIndex/Pages/ECoyote.aspx.

Philo, Chris. 2012. "A 'New Foucault' with Lively Implications – or 'the Crawfish Advances Sideways.'" *Transactions of the Institute of British Geographers* 37: 496–514.

Pimlott, Douglas H. 1961a. "Wolf Control in Canada." *Canadian Audubon*, 145–52.

– 1961b. "Wolf Control and Management in Ontario." Douglas H. Pimlott fonds, University of Toronto Archives. Acc. no. B1995-003, box 010.

– 1966. "Review: *Never Cry Wolf*." *The Journal of Wildlife Management* 30, no. 1: 236.

– 1968. "Deer and Wolves – The Fallacy of the Wolf Extermination Panacea." *Annual Meeting of the St Catharines and Lincoln County Game and Fish Protective Association*. Douglas H. Pimlott fonds, University of Toronto Archives. Acc. no. B1995-0003, box 010, 26 February.

Pimlott, Douglas H., J.A. Shannon, and G.B. Kolenosky. 1977. *The Ecology of the Timber Wolf in Algonquin Provincial Park*. 3rd printing. Ministry of Natural Resources.

Pluskowski, Aleksander. 2006. *Wolves and Wilderness in the Middle Ages*. Rochester, NY: The Boydell Press.

Premier's Office Files. 1954–1957. "Wolf Bounty." Provincial Archives of Manitoba. Acc. no. GR0043.

Probyn-Rapsey, Fiona. 2016a. "Eating Dingoes." *Australian Zoologist* 39, no. 1: 39–42.

– 2016b. "Five Propositions on Ferals." *Feral Feminisms* 6: 18–21.

Proulx, Gilbert, and Dwight Rodtka. 2015. "Predator Bounties in Western Canada Cause Animal Suffering and Compromise Wildlife Conservation Efforts." *Animals* 5: 1034–46.

Pynn, Larry. 1994. "BC Wolves to Be Moved to Yellowstone." *The Vancouver Sun*, 10 May, B3.

– 2012. "Contest Offers Cash Prizes for Wolf Kills in Northeastern BC" *Ottawa Citizen*, 20 November. https://ottawacitizen.com/News/Canada/contest-offers-cash-prizes-for-wolf-kills-in-northeastern-bc/wcm/9e5ac221-5c3a-4cac-a48d-84d893fa493a.

– 2020. "The Lone Wolf that Was Loved to Death." *Hakai Magazine*, 27 October. www.hakaimagazine.com/features/the-lone-wolf-loved-to-death.

Raoul, F. 1928. "Is the Wolf as Bad as Painted?" *Forest and Outdoors* 190.

Rath, Richard Cullen. 2003. *How Early America Sounded*. Ithaca: Cornell University Press.

Reid, J.A. 1920. "Terrible Slaughter of Deer." *Rod and Gun in Canada* 22, no. 3: 328.

Reo, Nicholas J., and Laura Ogden. 2018. "Anishnaabe Aki: An Indigenous Persective on the Global Threat of Invasive Species." *Sustainability Science* 13: 1443–52.

Richardson, L. 2015. "New York Needs Coyotes." *Slate*, 31 July. www.slate.com/articles/health_and_science/science/2015/07/coyotes_in_new_york_and_chicago_urban_ecology_of_rats_geese_deer_feral_cats.html.

Ritvo, Harriet. 1987. *The Animal Estate: The English and Other Creatures in the Victorian Age*. Cambridge, MA: Harvard University Press.

– 2017. "Invasion/Invasive." *Environmental Humanities* 9, no. 1: 171–4.

Robbins, Jim. 2020. "A Natural Classroom, Run by Wolves." *The New York Times*, 27 March. www.nytimes.com/2020/03/27/opinion/sunday/yellow-stone-wolves.html?auth=link-dismiss-google1tap.

Roberts, Charles G.D. 1904a. "The Homeward Trail." In *The Watchers of the Trails: A Book of Animal Life*, 351–61. Boston: L.C. Page & Co.

– 1904b. "The Passing of the Black Whelps." In *The Watchers of the Trails: A Book of Animal Life*, 323–48. Boston: L.C. Page & Co.

– 1904c. *The Watchers of the Trails: A Book of Animal Life*. Toronto: The Copp Clark Company.

– 1907. "The Grey Master." In *Kings in Exile*, 143–78. London, Melbourne, and Toronto: Ward, Lock & Co., Limited.

– 1912. "The Lone Wolf." In *Kings in Exile*, 237–68. New York: The MacMillan Company.

– 1922. "The White Wolf." In *Hoof and Claw*, 66–89. New York: The MacMillan Company.

– 1925. "Mixed Breed." In *They Who Walk in the Wilds*, 99–121. London: The MacMillan Company.

– (1909) 1966. "On the Night Trail." In *Haunters of the Silences*, 218–34. London: Duckworth & Co.

Rod and Gun. 1902. "Our Medicine Bag." Vol. 4, no. 4: 127.

- 1903. "Guardians of Game." Vol. 4, no. 9: 333–5.
- 1904. "Our Medicine Bag." Vol. 5, no. 10: 517.
- 1906a. "Destruction of Deer by Wolves." Vol. 9, no. 10: 137.
- 1906b. "The Indians and Big Game in the West." Vol. 8, no. 4: 226–8.
- 1906c. "Our Medicine Bag." Vol. 7, no. 11: 1238–40.
- 1907. "A Life and Death Struggle." Vol. 8, no. 10: 878.
- 1909a. "Our Medicine Bag." Vol. 10, no. 11: 1090, 1093–4.
- 1909b. "Wolves in British Columbia." Vol. 11, no. 7: 611.
- 1912a. "Our Medicine Bag." Vol. 14, no. 1: 61–2.
- 1912b. "Our Medicine Bag." Vol. 14, no. 3: 360.
- 1913. "Our Medicine Bag." Vol. 14, no. 10: 1130.
- 1928. "Ontario Hunters' Annual Meeting: Protective Association Asks for Higher Wolf Bounty." Vol. 29, no. 11: 912–14.
- 1947. "Vicious Black Wolves on Prowl in Manitoba." Vol. 48, no. 9: 5.
- 1950. "Letters: What Good Is Mr Wolf." Vol. 52, no. 1: 42.
Roosevelt, Theodore. 1920. "Nature Fakers." In *Roosevelt's Writings: Selections from the Writings of Theodore Roosevelt*, edited by Maurice Garland Fulton, 258–66. New York: The MacMillan Company.
Rose, Nicholas. 2006. *The Politics of Life Itself: Biomedicine, Power, and Subjectivity in the Twenty-First Century*. Princeton: Princeton University Press.
Rosiek, Jerry Lee, Jimmy Snyder, and Scott L. Pratt. 2019. "The New Materialisms and Indigenous Theories of Non-Human Agency: Making the Case for Respectful Anti-Colonial Engagement." *Qualitative Inquiry* 26, nos. 3–4: 1–16.
Rotundo, Anthony. 1993. *American Manhood: Transformations in Masculinity from the Revolution to the Modern Era*. New York: Basic Books.
Runtz, Michael. 1997. *The Howls of August: Encounters with Algonquin Wolves*. Erin, ON: Boston Mill Press.
Rutherford, Stephanie. 2007. "Green Governmentality: Insights and Opportunities in the Study of Nature's Rule." *Progress in Human Geography* 31, no. 3: 291–307.
- 2011. *Governing the Wild: Ecotours of Power*. Minneapolis: University of Minnesota Press.
- 2016. "A Resounding Success? Howling as a Source of Environmental History." In *Methodological Challenges in Nature-Culture and Environmental History Research*, edited by Jocelyn Thorpe, Stephanie Rutherford, and L. Anders Sandberg, 43–54. New York: Routledge.
- 2019. "Of Bounty and Beastly Tales: Wolves in the Canadian Imagination." In *Dog's Best Friend? Rethinking Human-Canid Relations*, edited by John

Sorenson and Atsuko Matsuoka, 337–53. Montreal and Kingston: McGill-Queen's University Press.

Rutter, Russell J., and Douglas H. Pimlott. 1968. *The World of the Wolf.* Philadephia and New York: J.B. Lippincott Company.

Rutter, Russell J., and Dan Strickland. 2002. *The Raven Talks about Wolves: Essays on Wolves from Alqonquin Park's Popular Newsletter, The Raven, 1963–2001.* Whitney, ON: The Friends of Algonquin Park.

Sandlos, John. 2000. "From within Fur and Feathers: Animals in Canadian Literature." *TOPIA: Canadian Journal of Cultural Studies* 4: 73–91.

Sax, Boria. 2000. *Animals in the Third Reich: Pets, Scapegoats, and the Holocaust.* New York: Continuum.

Schaefer, Donovan O. 2017. "You Don't Know What Pain Is: Affect, the Lifeworld, and Animal Ethics." *Studies in Christian Ethics* 30, no. 1: 15–29.

Scharff, Virginia J., ed. 2003. *Seeing Nature through Gender.* Lawrence: University of Kansas Press.

Seigworth, Gregory J., and Melissa Gregg. 2010. "An Inventory of Shimmers." In *The Affect Theory Reader*, edited by Melissa Gregg and Gregory J. Seigworth, 1–25. Durham, NC: Duke University Press.

Serrouya, R., D.R. Seip, D. Hervieux, B.N. McLellan, R.S. McNay, R. Steenweg, D.C. Heard, M. Hebblewhite, M. Gillingham, and S. Boutin. 2019. "Saving Endangered Species Using Adaptive Management." *Proceedings of the National Academy of Sciences* 116, no. 13: 6181–6.

Seton, Ernest Thompson. 1892. *Triumph of the Wolves (aka Awaited in Vain).* Oil on canvas, 53" × 79", Seton Memorial Library and Museum, Cimmaron, NM. https://ernestthompsonseton.com/seton-epic-paintings-1893-to-1895-biography.

– 1901. "Tito: The Story of the Coyote that Learned How." In *The Lives of the Hunted*, 263–351. New York: Charles Scribner's Sons.

– 1905a. "Badlands Billy: The Wolf that Won." In *Animal Heroes*, 109–65. London and Tonbridge: Bradbury, Agnew & Co. Ltd.

– 1905b. "The Winnipeg Wolf." In *Animal Heroes*, 287–320. London and Tonbridge: Bradbury, Agnew & Co. Ltd.

– 1937. " Wosca and Her Valiant Cub or the White Wolf Mother." In *Mainly about Wolves*, 1–26. London: Methuen and Company Limited.

– (1898) 2009. *Wild Animals I Have Known.* Champaign, IL: bookjungle.com.

Seton, Julia Moss, and Ernest Thompson Seton. 1966. *The Gospel of the Redman.* New Mexico: Seton Village.

Shankovich, Deborah L. 1998. "Wolfdogs Have Become this Man's Best Friends." *Pittsburgh Post-Gazette*, 5 November, W-1.

Shore, Randy. 2018. "BC's Selkirk Mountains' Gray Ghost Caribou Herd 'Functionally Extinct.'" *Vancouver Sun,* 17 April. https://vancouversun.com/news/local-news/b-c-s-selkirk-mountains-gray-ghost-caribou-herd-functionally-extinct.

Shrapnel, E.S. 1907. "Hunted by Wolves." *Rod and Gun and Motor Sports in Canada* 8, no. 10: 849–53.

Shukin, Nicole. 2009. *Animal Capital: Rendering Life in Biopolitical Times.* Minneapolis: University of Minnesota Press.

Sime, J.A. 1955. "Predator Control Training Report by BC Game Commission from November 7th to November 19th, 1955." Parks Canada Universal – Predator Control – Training for Park Wardens File U300. Library and Archives Canada, November.

Simoni, Stephanie. 2014. "Coyotes Taking Over East Haven Backyards." East Haven, CT: *News 8 WTNH.com,* 10 November.

Simpson, Leanne Betasamosake. 2017. *As We Have Always Done: Indigenous Freedom through Radical Resistance.* Minneapolis: University of Minnesota Press.

Sinclair, Rebekah. 2011. "Of Mites and Men: Animality, Bare Life and the Reperformance of the Human in *The Open.*" *Golden Caboose.* https://studylib.net/doc/14592620/of-mites-and-men--animality--bare-life-and-the.

Singh, Neera M. 2018. "Introduction: Affective Ecologies and Conservation." *Conservation & Society* 16, no. 1: 1–7.

Skoglund, Annika, and David Redmalm. 2017. "'Doggy Biopolitics': Governing via the First Dog." *Organization* 24, no. 2: 240–66.

Slaby, Jan. 2019. "Affective Arrangement." In *Affective Socities: Key Concepts,* edited by J. Slaby and C. von Scheve, 109–18. New York: Routledge.

Smalley, Andrea L. 2017. *Wild by Nature: North American Animals Confront Colonization.* Baltimore: Johns Hopkins University Press.

Smart, James. 1945. Parks Canada File U266 Universal Wolves. Library and Archives Canada, 17 June.

Smith, Anthony D. 2010. *Nationalism: Theory, Ideology, History.* 2nd ed. Cambridge: Polity Press.

Smith, Linda Tuhiwai, Eve Tuck, and K. Wayne Yang. 2019. "Introduction." In *Indigenous and Decolonizing Studies in Education: Mapping the Long View,* edited by Linda Tuhiwai Smith, Eve Tuck, and K. Wayne Yang, 1–23. New York: Routledge.

Spears, Tom. 2015. "Packs of Gatineau Park: Not Quite Wolves, Not Quite Coyotes." *Ottawa Citizen,* 22 October.

Srinivasan, Krithika. 2014. "Caring for the Collective: Biopower and Agential Subjectification in Wildlife Conservation." *Environment and Planning D* 32, no. 3: 501–17.

– 2019. "Remaking More-than-Human Society: Thought Experiments on Street Dogs as 'Nature.'" *Transactions of the Institute of British Geographers* 44, no. 2: 376–91.

Steffen, Will, Wendy Broadgate, Lisa Deutsch, Owen Gaffney, and Cornelia Ludwig. 2015. "The Trajectory of the Anthropocene: The Great Acceleration." *The Anthropocene Review* 2, no. 1: 81–98.

Steinhart, Peter. 1995. *The Company of Wolves.* New York: Vintage Books.

Straight, Lee. 1950. "The Wolf Menace as Experts See It." *Rod and Gun in Canada* 52, no. 4: 16–17, 35.

Strickland, Dan. 1999. "The Wolfian Trilogy Part 2: Thinking Things Through." In *The Raven Talks about Wolves*, 43–6. Whitney, ON: The Friends of Algonquin Park.

– 2004. *Wolf Howling in Algonquin Provincial Park: Algonquin Park Technical Bulletin No. 3.* Whitney, ON: The Friends of Algonquin Park and Ontario Parks.

Stronen, Astrid Vik, and Paul C. Paquet. 2013. "Perspectives on the Conservation of Wild Hybrids." *Biological Conservation* 167: 330–95.

Stronks, Rick. 2013. Personal communication, 21 August.

Struzik, Ed. 1998. "A Howling Success. Alberta Wolves Have Made Themselves at Home in Yellowstone to the Delight of Biologists and the Chagrin of Ranchers." *Edmonton Journal*, 15 June, A1.

Subramanian, Meera. 2019. "Anthropocene Now: Influential Panel Votes to Recognize Earth's New Epoch." *Nature*, 21 May. www.nature.com/articles/d41586-019-01641-5.

Sullivan, Sean. 2011. "Wolf-Dog Hyrbid has BC Island in 'Lockdown'; Marauding Killer." *National Post*, 19 February, A13.

Sundberg, Juanita. 2014. "Decolonizing Posthumanist Geographies." *cultural geographies* 21, no. 1: 33–47.

Sun Valley Wolf Kennels. 2015a. *Available Litters (upcoming)/Puppies for Sale.* http://sunvalleywolfkennels.com/puppies-available-now.

– 2015b. *High Content Wolf Cubs.* http://sunvalleywolfkennels.com/98-wolf-content-cubs.

Swaisgood, Ronald R., and James K. Sheppard. 2010. "The Culture of Conservation Biologists: Show Me the Hope!" *BioScience* 60, no. 8: 626–30.

TallBear, Kim. 2011. "Why Interspecies Thinking Needs Indigenous Standpoints." *Society for Cultural Anthropology.* 18 November. https://culanth.org/fieldsights/why-interspecies-thinking-needs-indigenous-standpoints.

Theberge, John B. 1973. "Wolf Management in Canada through a Decade of Change." *Nature Canada* 2, no. 1: 3–10.

– 1979. "The Man, the Wolf and the Ethic." The Douglas H. Pimlott fonds, University of Toronto Archives. Acc. no. B9 5003, box 003, file 09.

– 1998. *Wolf Country: Eleven Years Tracking the Algonquin Wolves.* Toronto: McClelland & Stewart Ltd.

Thiessen, George J. 1914. "Along the Trap Line: Fox, Wolf, Lynx and Marten." *Rod and Gun*, 935.

Thompson, Melanie S. 2007. "Placing the Wild in the City: 'Thinking with' Melbourne's Bats." *Society and Animals* 15: 79–95.

Thompson, Samuel. (1884) 2011. *Reminiscences of a Canadian Pioneer for the Last Fifty Years: An Autobiography.* The Project Gutenberg. https://gutenberg. ca/ebooks/thompsons-reminiscences/thompsons-reminiscences-00-h.html.

Thorpe, Jocelyn. 2012. *Temagami's Tangled Wild: Race, Gender and the Making of Canadian Nature.* Vancouver: UBC Press.

Tidwell, Mike. 2000. "Taking with Wolves." *Washington Post*, 17 December.

Todd, Zoe. 2016. "An Indigenous Feminist's Take on the Ontological Turn: 'Ontology' Is Just Another Word for Colonialism." *Journal of Historical Sociology* 29, no. 1: 4–22.

Toronto Star. 1990. "Wolves Threatened by a Lust for Coyotes." 30 September.

– 1991. "Wolfdogs Arouse Fear – and Affection." 10 August, F6.

Traill, Catherine Parr Strickland. 1856. *Lady Mary and Her Nurse, or, a Peep into the Canadian Forest.* London, UK: Arthur Hall, Virtue & Co.

TripAdvisor. 2015. "Wolf Howl Is Non-existant" [*sic*]. 6 September. www. tripadvisor.ca/ShowUserReviews-g319818-r307625442-Algonquin_ Provincial_Park_Ontario.html.

Tsing, Anna. 2012. "Unruly Edges: Mushrooms as Companion Species." *Environmental Humanities* 1: 141–54.

Tuan, Yi-Fu. 1984. *Dominance and Affection: The Making of Pets.* New Haven, CT: Yale University Press.

Tuck, Eve, and K. Wayne Wang. 2012. "Decolonization Is Not a Metaphor." *Decolonization: Indigeneity, Education & Society* 1, no. 1: 1–40.

Turner, Frederick Jackson. 1893. "The Significance of the Frontier in American History." http://nationalhumanitiescenter.org/pds/gilded/empire/text1/turner. pdf.

Turner, Jenny. 2017. "Life with Ms Cayenne Pepper." *The London Review of Books* 39, no. 11 (1 June).

Usik, Katherine Anne. 2015. "The Hunt for Ma'iingan: Ojibwe Ecological Knowledge and Wolf Hunting in the Great Lakes." MA thesis, University of Iowa. https://ir.uiowa.edu/etd/1781.

van Dooren, Thom. 2014. "Mourning Crows: Grief and Extinction in a Shared World." In *The Handbook of Human-Animal Studies*, edited by Susan McHugh and Garry Marvin, 275–89. London and New York: Routledge.

– 2016. "The Unwelcome Crows." *Angelaki: Journal of the Theoretical Humanities* 21, no. 2: 193–212.

Vancouver Sun. 1997. "Canadian Wolves a Howling Success: Transplanted Wolf Packs Have Produced 11 Litters this Spring in Wilds of Yellowstone Park." 30 May, A.14.

Velasquez-Manoff, M. 2014. "Should You Fear the Pizzly Bear?" *New York Times,* 17 August. www.nytimes.com/2014/08/17/magazine/should-you-fear-the-pizzly-bear.html.

Veracini, Lorenzo. 2008. "Settler Collective, Founding Violence and Disavowal: The Settler Colonial Situation." *Journal of Intercultural Studies* 29, no. 4: 363–79.

Vowel, Chelsea. 2016. *Indigenous Writes: A Guide to First Nations, Métis and Inuit Issues in Canada.* Winnipeg: Highwater Press.

Vyhnak, Carola. 2009. "Meet the Coywolf." *The Toronto Star,* 15 August. www.thestar.com/news/gta/2009/08/15/meet_the_coywolf.html.

Wadiwel, Dinesh. 2015. *The War Against Animals.* Leiden, The Netherlands: Brill.

Wadland, John. 1978. *Ernest Thompson Seton: Man in Nature and the Progressive Era 1880–1915.* New York: Arno Press.

Walker, Brett L. 2013. "Animals and the Intimacy of History." *History and Theory* 52, no. 4: 45–67.

Wallace, W., K. Coates, and W.R. Morrison. 2015. *On the Frontier: Letters from the Canadian West in the 1880s.* Regina: University of Regina Press.

Walsh, Sue. 2015. "Nature Faking and the Problem of the 'Real.'" *ISLE: Interdisciplinary Studies in Literature and the Environment* 22, no. 1: 132–53.

Waterton, C., and K. Yusoff. 2017. "Indeterminate Bodies: Introduction." *Body & Society* 23, no. 3: 3–22.

Watts, Vanessa. 2013. "Indigenous Place-Thought & Agency amongst Humans and Non-Humans (First Woman and Sky Woman Go on a European World Tour!)." *Decolonization: Indigeneity, Education & Society* 2, no. 1: 20–34.

Way, Jonathan G. 2007. *Suburban Howls: Tracking the Eastern Coyote in Urban Massachusetts.* Indianapolis: Dog Ear Publishing.

– 2013. "Taxonomic Implications of Morphological and Genetic Differences in Northeastern Coyotes (Coywolves) (*Canis latrans* × *C. lycaon*), Western Coyotes (*C. latrans*), and Eastern Wolves (*C. lycaon* or *C. lupus lycaon*)." *The Canadian Field Naturalist* 127, no. 1: 1–16.

– 2016. "Why the Eastern Coyote Should Be a Separate Species: The
   'Coywolf.'" *The Conversation*, 11 May. https://theconversation.com/
   why-the-eastern-coyote-should-be-a-separate-species-the-coywolf-59214.
Way, Jonathan G., and William S. Lynn. 2016. "Northeastern Coyote/Coywolf
   Taxonomy and Admixture: A Meta-Analysis." *Canid Biology & Conservation*
   19, no. 1: 1–7.
Way, Jonathan G., Linda Y. Rutledge, Tyler Wheeldon, and Bradley N. White.
   2010. "Genetic Characteristics of Eastern 'Coyotes' in Eastern
   Massachusetts." *Northeastern Naturalist* 17, no. 2: 189–204.
Weaver-Hightower, Rebecca. 2018. *Frontier Fictions: Settler Sagas and
   Postcolonial Guilt*. Cham, Switzerland: Palgrave Macmillan.
Weisberg, Zipporah. 2009. "The Broken Promises of Monsters: Haraway,
   Animals and the Humanist Legacy." *Journal for Critical Animal Studies* VII,
   no. II: 22–62.
Welsh, Jennifer. 2014. "Humans Have Created a Top Predator that Is Taking
   Over the Northeast." *Business Insider*, 22 August. www.businessinsider.com/
   coywolves-have-taken-over-the-northeast-2014-8.
Wetherell, Margaret. 2012. *Affect and Emotion: A New Social Science
   Understanding*. London: SAGE Publications Ltd.
– 2014. "Trends in the Turn to Affect: A Social Psychological Critique." *Body &
   Society* 21, no. 2: 139–66.
White Earth Land Recovery Project. n.d. *Ma'iingan (The Wolf) Our Brother*.
   Accessed 27 July 2020. www.welrp.org/about-welrp/
   maiingan-the-wolf-our-brother.
Whittaker, M.W. 1911. "Strange Adventures with a Wolf." *Rod and Gun in
   Canada* 12, no. 11: 1425–7.
Whyte, Kyle. 2020. "Indigenous Environmental Justice: Anti-Colonial Action
   through Kinship." In *Environmental Justice: Key Issues*, edited by B. Coolsaet,
   266–78. New York: Routledge.
Wilde, Nicole. 2004. *Living with Wolfdogs: An Everyday Guide to a Lifetime
   of Companionship*. Santa Clarita, CA: Phantom Publishing.
Williams, F.V. 1915. "How Saunders Caught the Game-Hog." *Rod and Gun
   in Canada* 17, no. 6: 546–53.
Wilson, Matthew W. 1997. "The Wolf in Yellowstone: Science, Symbol, or
   Politics? Deconstructing the Conflict between Environmentalism and Wise
   Use." *Society & Natural Resources* 10: 453–68.
Wilson, P.J., S. Grewal, I.D. Lawford, J.N.M. Heal, A.G. Granacki, D. Pennock,
   J.B. Theberge, et al. 2000. "DNA Profiles of the Eastern Canadian Wolf and
   the Red Wolf Provide Evidence for a Common Evolutionary History

Independent of the Gray Wolf." *Canadian Journal of Zoology* 78, no. 12: 2156–66.

Winsa, Patty. 2011. "Compensation Rises for Coyote Kills." *Toronto Star*, 17 July. www.thestar.com/news/gta/2011/07/17/compensation_rises_for_coyote_kills.html.

Wisconsin Department of Natural Resources. n.d. *Cattail Hybrid*. Accessed 26 April 2021. https://dnr.wisconsin.gov/topic/Invasives/fact/CattailHybrid.html.

Wise, Michael D. 2016. *Producing Predators: Wolves, Work, and Conquest in the Northern Rockies*. Lincoln: University of Nebraska Press.

Wolch, Jennifer. 1996. "Zoopolis." *Capitalism, Nature, Socialism* 7, no. 2: 21–47.

– 2002. "Animal Urbis." *Progress in Human Geography* 26, no. 6: 721–42.

Wolfe, Cary. 2008. "Flesh and Finitude: Thinking Animals in (Post)Humanist Philosophy." *SubStance* 3, no. 117: 8–36.

– 2012. *Before the Law: Humans and Other Animals in a Biopolitical Frame*. Chicago: University of Chicago Press.

Wolfe, Patrick. 2006. "Settler Colonialism and the Elimination of the Native." *Journal of Genocide Research* 8, no. 4: 387–409.

– 2013. "The Settler Complex: An Introduction." *American Indian Culture and Research Journal* 37, no. 2: 1–22.

Worster, Donald. 1994. *Nature's Economy: A History of Ecological Ideas*. 2nd ed. Cambridge: Cambridge University Press.

Yamnuska Wolfdog Sanctuary. 2020a. *Our Wolfdogs*. https://yamnusk awolfdogsanctuary.com/wolfdogs.

– 2020b. *Visit the Sanctuary*. https://yamnuskawolfdogsanctuary.com/sanctuarytours.

Yellowstone National Park. 2020. *How Many Wolves Are in Yellowstone?* 6 March. www.yellowstonepark.com/things-to-do/how-many-wolves-yellowstone.

Yoon, Hyaesin. 2017. "Feral Biopolitics." *Angelaki: Journal of the Theoretical Humanities* 22, no. 2: 135–50.

Young, Stanley Paul. 1946. *The Wolf in North American History*. Caldwell, ID: The Claxton Printers, Ltd.

Yukon Wolf Management Planning Team. 1992. *The Yukon Wolf Conservation and Management Plan*. Yukon Renewable Resources.

Index